I0892976

Franciscans in Canada
Historical Essays

Franciscans in Canada
Historical Essays

Edited by
Paul-André Dubois and Robert Mokry, OFM

Translated by Robert Mokry, OFM

Academy of American Franciscan History
San Diego, California
2024

Chapters 1–4 from
Paul-André Dubois, ed., *Les Récollets en Nouvelle-France: Traces et Mémoire,*
Québec, QC, Presses de l'Université Laval, 2018.

and Chapters 5–6 from
Hamelin, Jean (dir.), *Les Franciscains au Canada, 1890–1990,*
Sillery, QC, Septentrion, 1990.

Published with permission of the publishers.

Academy of American Franciscan History
San Diego, California

Library of Congress Cataloging-in-Publication Data

For CIP data go to www.aafh.org.

Table of Contents

Introduction

Robert Mokry, OFM

Distinguished Professor of Canadian Religious History, Dr. Paul-André Dubois's work on the Recollects and his keen interest in the renewed Franciscan presence in Canada inspired me to pull together this collection of essays to provide an overview of some 400 years of Franciscan presence. My intent is to make available to the anglophone reader pertinent articles that permit a better understanding of why, how, and where the Franciscan Order came to be present: first, in New France, or regions of eastern Canada, as Recollects; and then, in the last century, re-established as the Order of Friars Minor (OFM) both in eastern and western Canada.

I have drawn from two major books. The first, *Les Récollets en Nouvelle-France: Traces et Mémoire*,[1] a compilation of scholarly works edited by Dubois, consists of four general categories: 1) the presence of the early friars—predominantly Recollects and less so the Capuchins—in various locations of eastern Canada; 2) the physical world of these friars; 3) the friars's ways of expressing themselves; and 4) physical reminders of the friars' presence. I have included, from the first part of this book, four articles that deal with the Recollects identity and work. Three are translations from French and one originally published in English.

The first translated article is Bernard Dompnier's "The Franciscans: Between Fidelity to Their Heritage and the Religious Challenges of the Modern Era (XVIth–XVIIth Centuries)." In fact, it does not deal with the friars's presence in Canada at all; rather it treats the religious environment during the Counter Reformation and the changing political situation in Europe which account for much of the Franciscan missionary action throughout the world, and more relevantly, in New France. It also presents a good picture of the developments in the Franciscan family, out of which the Recollects arose, who, despite the vagaries of time and the evolution of the Franciscan family, still have some bearing on our present Canadian Franciscan (OFM) identity.

1. Paul-André Dubois, ed., *Les Récollets en Nouvelle-France: Traces et Mémoire*, Québec, QC, Presses de l'Université Laval, 2018.

The second translation, written by Paul-André Dubois and Dorothée Kaupp, is:"The Recollects in New France: Portraits and Pictures." This well illustrated article uses numerous reproductions and visual aids to address the Recollects' first arrival in 1615, their return in 1670, and their continual presence, even under the British, until the last friar died in 1849. The article also briefly mentions the reappearance of the Franciscan family at the end of the 19th century and the mythical reintroduction of the ancient Recollects into Quebec's emerging politico-religious identity.

The third translated article,"The Work of a Recollect: Recollects and Military Chaplaincy in New France, 1670–1760," by Rénald Lessard, provides a picture of the development of the Recollect Order as military chaplains and the good relations this afforded them with the King. Military chaplaincy did not restrict the ordained friars; rather, it also allowed them to serve in parishes and undertake missionary work which opened the door to all members of the Order—priest and lay—to serve the emerging community in various apostolates. Much of the information contained in this article builds on an earlier detailed study, "L'œuvre des Récollets" prepared by the Franciscans Marion Habig and René Bacon which was included as a prefatory chapter to Fr. Odoric Jouve's magisterial work, *Dictionnaire biographique des Récollets missionnaire en Nouvelle-France, 1615-45–1670-1849.*[2] It should be noted that Jouve's biographical entries have been republished jointly in French and English by the Université Laval and the University of Toronto in the *Dictionary of Canadian Biography* and are available online (http://www.biographi.ca/en/index.php).

The fourth article, written in English by A.J.B. Johnston and titled "The Récollets at Louisbourg," speaks of the 18th century Recollect presence elsewhere in eastern Canada. Unlike the Parisian Recollects from the Province of St. Denis who first arrived and settled themselves principally in the town of Quebec, these friars, who arrived somewhat later came from Brittany and settled in what is now Newfoundland, Cape Breton, and Nova Scotia. Their presence provides a little-known picture of a diverse Recollect presence in Canada and of a Recollect unity-in-mission which contributes to a larger understanding of the Canadian Franciscan heritage.

The second book, from which I have included two major articles, is Jean Hamelin's edition of *Les Franciscains au Canada.*[3] Published as a centenary project in 1990, it consists of an important historical study of the reestablishment of the Franciscans, that is the Order of Friars Minor (into which the

---

2. Odoric-Marie Jouve, *Dictionnaire biographique des Récollets missionnaires en nouvelle-France, 1615-45–1670-1849 : province franciscaine Saint-Joseph du Canada,* Montréal, QC, Bellarmin, 1996.

3. Jean Hamelin, ed., *Les Franciscains au Canada, 1890–1990,* Sillery, QC, Septentrion, 1990.

Recollects were incorporated at the Leonine Union of 1897) in Canada, as well as numerous essays about apostolates undertaken by the St. Joseph's Province, renowned friars, and their contributions to French-Canadian society.

The fifth article of the compilation, titled "Historic Overview," presents the most complete study to date of the Franciscan presence and expansion throughout Canada, including important information about the missions to western anglophone Canada. Unfortunately, there is only passing mention of the friars' involvement in New Brunswick (and parts of the northeastern United States).

I have also included a sixth and final article, a translation similarly taken from Hamelin's book, titled: "Franciscans and Education." It deals with the impact of the friars' educational apostolate on Quebec's social development. I believe it provides an understanding of the role that the"Quiet Revolution" and society's reaction to a pre-Vatican II church played in Quebec, and it offers insights into the Church's present situation. It also refers to St. Joseph Province's early educational apostolate in western Canada which, although less extensive among anglophones than it was in Quebec, has left an enduring contribution.

It is useful for anglophone readers, seeking to understand the Order of Friars Minor's presence in Canada, to recall that despite linguistic, cultural, and geographic differences, the Order took root thanks to the many friars who came to anglophone regions from predominantly francophone eastern Canada. These friars ministered to and fostered local vocations, were instrumental in the west's attaining various stages of independence, and many of them stayed on in ministry long after the west attained autonomy. The short years of western Franciscan autonomy, as a Custody and then as the Province of Christ the King, is but a brief episode in the long history of the Franciscan Order in Canada that goes back to the seventeenth century and now continues in the single Canadian OFM Province of the Holy Spirit.

Introductory Comments

PAUL-ANDRÉ DUBOIS

The Franciscan presence in Canada is intimately linked to the country's history. Only a few years after the founding of Quebec City, the first Recollects set foot on Canadian soil and began their ministry. The grand narrative of the Catholic origins of French Canada has magnified this presence, while being careful not to criticize its shortcomings. Still, it must be admitted that the first sons of Saint Francis in Canada showed heroic dedication to those they encountered, whether in the fledgling settlement of Quebec, or in the native posts and villages they visited. Pioneer missionary Brother Gabriel Sagard's writings[1] show just how much hope the French priests of the seraphic order had in this work; they were eager to follow in the footsteps of the Franciscan missionaries in New Spain. However, the abrupt end of the Franciscan adventure in New France in 1629 led to a long period of dormancy for the Recollects in the French colony. The Order of St. Francis returned to their missionary efforts in Canada in 1670, despite not being invited to return by the Bishop of Quebec and the colonial administration for missions to the Aboriginals. The role of the Recollects was limited, though a few served, notably among the Micmacs; all in all, the Jesuits, and to some extent the secular clergy of the Seminary of Quebec, monopolized this apostolic field. One reason, perhaps, was that it was well known that the Recollects were poor linguists. No doubt informed by the Jesuits, who never missed an opportunity to scratch their rivals in the process, Intendant Jean Bochart de Champigny maintained that the "difficulties these fathers have in learning the language of the Savages means that few are suitable for the savage missions."[2]

According to Champigny's 1702 memoir, this difficulty was due to the advanced age of the Recollects when they arrived in New France, as well as their great mobility, which enabled them to move easily from one place to another, or to leave their post to travel to France on various business matters,

1. Brother Gabriel Sagard, *Le grand voyage au pays des Hurons* (Paris, 1632) ; *L'histoire du Canada* (1636)

2. « Mémoire de l'estat présent de la Nouvelle France laissé par le Sr de Champigny à Monsieur de Beauharnois, intendant pour sa Majesté au dit pays, ce 11 novembre 1702 » (Collection de la famille Beauharnois, C-2925, p. 150–229), MG18-G6, vol. II, f. 245.

implicitly deemed futile by the colonial administration. However, mastery of Native languages requires not only intelligence and youth, but also perseverance, which presupposes stability in the same place. The opening of a novitiate at the Quebec convent was intended to remedy this shortcoming, according to the Recollects, by stimulating local recruitment.

In fact, while local recruitment was a real success thanks to the open-mindedness of the Recollects and the favorable conditions they offered to the sons of families from Quebec City and the surrounding area to enable them to enter the priesthood, the great work of the sons of Saint Francis in New France was undoubtedly chaplaincy within the army and a significant presence in remote Canadian parishes of recent foundation. Accustomed to Franciscan poverty, the Recollects were ideally suited to these thankless tasks, which the diocesan secular clergy sometimes shied away from, given the sacrifices involved in missionary life among Canadian settlers. This sustained presence in the urban world, thanks to three convents (in Quebec, Trois-Rivières and Montreal), as well as in the rural world as parish priests, inscribed the Recollect presence in the culture and imagination of Canadians throughout the 18th century to today.

The synthetic work of Odoric-Marie Jouve, Archange Godbout, Hervé Blais and René Bacon is still very important in the field of Franciscan studies in Canada. First and foremost, the *Dictionnaire des missionnaires récollets* presents factual data as accurate as possible on each of the Récollet missionaries from the first religious to arrive in New France to the last survivors of the order in Canada at the beginning of the 19th century.[3] This is unquestionably a collective work, spread over decades of patient research in the most diverse sources, at a time when historical research had few research instruments and few technological tools at its disposal to enable a broad sweep of historical sources. The magnitude of the task accomplished by these Franciscan historians is staggering. Following in their footsteps, historian Caroline Galland has produced a remarkable synthesis that completes this book, giving as complete a picture as possible of this part of Canadian socio-religious history.[4] The present work, which paints an original picture of the Franciscan presence in Canada, is certainly an invitation to pursue historical research in this field, where large swathes of history have yet to be discovered.

---

3. Archange Godbout, Hervé Blais and René Bacon, Dictionnaire biographique des Récollets missionnaires en Nouvelle-France. Montréal, Bellarmin, 1996, 903 p.

4. Caroline Galland, *Pour la gloire de Dieu et du Roi. Les récollets en Nouvelle-France aux XVII*[e] *et XVIII*[e] *siècles,* Paris, Cerf, 2012, 528 p.

CHAPTER 1

The Franciscans: Between Fidelity to Their Heritage and the Religious Challenges of the Modern Era (XVIth–XVIIth Centuries)[1]

BERNARD DOMPNIER, BLAISE-PASCAL UNIVERSITY, CLERMONT-FERRAND, FRANCE

The history of the Friars Minor is undoubtedly the most complex of all those religious orders which, over centuries, fragmented into various branches and experienced almost complete reunifications; indeed, the friars had several branches that lasted only a short time. The modern era provided ample opportunity for the Franciscans to produce various understandings and implementations of the Rule left by their founder, which had already become apparent in the decades following the death of the Poverello of Assisi. The modern era opened with the separation of the friars into two great families—Conventuals and Observants—which the Pope ratified in 1517 with the Bull *Ite et vos*. Then in 1619, a century later, the Capuchins, who had appeared in the first half of the sixteenth century, obtained in their turn total independence from the Order and were placed under the authority of their own Minister General. Moreover, within the Observants, reform movements developed which began to recognize a relative autonomy—the Discalced in Spain, the *Riformati* in Italy, and the Recollects in France, "Belgium," and Germanic regions.

It is true that Francis of Assisi's legacy for those who claimed to be his disciples favored varied and quite divergent responses, since it is more of a spiritual message than an institutional outline. The prescriptive documents

1. Translation of: Bernard Dompnier, « Les Franciscains entre fidélité à leur héritage et défis religieux de l'âge moderne (XVIe–XVIIe siècles) », in *Les Récollets en Nouvelle-France : Traces et Mémoire*, ed. Paul-André Dubois (Québec, QC : Les Presses de l'Université Laval, 2018), 61–107.

Luciano Borzone (Genoa, 1590–1645), *Saint Francis in ecstasy*, c.1630–1639. Oil on canvas, 117 × 96 cm, private collection.

left by the Poverello, who never wanted to found a religious order in the usual sense of the term, are few and brief. The Friars Minor's principal guide is the personal example of Francis, who had himself followed in the footsteps of Christ. Without going so far as to consider the founder's message as intrinsically anti-hierarchical, it must at least be agreed that the Franciscan charism is not inclined to an overly rigid organization.

Of course, any religious order needs a minimum of norms to regulate common life, especially when the order increases in size, and enough authority to assure respect for the norms. Whatever their hopes were for a liberal renewal of their founder's message, the Friars Minor could not escape this necessity. Moreover, religious orders base their systems of governance more or less directly on the patterns that prevail in the Church. As we know, strong hierarchical ideas about the exercise of authority prevailed for a long time in the Church, and they were imposed all the more after the Council of Trent.

Understanding the Franciscan family's complex history calls for considering two main elements. The first is that of the internal tensions arising from Francis's message. As in all orders, the Friars Minor's reform movements always demanded an absolute fidelity to the Rule of Francis and advocated, without any concessions, a return to the fundamental first directives. To reform an order is always to propose a return to the origins, with the conviction that over time the primitive fervor has been relaxed and that the initial ideals have even been betrayed.

A second element in interpreting the major aspects of Franciscanism's evolution into the modern era is the necessity to see this evolution in relation to the external religious contexts, whether they were the needs and appeals of the Church, or different currents of spirituality. Although radically different from the first, this second element exerts an influence on the rereading of the Rule and Franciscan origins, since this is done by men who are part of an environment and who share aspirations that are no longer those of the thirteenth century. For the era in question, the desire to return to the origins is formulated in a language that reflects the sensibilities of "modernity" with its religious expectations and notions of Christian perfection.

Franciscan historiography has long been the almost exclusive domain of the friars and has not always been free of biases which put one or another of its dimensions in the best light. The noteworthy revival that Franciscanism experiences today is accompanied by particular attention to defining the specifics of each of the branches of the Order, according to their own identities.[2] In line with these works, we propose, in the following pages, to point out the challenges confronting Franciscans rather than providing a general history of Franciscanism in the modern era. Among the challenges and responses that the Friars Minor must face, we will pay particular attention to those faced by the Recollects, even if our knowledge of them remains sketchy.

DIFFERENT WAYS OF LIVING UNDER THE SAME HABIT

If we try to sketch a picture of all the Friars Minor in the modern era, we are immediately struck by the obvious diversity in the ways of thinking about fidelity to Francis of Assisi. There are many ways to wear a habit, even literally, since the color and shape vary according to the branches of the Order, not to mention the length of the capuche or whether shoes are worn, which also allow the friars to indicate their differences. Despite this, all the friars are convinced that they are being perfect imitators of Francis, and that includes their particular way of dressing. In the Father's house, there are many

2. This in particular is the approach taken in the two volume collection coordinated by Frédéric Meyer and Ludovic Viallet, *Identités franciscaines à l'âge des Réformes* (Clermont-Ferrand, PUBP, 2005), and *Le silence du cloître, l'exemple des saints XIVe–XVIIe siècles* (Clermont-Ferrand, PUBP, 2011). Stimulating reflections for a historiographical revival are found in Ludovic Viallet, « Héritages de l'Observance et aspirations réformatrices chez les Franciscains au début du XVIe siècle », in *Les Récollets. En quête d'une identité Franciscaine*, eds. Caroline Galland, Fabien Guilloux and Pierre Moracchini (Tours, PUFR, 2014) 29–37.

St. Francis's attire, from several originals.[a]

dwellings places,[3] and that goes for the Franciscans, too. We will consider, during the modern era, at least four kinds of friars from the branch of the Strict Observance of which the Recollects are part.[4]

---

[a]On the Recollects, Frédéric Meyer, *Pauvreté et assistance spirituelle. Les Franciscain Récollet de la province de Lyon aux XVIIe et XVIIIe siècles*, Saint-Étienne, PU, 1997; Caroline Galland, *Pour la gloire de Dieu et du Roi. Les récollets de Nouvelle-France aux XVIIe et XVIIIe siècles*, Paris, Le Cerf, 2012; Caroline Galland, Fabien Guilloux et Pierre Moracchini, *Les Récollets*. As a guide for future work: Frédéric Meyer, « Pour faire l'histoire des Récollets en France (XVIe–XIXe siècles) », *Chrétiens et sociétés*, 2, 1995, p. 83–99.

3. John 14:2.

4. For a comprehensive overview of the Franciscan family and its components at various times in history, we rely primarily on *Dizinario degli Istituti de perfezione*, eds. Guerrino Pellicia and Giancarlo Rocca (Rome Edizioni Paoline, 1974-1997, 9 vols). See especially the entries for: " Cappuccini (II. collar. 203–252), « Conventuali (III, col. 1–94), « Francescanesimo (IV, col. 446–464), « Frati Minori (IV, col. 823–838), « Frati Minori simplicer dicti (IV, 839–911), « Osservanti (VI, col. 1022–1035), " Recolletti (VII, col. 1307–1322). A lovely overview, which stops unfortunately at the beginning of the modern era, was recently put forth by Grado Giovanni Merlo, *Au nom de saint François. Histoire des Frères mineurs et du franciscanisme jusqu'au début du XVIe siècle* (Paris, Le Cerf, 2006 [original ed. in Italian, Padua, Editrici Francescane, 2003]). For a quick survey of all the Friars Minor, we also have the old work of Achille Leon, *Histoire de l'ordre des Frères mineurs. Saint François d'Assise et son œuvre* (Paris, Éditions franciscaine, n.d. [1954]). On

THE STRICT OBSERVANCE

This term is used to designate the three reforms that were born within the Observants in the sixteenth century. The movement first originated in the Iberian Peninsula, a little before 1500, with John of La Puebla; but its rise is mainly the work of Peter of Alcantara (1499–1562), who went beyond the Observants of John of La Puebla's Discalced reform. Then, Italy, in its turn was won over by this desire for reform. The houses of recollection that were opened there and were represented by a protector in Rome obtained the right to form separate custodies in 1532 and were soon transformed into provinces in their own right. The Recollects were the French counterpart of this reform movement.[5] The first attempts to establish houses of recollection in the kingdom were made in 1533, then in 1570, but it was not until 1583 that they were established in a lasting way at Murat and Rabastens, houses that belonged to the Aquitaine Province, which were undoubtedly the most sensitive to the Spanish influence. The beginnings were difficult, as evidenced by the Duke of Nevers's failure to install a community of Italian *Riformati* in his city. The second half of the sixteenth century was marked by a strong xenophobia, and it was only around 1600 that the Recollects took root, more particularly in 1595, when the General of the Order[6] promulgated their first statutes; and then in 1597 when they were granted a friary in each of the three great provinces of northern France. Finally, in 1601 the pope authorized them to place themselves under the authority of a Commissary General, who was responsible for France and the Belgo-Rhine area. The first two French provinces were established in 1612. The name Recollects, chosen by the friars, is derived from the Portuguese and Spanish terms *(recohimento, recogimento)* which means recollection and withdrawal, and reflects the importance that this reform gives to mental prayer to which the friars were to devote at least two hours a day away from the tumult of the world.

The three groups just mentioned formed the Strict Observance and shared the same demands regarding spiritual life, a characteristic which they had in

---

the Friars Minor in France, *Mouvements franciscains et société française XIIe–XXe siècle,* ed. André Vauchez (Paris Beauchesne, 1984).

5. On the Recollects, see Frédéric Meyer, *Pauvreté et assistance spirituelle. Les Franciscains Récollets de la province de Lyon aux XVIIe et XVIIIe siècles* (Saint-Étienne, PU, 1997); Caroline Galland, *Pour la gloire de Dieu et du Roi. Les récollets de Nouvelle-France aux XVIIe et XVIIIe siècles,* Paris (Le Cerf, 2012); Caroline Galland, Fabien Guilloux and Pierre Moracchini, *Les Recollets.* For a guide to future work, see: Frédéric Meyer, "Pour faire l'histoire des Récollets en France (XVIe–XIX siècles)," *Chrétiens et sociétés,* 2, 1995, 83–99.

6. In fact, they adopted the regulations used by their Spanish and Italian counterparts. But each Recollect province then saw to its own statutes.

A Friar Minor of the Strict Observance: a Recollect without mantle.

common with the Capuchins. But, unlike the latter, they remained within the Order of Friars Minor, participated in General Chapters, and recognized the authority of the Minister General. Like the Discalced Spanish and the *Riformati* Italians, with whom they were not organically linked, the Recollects had the status of a congregation within the Order.[7] The Recollects' initial objective was not to found new friaries but to reform those of the Observants. Despite royal support, their plans only succeeded partially, contrary to what was seen in the Germanic world, where Observance shifted almost entirely to Recollection. In France, a number of brothers subscribed individually to recollection, but the movement was not intentionally imposed. It was recognized and organized later than in Spain and Italy, and it did not immediately establish a policy of creating new friaries. This difference in timing had serious consequences for the Recollects. They missed their chance to take advantage of the favorable situation for establishing new religious houses. By around 1630, cities began to realize that they could no longer accept new orders since the number of mendicants they housed had reached a critical

7. On the relationship between the movements of the Strict Observance and their self-perception, Frédéric Meyer, « L'unité de la Stricte Observance franciscaine. Mythes et réalités (XVIe–XIXe siècles) » in *Les communautés régulières face à leur passé* (Saint-Etienne, PU), 275–297.

An Observant Friar Minor without mantle.

threshold. The Capuchins, however, who were very close to the Recollects in lifestyle, apostolate, and spirituality, were able to take full advantage of the permission given to them in 1574 to cross the Alps, and they began immediately to establish a tight-knit network of friaries. The Recollects' upsurge began a generation after that of the Capuchins, which resulted in them often being refused entry into important cities and in their having to settle for cities which provided lesser support. Due to this initial delay, the Recollects appear as an Order established more in towns than in the great cities.[8]

THE OBSERVANCE FAMILY CONNECTIONS

The Observants, on which the Recollects were legally dependent, formed one of the two main branches of the Order of Friars Minor. Appearing in the fourteenth century, the Observance movement experienced a remarkable development in the fifteenth, as is illustrated by leading personalities such as Bernardine of Siena and John Capistran. The friars who subscribed to it shared a demand for fidelity to the primitive Rule (they viewed themselves as *observantes Regulam,* hence their name) and, in doing so, they followed more or less directly in the wake of the Italian Spirituals who, since the thirteenth

8. Frederic Meyer, *Pauvreté et assistance spirituelle,* 51–52.

century, had distanced themselves from the "Community" (that is to say, those who were referred to as Conventuals). The observance movement, which originally presented itself differently in different countries, began to be united in 1451 by commonly adopting the so-called Barcelona statutes. The bull of 1517, by which the office of Minister General of the Order passed to the Observants, is their charter of union and decrees their separation from the Conventuals: it brings them together into a single entity and makes them the principal branch of the Friars Minor. Thereafter the Conventuals had to be content to have a Master General at their head. The union, however, remained rather theoretical since the two Observant families which existed before 1517 continued their relatively autonomous existence: those of Italy, Austria, Hungary, and Poland are called Cismontanes, while the others are called Ultramontanes. In total, there were about 1,300 Observant convents at the beginning of the sixteenth century; in 1580 there were 2,100, populated then by 35,000 religious; a century later, the number of friars is about the same.[9]

The Conventual counterpart

The Conventuals are the least well-known component of the Order of Friars Minor, probably because religious historiography always favors what is new (even as a claim to return to tradition) as well as disputes and "heroes" rather than men who live quietly, in the shadows, sometimes in mediocrity too, and who leave fewer traces in the archives. Generally, the Conventuals represent the part of the Order that accepted the relaxations of the Rule (or "developments") that have been granted by various popes. They are directly in line with the attitude of one of Francis's first companions—Brother Elijah—who wanted to temper poverty with apostolic expediency. The 1322 bull, *Ad conditorem* of John XXII, which authorized collective ownership, definitively confirmed the choice made by this component of the Order. In the conflicts that set Conventuals and Observants in permanent opposition, successive popes granted advantages sometimes to one, sometimes to another. Even if the bull of 1517 seems to indicate the Observants' triumph, at the beginning of the seventeenth century, the Conventuals also succeeded in having a Minister General, which placed them on an equal footing with their rivals. Although well established in Italy, they disappeared from the Franciscan panorama in Spain in 1566, when the king imposed the integration of all Conventuals into the Observance movement. In France, following the bull of 1517, four of the Conventuals' five provinces switched to Observance; only

9. For the French situation, see Jean-Marie Le Gall, « Pour une cartographie des Observances. Bilan provisoire », eds. Frédéric Meyer and Ludovic Viallet, *Identités franciscaines,* 211–235.

A Friar Minor Conventual.

the Province of Provence and a number of friaries in Burgundy remained. These friaries were formed into a second Conventual Province called Saint Bonaventure. In the French kingdom, both Observants and Conventuals continued to be referred to as Cordeliers, which had been the traditional way of referring to the Friars Minor, and this was sometimes a source of confusion, especially for historians.

THE CAPUCHINS: EMANCIPATED FRIARS

In many respects, the same requirements as those of the Recollects and the Strict Observance as a whole were central to the Capuchins' approach. They presented themselves as defenders of complete respect for the Rule, especially in terms of poverty or the intensity of the spiritual life.[10] The

10. On the Capuchins, the studies relating to France are almost all devoted to one of the provinces of the order. See in particular, Théorime of Saint-Just, *Les Capucins de l'ancienne province de Lyon* (Saint-Étienne, Petit Messager de saint François, 1951–1957, 3 vols.); John Mauzaize, *Le rôle et l'action des Capucins de la province de Paris dans la France religieuse du XVIIe siècle* (Lille ANRT, 1978, 3 vols.); Bernard Dompnier, *Enquête au pays des frères des anges. Les Capucins de la province de Lyon aux XVIIe et XVIIIe siècles* (Saint-Étienne, PU, 1993).

Capuchins' beginnings go back to Matthieu de Bascio, an Observant intent on perfectly imitating Francis of Assisi, and to the two brothers who quickly joined him—Louis and Raphael of Fossombrone. They formed the first group of "Hermit Friars Minor." This name emphasizes their ideal of retreat from the world, which in the long term characterizes their reform. Even when they were fully engaged in apostolic activities, the Capuchins refused to hear the confession of diocesan priests or to provide spiritual direction for people in the world,[11] both of which were ministries that the Recollects agreed to take on. The Capuchins' papal recognition of 1528 placed them under the Conventuals' jurisdiction to protect them from the vindictiveness of the Observants, who considered them disobedient, and it also authorized them to welcome friars wishing to share an "austere and eremitic life." The following year, their Constitutions of Albacina provided the first codification of the community's decisions. During the particularly chaotic first decades of their existence, the Capuchins often risked disappearing entirely. They struggled to overcome internal dissensions which arose when, because of suspicion of heretical teachings, Louis de Fossombrone was removed from the leadership of the congregation and when their vicar general, Bernardin Ochino, fled to Geneva in Protestant lands to escape the Inquisition. Because of this turmoil, the Capuchins were prohibited for several decades to expand outside of Italy; the ban was only lifted in 1574. From that moment on, their development was dazzling, especially in France and Switzerland, countries where they were on the front line of the Counter-Reformation conflicts. Later, after 1648, they also established themselves firmly in the territories of the [Holy Roman] Empire. Their center of gravity, however, remained in Italy. In 1643, they had more than 800 convents in the peninsula compared to 300 in France, 88 in Spain and 200 in the rest of Catholic Europe. A witness to their success in establishing themselves, which is also a reason for it, is that their recruitment level reached a high that was rarely attained by orders of this time. In this same year 1643, the Capuchins numbered more than 11,000 in Italy, 5,000 in France, 1,600 in Spain, and 3,000 friars in other countries – the total membership exceeded 20,000.

To complete the overview

For a complete picture, it is also necessary to mention the Third Order Regular which has existed since the thirteenth century but experienced a marked revival in France in the seventeenth century with the "Picpus

11. On the exercise of this office by the Recollects, see Pierre Moracchini, « Les Récollets français et la *Cura monialium* », in *Les Recollets,* eds. Caroline Galland, Fabien Guilloux and Pierre Moracchini, 127–144.

Capuchin nun with the large black veil used when going to communion.

Fathers,"[12] who were grouped into thirty-five friaries in 1640, mainly in Normandy and Lorraine. They were under the umbrella of the Observants, to whom they were close regarding their way of life, but nevertheless they had the peculiar right to own property, like the Conventuals. The history of Franciscan women is less complex than that of the first order; in general, their divisions broadly follow those of the men. The Poor Clares are divided into

12. Translator's note: Our author refers to an early 18th century reform movement among the Observants (Recollects), which, under the leadership of Friar Charles de Picpus from the Paris friary, established its identity on the spirituality of penance which was most visible in those who went begging. Charles de Picpus's 1710 manual entitled *Le questeur religieux* directed that whoever wanted to join this Third Order Regular group should redeem his faults by carrying many crosses, and in particular the crosses of "opprobrium, affronts, scorn, rejection, heat and cold, lack of clothing and all the other inconveniences that are attached to and inseparable from begging." Cf. Fabienne Henryot. « La quête franciscaine aux XVIIe et XVIIIe siècles : théories et pratiques d'une économie de l'Évangile » in *Religione e istituzioni religiose nell'economia europea. 1000–1800, XLIII Settimana di Studi de la Fondazione Istituto internazionale di storia economica "F. Datini,"* May 2011, Prato, Italie. pp.293–305. ffhal-00804632v2. For the online version see: https://hal.archives-ouvertes.fr/hal-00804632/document. These Picpus Fathers should not be confused with the Congregation of the Sacred Hearts of Jesus and Mary which was established toward the end of the 18th century, during the French Revolution, and are called as such because their first house was located on the Rue de Picpus in Paris, France.

two main families: the Urbanists and the Colettines. The former followed the Rule given by Pope Urban IV in 1263, which granted them the right to own property. The latter, who subscribed to the reform of Colette of Corbie in the fifteenth century, opted for the stricter Rule of 1253. Other Poor Clares also attached themselves to the Capuchins. Their few monasteries were mainly in Italy and, to a lesser extent, in France. And last of all and only in Italy, there are still some communities of Alacantarines, which were established not earlier than 1631.

The separation of the various branches of the Friars Minor, done for the sake of clarity, should not suggest that their development was without tensions and conflicts. Each tends to consider itself as the only legitimate guardian of the Franciscan heritage. Thus, when Brother Charles Rapine wrote the history of the Recollects in 1631, he did not fail to point out that the Capuchins, unlike them, broke with the lineage by establishing themselves as an entirely different order. At another level, as already mentioned, arguments over dress took a particularly nasty turn in the 1620s when the Capuchins and Recollects fought about the style of their capuches.[13] The question is not so innocuous as it seems: the habit is a symbol of fidelity to Francis, but it also indicates which group of friars is begging when they go from house to house. If the capuches are too similar, the faithful's alms might end up in a bag for which they were not intended. As this example shows, rivalries are exacerbated by each of the branch's arguments for its right to exist which are linked with different interpretations of the Rule. In the sixteenth century in particular, the Italian Observants had to deal with a real hemorrhage of friars who went to the Capuchins, and whom the Roman authorities easily permitted to change orders, since they opted for a more severe rule.[14] In seventeenth-century France, establishing new friaries became the major point of contention between the Friars Minor. Establishing a new community that begs alms meant that those friars already present in the city would have to share the faithful's generosity and that could eventually lead to a reduction in the size of their communities. When the Capuchins were the first to arrive in a city, which was often the case, they sometimes tried to convince the municipal authorities to prevent the Recollects from settling there. Nor could the Recollects count on the support of the Observants, who had not forgotten the time when these troublesome friars tried to take over their friaries.[15] Seventeenth-century France seemed to have an overabundance of Friars

13. Meyer, *Pauvreté et assistance spirituelle,* 131–133.

14. Bernard Domnier, « Les séductions de la vie capucine entre XVIe et XVIIe siècle. Autour des demandes de changement d'habit », in *Identités franciscaine,* eds. Frédéric Meyer and Ludovic Viallet, 185–207.

15. Meyer, *Pauvreté et assistance spirituelle,* 52–63.

Minor, which created a situation that was not conducive to peaceful relations between them.

SHARING LINES

Considering several fundamental issues not only permits us to identify the distinctive features of each of the constituent groups of the Franciscan family but it also emphasizes the major options of the whole Order. It is in this way that we see the Friars Minor's unity and diversity.

POVERTY

As a whole, the Franciscans distinguish themselves from most other orders by a particularly demanding poverty. This obviously concerns their use of money as well as the building and design of friaries and even their habit. The most austere friars wore threadbare and patched habits and went without shoes and used clogs or sandals. In 1563 the Council of Trent granted collective possession of property to all mendicants, with the explicitly stated exception of the Observants and the Capuchins.[16] Thereafter, the Conventuals saw their position on ownership strengthened and practiced poverty with less severity. The Capuchins and Observants lived on alms, although mendicancy and poverty were not the same for each. The Observants, who had long been living in cities and often in large friaries, did not have to contend with the problems created by building new friaries in new locations. They also benefitted from a strong network of benefactors who left bequests in exchange for burial in their churches, or who contributed to the decoration of their churches, and who paid for masses said by the friars. The Observants also had the right to amass alms. All of this ultimately ensured them of a relative material security. The Recollects and Capuchins lived in a poverty that often bordered on destitution. This situation should not be attributed to a lack of support from the social elites since over time these two families, especially the Capuchins, found a good part of their vocations from among them. Rather it is a question of choice to live poverty to the fullest, which was precisely stated in their respective Constitutions. The Recollects' constitutions formally forbade "storing up wheat during the harvest, since this is contrary to most

---

16. « The holy council grants permission to own goods and money, in the future, to all monasteries and houses, both men and women, even Mendicants and those who, by their constitutions, could not possess any . . . with the exception of the houses of the religious of St. Francis, Capuchins, and those called Minors of the Observance." This is a translation of Albert Michel, *Les décrets du concile de Trente* [Charles-Joseph Hefele, *Histoire des conciles d'après les documents originaux*, trad. fr. Henri Leclercq, X] (Paris, Letouzey and Ané, 1938), 601.

high poverty."[17] Their conventual buildings, often rudimentary constructions, were sparsely furnished. The friars' daily subsistence was ensured mainly, if not exclusively, by begging, hence it was necessary to stop receiving novices when the faithful's charity did not permit the upkeep of a larger community. The Capuchins were forbidden to receive alms in money and the mere handling of coins was a fault; the principle was similar for the Recollects ("receive neither silver nor money, neither by us nor by any person as a go-between"[18]), but the practice was a little bit more flexible since it explicitly allowed the use of "spiritual friends" to buy what was provided for in the begging:

> Since we have two main means of providing for our needs, the first by begging for things in kind, the other by having others pay merchants for the cost of goods, we undoubtedly want always to try the first, even if we foresee that what we are asking for cannot be had without money.[19]

For the Recollects, however, the guardian of the friary could only ask the friend to make a precise purchase and not generally delegate this power to friends. The brothers who took the liberty to accept or solicit money on their own initiative were punished as "appropriators." The same Constitutions also expressed a "horror of financial offerings that could be made in the churches . . . for masses, sermons, confreries and pardons; and for the coffers, boxes and bowls which could be placed there to receive the said offerings."[20] The Capuchins were no less insistent in this regard, even if, on both sides, the practice of accepting offerings for masses gradually took root.

Beyond the rejection of property itself, the most austere Franciscans advocated the use of property in a poor way; that is to say, they barred everything that resembled appropriation. Consequently, they refused provisions, there were no locks and keys (especially in the friars' cells), and even cloakrooms were reduced to a minimum. The Capuchins had only two tunics; and it was the same for the Recollects who were "clothed with worn habits," and even when these were new, had to cover them with "old pieces taken from tunics or habits that were worn out."[21] These different requirements were

---

17. Unless otherwise stated, our references to the Recollects' Constitutions refer to the book entitled *Les statuts généraux de Barcelone pour la famille cismontaine de l'ordre de N. Père Sainct François, reveus, reçues et approuvez en la Congrégations générale tenue à Ségovie l'an 1621 [...] Traduits de latin en françois, et accomodez à l'étroite Observance et aux usages de Récollets de la province de S. Denys en France, du consentement de toute la mesme province [...] et tout de nouveau en [...] l'an 1660* (Rouen, Jean Machuel, 1663); here, p. 120.

18. *General Statutes*, p. 57.

19. *General Statutes*, p. 58.

20. *Ibid.*, pp. 61–62.

21. *Ibid.*, p. 84.

Friar minor Capuchin without mantle.

justified spiritually, as explained in the Capuchins' Constitutions where the detachment from goods is presented as a way to perfection: the friars must "be poor of earthly things so that they may be rich in divine grace, holy virtues and heavenly riches."[22] The distance from the world cultivated by "disappropriation" as well as contempt for the body, to which only minimal care was granted, were further coupled with an annihilation of one's own will which ensured total obedience to superiors. Poverty was thus the key to the imitation of Francis and, through him, of Christ.

COMMUNITIES

Many Franciscan friaries were located at the gates of cities, especially if they were recent establishments. The first explanation for the location of these friaries is that walls encircled the dense urban space; but, more generally, this location was a choice that permitted the friars to preserve a spirit of withdrawal—or recollection—without reducing the possibilities of apostolates and begging. The size of communities varied considerably, even within the same

22. Constitutions of 1643, ch. 4, cited from the French edition: *Les Constitutions de FF. Mineurs Capucins de S. François, approuvées et confirmées par nostre Saint Père le Pape Urbains VIII* (Paris, Denys Thierry, 1645), 32.

religious family. Generally speaking, however, small friaries were favored by the branches of the Order which observed the strictest poverty, since they permitted finding sustenance without imposing lengthy excursions on those begging. Capuchins and Recollects thought that the optimal number of friars was twelve, and that the community could thus be "fed with . . . daily alms without tiring the begging friars by having them go continuously to the countryside and without harassing the benefactors too much."[23] There were, however, exceptions in large cities, such as the Capuchin friary in Palermo which had 100 friars in 1650. The Observants, and especially the Capuchins and Recollects, also had small houses, which were not subject to the same regime as ordinary friaries. They were intended for friars who wanted, more or less permanently, to devote themselves to recollection and an intense spiritual life, and they are called houses of recollection, hermitages or hospices.[24] Among the Capuchins in particular, they are also sometimes called missions and are associated with the apostolates in territories where it was not possible to maintain a community because of hostile opposition to begging, for example where the majority of the population was Reformed church.

Contrary to a prevailing image that the Franciscans were always on the road, begging or carrying out an apostolate, the majority of the friars were quite stable. Although the Capuchins were less stable than the Conventuals (who did not change friaries during their lifetime), most of the Capuchins never went beyond the limits of the province in which they took their habit, and seldom even beyond the custody, or internal subdivision, of the province where they were recruited. Changes in assignment were made at chapters, and only exceptionally were there transfers from one custody to another. Only the friars who had important administrative responsibilities in the Order (members of the general or provincial curias, custodies attending general chapters . . .) or who held preaching commitments throughout the kingdom were allowed to make journeys without returning the same evening to their usual residence. The Franciscans were first and foremost the men of a particular territory, which was usually that of their birthplace. Local patriotism was apparent even among themselves, as was evidenced by the conflicts between Capuchins of different "nations" within the same province; for example, between the Burgundians and the Francs-Comtois when they both belonged to the Lyon Province. A large number of friaries and friars confined to a particular region was advantageous for apostolates: preachers and missionaries knew their audience and their devotional practices; and when

23. *General Statutes*, p. 79.

24. See in particular Benedikt Mertens, « Retraite annuelle et survivance du rêve de la solitude chez les Frères mineurs de la première moitié du XVIIe siècle », in Ludovic Viallet and Frédéric Meyer, *Le silence du cloître,* 157–175.

necessary, they could also speak the local dialects. The general practice, if not the rule, was largely *stabilitas.*

STUDY

Although he presented himself as illiterate, Francis of Assisi nevertheless authorized Antony of Padua to teach, and *studia* were quickly established within the Order. But the entire history of the Friars Minor is fraught with an ambivalent approach to study. For some friars, study appeared to be a violation of the rule of poverty and a source of pride. For them, the call to conversion, which is at the heart of the friars' preaching, does not require the accumulation of knowledge, but rather a spirit of prayer. In opposition to them, there was also a current of thought within Franciscanism that was favorable to acquiring knowledge and which was seen as indispensable for the apostolate. During the modern era, this requirement was reinforced to fight effectively against Protestantism. The Capuchins, who had not at first set up study centers, established them in the sixteenth century. Comparing successive versions of their Constitutions bears witness to their evolution.[25] Those of 1536 and 1552 comment only on the major themes of chapter 9 of the Rule of St. Francis, relating to preachers, who were to proclaim Christ crucified and to teach "vices and virtues, punishment and glory" while relying on Scripture. The question of studies only appears at the end of this chapter of the Constitutions where, regarding the qualities required of students, it is insisted that priority be given to their spiritual formation. In the Constitutions of 1575, the structure of the chapter did not change, but the passage on the content of studies was expanded by a few lines. The study of "sciences necessary for understanding scholastic theology" (this is the first subtle mention of a theological formation) was added to the requirements of a knowledge of grammar and Holy Scripture. There was also a marginal reference to the Council of Trent's decree concerning the "reforms on teaching and preaching."[26] The 1608 edition, however, profoundly reworked the structure of chapter 9. It now began with prescriptions relating to studies,

25. For this comparison, we use *Constititutions ordinis Fratrum Minorum Capucinorum saeculorum decursu promulgatae,* I. *Constitutions antique* (Roma, Curia generalis OFM Cap, 1980). According to the Constitutions of Albacina already mentioned, the order revised these legislative texts in 1536, 1552, 1575, 1608, 1638, 1643. The last Constitutions remained in force until 1909.

26. Albert Michel, *Les décrets du concile de Trente,* p. 6061. The bull *Triumphantis* of March 14, 1587, comes a bit later to encourage the Capuchins to study scholastic theology to combat doctrinal errors (For the legislative evolution of the order, Venantius a Lisle-en-Rigault, *Monumenta ad constitiones ordins Fratrum Minorum Capuccinorum pertinantia* (Roma, Curia Generalis, 1916); 471.

firmly emphasized the importance for the friars to make use of studies to save souls, and again referred to the decrees of the Council of Trent.[27] The place given to study evolved in accordance with the Order's increasing commitment to the Catholic counter reformation. Formation requirements responded to the needs of an apostolate, and thus only the brothers who participated in an apostolate to save souls received a complete course of studies. The Capuchins thus distinguished two permanent categories among their clerical brothers: the simple priests (*sacerdotes*), whose formation was reduced (since the Order did not hear confession of the laity, the study of moral theology was unnecessary); and preachers (*praedicatores*), who alone were entitled to a complete course in philosophy and theology. In seventeenth-century France, the preachers became more numerous than the simple priests, undoubtedly a sign that studies enjoyed greater favor, but also that the title of preacher was more sought-after. In the Recollect provinces, the houses of studies also welcomed only a part of the newly professed—those who were "of not too advanced an age, of good morals, of good mind and capable of learning what the Order wants them to study."[28] Although the documentation is less abundant than for the Capuchins, everything seems to indicate that the two families adopted a similar attitude.

Recitation of the office and mental prayer

The Rule of St. Francis counsels the friars to adopt the Roman office both in content and *ritus servandus*. Although it does not specify singing, choirs are probably taken for granted since small communities quickly dispensed of them which would indicate that it was usual elsewhere. In the fifteenth century, the practice of mental prayer developed and was often accompanied by a decline in singing in favor of a simple recitation of the office. From that moment on, a kind of rule developed: the more radical the reform, the less music, including ecclesiastical singing, was practiced.[29] Thus, the reform movements that were part of the Strict Observance tend to replace singing by simple chanting. This was the case with the Recollects, whose Constitutions generally do not discuss the question very much. The Province of Lyon's

---

27. *Constitutions ordinis,* I, pp. 263–264. The next edition of the Constitutions, in 1638, provides further details: the study of philosophy for three years, theology for four: the latter will favor St. Bonaventure or St. Thomas (*Constitutiones ordines,* I, p. 393).

28. *General Statutes,* p. 106.

29. On these questions, Fabien Guilloux, *Les Frères mineurs et la musique en France (1550–1700),* Doctoral thesis, University of Tours, 2006. See also by the same author, "Les livres de chants des Récollets," in *Les Recollets,* eds. Caroline Galland, Fabien Guilloux and Pirre Moracchini, 277–302.

Constitutions of 1630 specify, however, that the masses celebrated in the friary churches, with the exception of a few high feasts—are low masses without singing.[30] As for the office itself, the order had been clearly defined as early as the statutes of 1595: "Although the rite of the singing of the office is pious and was instituted and introduced by our holy fathers, yet so that the friars of our houses of retreat can devote themselves more freely to prayer and contemplation, they should be chanted devoutly."[31] However, as this text suggests, the practice varied according to the types of houses.

Details abound about mental prayer and are precisely codified. Depending upon the province, the friars devoted themselves to between two and a half to three hours per day, divided into three sequences, of which the two longest were after Lauds and after Vespers or Compline. Prayer took place in the church and began with a friar reading for a "half-quarter of an hour" at the pulpit from a book meant to evoke piety. Each friar then knelt in his place and began his silent meditation. The statutes added that "at the time of mental prayer, the friar is not allowed to pray vocally, or to read a book, or to leave without the permission of the one who presides over the choir."[32] To the third sequence of daily mental prayer, which was the shortest and at the end of the day, just before Prime, was added an examination of conscience. In the seventeenth century, however, the daily time devoted to meditation was decreased, while there was corresponding increase of singing the office.[33] The chapter of 1686 prescribed the use of plainchant on Sundays and feasts in large friaries, and the chapter of 1698 extended it even further.

In this regard, the Capuchins' practice of not singing the office but chanting it appears very close to that of the Recollects.[34] Their Constitutions, moreover, asked them to give themselves to mental prayer twice a day for an hour each time and reminded them that to pray was "to speak to God with the heart." This was why it was necessary to "strive to make prayer more mental than vocal. Devotional services, which had been added to daily prayer, were also prohibited "so that the friars would have more time to devote

30. « Omnes missae Etiam conventuales, quibusvis diebus submissa voce, almost privatae (ut jam dictum est) sine nota, sine ullo CantuSine altiori tono (ut loquemur) celebrentur » (*Constitutions and statua Fratrum Minorum Recollectorum provincial Sancti Francisci in Gallia,* Lyon, Jean Aimé Candy, 1630, p. 84).

31. Quoted by Achille Léon, *History of the order,* 86.

32. General *Statutes,* pp. 47–48.

33. On these developments, see Frédéric Meyer, *Pauvreté et assistance spirituelle,* 229–231.

34. In addition to the works of Fabien Guilloux already mentioned, see Jean Mauzaize, *Le rôle et l'action,* I., 283–306.

Lodovico of Gimignani (1643–1697), *Saint Peter of Alcantara in ecstasy before the Cross* (detail), seventeenth century. Oil on canvas, Palais Fesch, Fine Arts Museum, Ajaccio, Corsica.

themselves to personal and mental prayer which was much more fruitful than vocal."[35] Bovius, their chronicler, justified meditation by the desire to conform to the ancient anchorites' practice. But, as with the Recollects, the singing of the office made at least a modest breakthrough in the seventeenth century which was probably indicative of a reduction in the time devoted to mental prayer.

The sway of asceticism

The statutes and constitutions of the Recollects and Capuchins clearly indicated that these two reforms put forth an ascetic interpretation of Franciscanism which resounded of contempt for the body and the world that the Catholic Reformation had established as a condition for salvation. Significantly the iconography of Francis of Assisi made him a hermit with an emaciated body and livid complexion, meditating on a skull in the solitude of the woods or mountains, or weakened after an ecstasy and appearing as an

35. Translations from *Constitutiones ordinis*, I. pp. 164–165 (Constitutions of 1575). This text has few differences from those of 1536 and 1552.

"exhausted figure with a death pallor."[36] The models that these two reforms chose to honor and exalt corresponded to the same ideal. The first beatified Capuchin was not a minister general, a fearless missionary, or an illustrious preacher, but the humble brother Felix Cantalice, who for forty years walked the streets of Rome collecting alms for his community. He was an illiterate friar, dressed in a patched habit, who fed on bread scraps and spent his nights in prayer in the friary church. He died in 1587 and was beatified in 1622.[37] The Recollects, in the absence of a saint or blessed from their ranks,[38] willingly saw themselves reflected in Peter of Alcantara, a key figure of the Strict Observance in Spain, who was also beatified in 1622 and who can also be considered an ascetic hero. To convince themselves, they only had to leaf through the biography published by François Courtot in 1670. The tone was established in the portrait presented in the "Preface to the reader":

> Because he always went about bare headed, the sun had burned his skin and had tanned him so much that he had a dark complexion close to that of a Negro. He had sunken eyes, his forehead was full of wrinkles, his lips were pursed. He was so much skin and bones that he was taken for a skeleton. There was almost no flesh on his arms and legs, his hands and feet resembled tree roots spread out and dried by the sun. His great austerities had made him so dissimilar to other men that he had only their most general facial features and characteristics. . . . He surpassed what we read of the old anchorites and new cenobites by his austerities. . . . I believe that his special character resides in making the religious of St. Francis know that the perfection to which their holy rules can raise them is boundless, limitless, without measure.[39]

Throughout this work, we are frequently brought back to his increasing practice of scourging. It is explained that, shortly after his profession, he

> built a little out-of-the-way cell with tree branches and dirt, to which he would retire during the day and practice the greatest mortifications, without fear of being seen or heard by other religious.

---

36. Émile Mâle, *L'art religieux de la fin du XVIe siècle, du XVIIe siècle et du XVIIIe siècle. Étude sur l'iconographie après le concile de Trente,* Paris, Armand Colin, 1972, p. 200.

37. His canonization did not occur until 1712. About Felix de Cantalice as a model of Capuchin life, see Bernard Domnier, « Félix de Cantalice ou la vie religieuse comme art de la *simplicitas* » in *Les arts de la simplicitas. Rome à la fin de la Renaissance*, ed. Carlo Ossola.

38. The first Recollect canonized is Joachim de Sainte-Anne, martyred in England in 1679 and raised to the altars only in 1970, after being beatified in 1929.

39. Francis Courtot, *La vie de saint Pierre d'Alcantara, religieux de l'ordre de saint François, tirée de differens auteurs,* Paris, Antoine Bertier, 1670, "Avis au lecteur," no pagination.

> But despite the efforts he made to conceal himself, we heard him shouting his prayers in loud cries several times, we saw him use the discipline pitilessly, we even saw that he carried a tin cilice pierced in several places so that the inward turned points constantly tore his skin.[40]

With such a model, there is no doubt that, as a historian of the Friars Minor wrote, there was an "increase of austerities" in the Reformed branches during the period from 1550 to 1650.[41]

The quest for personal salvation was the friars' main motivation: the observance of the Rule constituted a sure path to perfection by the austerities it imposed as well as by the intensity of the spiritual life it proposed. The ideal that animated these reforms was effectively to make the friars "brothers to the angels"[42] by having them flee the world and live entirely turned towards divine contemplation. The pages of the Recollects' Constitutions, devoted to leaving the friary, indicated the real shame that outside contact represented: journeys and pilgrimages were described as sources of "scandals, annoyances and great threats to the regular discipline." Superiors were also asked "to preserve a spirit of contemplation for the friars, as well as a true detachment from secular affairs, visits to relatives, friendships, walks, and recreation. Every friar was obliged to this and would rarely leave the friary."[43] In a way, the prevailing climate during the Catholic Reformation tended to make all orders embrace the monastic ideal, even if they had an apostolic dimension. Within Franciscanism, the Capuchins and the Recollects were certainly the most affected by this dominant conception of religious life. Their interpretation of Francis was more permeated with this notion than was that of the friars in the older branches of the Order: if there was any truth in this notion of Francis, it is doubtful that it was attained.

A more nuanced reality

Without taking away anything from the overall picture that has just been presented, it is necessary, nevertheless, to add some nuances to times and locations. Religious historiography has always cautioned against implementing initial high ideals or those that animated phases of reform. It has often emphasized that periods of "decadence" alternate with these moments of religious scrupulosity. This is too simplistic. Considering the history of orders

---

40. Francis Courtot, *La vie de saint Pierre d'Alcantara,* 15.

41. Achille Leon, *Histoire de l'ordre,* 72.

42. The formula is borrowed from the Capuchin Bernardi of Paris, *Le parfait novice instruit des voyes qu'il doit tenir pour arriver à la perfection de son estat* (Paris, Denys Thierry, 1648), 484.

43. *General Statutes,* p. 123.

in terms of a swinging of the pendulum with its highs and lows arises mostly from the ways we have thought about writing this history: that is, to draw lessons from past models for present and future generations. Consequently, the only periods really worthy of interest were those of intense fervor in perfect conformity to the founder's charisma—those "glorious pages" which stood out in a long history, most of which should have been dealt with more humbly.

Such an approach to the past is profoundly unfair to the thousands of religious who have not had the chance to live with founding "heroes" or reformers, but who have nevertheless chosen the same habit and followed the same Rule. Their assumed individual and collective faults are baseless: individually, each of these "unknowns" has often adapted to the regular life prevalent at the time of his profession; collectively, they merely adapted to new contexts that generally allowed the common heritage to be saved and transmitted.

At the same time, we have to recognize, without any moral judgement, how those generations struggled to renew original ideals and to transmit them to the following generations. Bit by bit, fervor frequently turned into a series of formal observances which blurred the profound significance of the reform. Moreover, the very success of the reform was often a pitfall for them because it required contending with various challenges. The friars who had already taken the habit and a specific lifestyle had to undertake a new way of living in accord with the expectations of a disproportionately large number of new recruits. They struggled to avoid slipping into "monasticism"[44] and to safeguard the equality between lay brothers and priests, which was fundamental to Franciscan life. In this regard, it is probably not insignificant that, among the Recollects, in 1625, the lay brothers lost the "passive voice" that allowed them to be elected to functions of responsibility.

Among the Capuchins, the French provinces struggled a few years later to maintain the same rights for all brothers, priests or non-priests, to which the Order's authorities wanted to return.[45] For the French Capuchins, many of the transformations just mentioned became evident from the 1660s and 1670s onwards. The adoption of conventional explanations of vocations wiped out the distinguishing features of the Capuchin experience. The heated historiographical activity of the same time indicated a somewhat desperate attempt to preserve the original memory of the [Capuchin] Order. Although it is not the only explanation, the great demographic crisis that the Capuchins

44. By this we mean the adoption of communal rules of functioning, which reduce the defining qualities of the order into a standard model that implicitly imposes the experience of a number of friars on each friary.

45. Bernard Domnier, « Humilité, égalité fraternité. Le conflit du 'suffrage universel' chez les capucins du XVIIe siècle », in *Temps, culture, religion. Autour de Jean-Pierre Massaut* (Brussels, Nauwelaerts, 2004), 208–223.

experienced in the 1630s certainly played a decisive role in changing their situation. The friars' care of plague victims contributed to the disappearance of a large part of the older religious who had been in contact with the friars who introduced the Order into France. Consequently, the many novices who flocked to the doors of the friaries to fill the vacant places (as the Order's apostolate to the "infected" increased in popularity) were undoubtedly deprived of formators who could pass on the Capuchin community's identity. As the saying goes, the success of an order is not without its price.

As the above example shows, an order also lives with the different circumstances of the times in the country where it is expanding, especially in an era when communications are relatively slow. The same religious family adapts, either by choice or necessity, to the context in which it is immersed. The historian's account, whose task is limited to accounting for and trying to understand the processes at work, has no place for moral assessments. The survival of the Order, which must be accepted by the society in which it develops, depends fundamentally on its ability to adapt, which is all the more apparent for the communities who obtain their sustenance principally from the generosity of the faithful. It should be added that the Friars Minor are particularly experienced in the diverse ways of living their ideal. Since the Middle Ages, the many branches of the Order have often been linked to territories. This is clearly shown by the Observant development which was a pluralistic phenomenon made up of multiple initiatives that appeared in various countries, driven by similar demands, but also finding particular forms of expression.[46] In the modern era, the Strict Observants also took on different expressions in Spain, Italy and France despite their similar features. It is certainly possible to write a history of the Capuchins who—like the Observants—were widespread throughout the Catholic world, which is based on their Constitutions and General Chapter decisions which reflect the unity and foundational elements of the Order; however, the diversity of ways of understanding and living their common identity should not be overlooked.

Even between the two countries where the Order was the oldest and most firmly rooted—Italy and France—many differences can be observed. In Italy, friaries were often smaller than in France, clericalization was more prevalent, and acceptance of the Baroque culture was quicker.[47] Most importantly, there

---

46. Once again, we must refer here to Frédéric Meyer and Ludovic Viallet, *Identités franciscaines.*

47. French Capuchin, Archange de Bourbon-Lancy's, portrayal of his illustrious Italian colleague, Marc d'Aviano, during his passing through Lyon in June 1681, conveys an interesting example of this difference (Bernard Domnier, « Quand passe un thaumaturge (Lyon, 1681). Autour des perceptions de la réputation de sainteté », in *Foi, fidélité, amitié en Europe à l'époque moderne. Mélanges offerts à Robert Sauzet* (Tours, PU, 1995, t. I), 159–170.

were profoundly divergent interpretations between the two countries on the Franciscan call to apostolates: the French Capuchins were on the front line in both foreign and internal missions; their Italian brothers were extremely reserved regarding their presence among populations that had to be educated and converted.

PRESENCE IN THE WORLD. THE FRANCISCAN APOSTOLATE

The Franciscans certainly have a very ancient apostolic tradition, since the Rule of 1223 already provided for the friars to go among the Saracens and other infidel. Admittedly, it was not strictly speaking a sending out by order since it was an individual initiative, but nevertheless the superiors had to approve these trips. The situation changed considerably in the modern era due to particularly new challenges. In less than a century, between the mid-fifteenth and the middle of the following century, the known world expanded considerably and consequently it was necessary to bring the Catholic faith to the newly discovered peoples; evangelization was even used to justify conquests. This new situation was an incentive for the Friars Minor, among whom were millennialists. Their vision was linked to a reconfiguration of the world and they saw themselves as instruments for the regeneration of the Church[48] who were to work as quickly as possible for the conversion of the Gentiles. A second challenge concerned the old Christian lands, where the Protestant Reformation's expansion called for the beginning of a spiritual renewal of [Catholic] territories and populations. Heresy was certainly a familiar phenomenon to men of the Church, but the movement launched by Martin Luther broke with everything that was known until then both by the extent of its expansion, hastened by printed communication, and by a strongly rooted societal support of princes. The result was a defiance of pontifical authority and supporters to which Rome was not accustomed. The importance of both challenges necessarily led to revising the ideas and methods of undertaking apostolates; the modern era would be the first blossoming of missions.

THE PLAYERS AND THEIR STAGE. THE NEW WORLDS

At the risk of oversimplification and to put the missions within a global context at the same time as identifying their particular characteristics, we present only a few aspects of the rich history of Franciscan missions in the

48. Georges Baudot, *Utopie et histoire au Mexique. Les premiers chroniqueurs de la civilisation mexicaine* (Toulouse, Privat, 1977).

modern era.[49] When the kings of Spain and Portugal established their respective empires, they laid the foundations for an ecclesiastical infrastructure which was a task expected of them under the so-called "patronage" system. The majority of missionaries and parish priests were provided by the religious of the peninsula among whom were twelve Franciscans (the same number as the Apostles) who were present in Mexico as early as 1524, and the first archbishop of Mexico was a Franciscan (1528). Even if they were not the only ones, reform-loving friars swelled the ranks of the religious who crossed the ocean. They were particularly motivated by the hope of implementing their idea of renewing religious life more easily by distancing themselves from provincial authority. The Franciscan, Luis de Bolanos, and his companions should be given credit for beginning the first "reductions"[50] in Paraguay in 1580. The history of the missions in the Spanish and Portuguese empires was not only recorded in heroic accounts but reached into the depths of everyday realities. The development of missions was often linked with the Franciscans, some of whom were opposed to the greedy diocesan priests who loved comfort and luxury and who aligned themselves with the colonists and were hard on the Indians. The friars' opposition to the dominant clergy's behavior gave rise to the creolization of their recruitment.

In the territories where France undertook discovery and colonization expeditions, Recollects and Capuchins, along with the Jesuits, were the first to be present, if we discount a few diocesan priests who appear sporadically. The Recollects took part in Champlain's venture and settled in Quebec City and along the St. Lawrence after 1615.[51] This missionary experience was unpredictably short-lived, but that indicates all the more the Order's availability for distant apostolates. A few years earlier, in 1612–1615, the Capuchins, Yves d'Évreux and Claude d'Abbeville, had taken part in the short-lived Maragnan expedition to Brazil, which marked the French branch

---

49. Franciscan missions are put in perspective in Alain Milhou, « L'Amérique », in *Le temps des confessions (1530–1620)* [« Histoire du christianisme », 8], ed. Marc Venard (Paris, Desclée, 1992), 693–785. For many useful points about the French missions, see Guillaume de Vaumas, *L'éveil missionnaire de la France (d'Henri IV à la fondation du Séminaire des Missions Étrangères)* (Lyon, Imprimerie Express, 1942).

50. Translator's Note: Reductions were mission settlements established for indigenous people. According to the on-line *Catholic Encyclopedia*, "The kings of Spain having the conversion of the native peoples sincerely at heart, missionaries accompanied even the earliest expeditions to La Plata, and churches and parishes were founded in the new colony as soon as possible. Here, as elsewhere, the first pioneers of the Faith were sons of St. Francis." —https://www.newadvent.org/cathen/12688b.htm

51. Caroline Galland, *Pour la gloire de Dieu et du Roi.*

Claude d'Abbeville, *History of the Capuchin Fathers' mission on the Island of Maragnan and surrounding lands,* Paris, François Huby; 1614, frontispiece, engraving, 15.3 × 9.4 cm, John Carter Brown Library.

of the Capuchin Order's beginning commitment to the missions.[52] In the decades that followed, the Capuchins multiplied their apostolates. They gained the right to evangelize many territories through the favor of the Roman Congregation of *Propaganda Fide,* which was founded in 1622 to ensure the guardianship of the missions throughout the world, and because of their human resources, which significantly increased their differences from the Recollects. Thanks to Fathers Joseph of Paris and Pacific of Provins's close relations with the Congregation, they had a strong presence in the Levant (Constantinople, Saïda, Persia), where they wanted to establish a departure point for Armenia, India and Ethiopia. They also began missions to the Antilles (1637), Senegal (1634–1639), and again, to Cayenne.[53] In many

52. Andrea Daher, *Les Singularités de la France équinoxiale. Histoire de la mission des pères capucins au Brésil (1612–1615)* (Paris, Honoré Champion, 2002).

53. Today, historiography gives more attention to Jesuit missions (especially because of the quality of the sources), which tends to give an unbalanced picture of the presence of the various religious orders. For the details of the missionary enterprises of the Capuchin order, by territory, see: Clemente Da Terzorio, *Le missioni Dei Minori Cappuccini, Sunto Storico,* Rome Tipografia pontificia, 1913–1938, 10 vols.

cases, their settlements were not long-lasting, but the Capuchins were not discouraged and were always ready to send manpower elsewhere. The support given by the Congregation of the *Propaganda Fide* is surprising because it was known that the Congregation was not very favorable to religious missions. It considered religious insufficiently submissive to bishops and to itself. It could not, however, during the first years of its existence while it lacked staff, ignore the enthusiasm, zeal, and effectiveness of the Capuchins; and Joseph of Paris also knew perfectly well how to promote the friars.[54]

Is there a Franciscan approach to the missionary apostolate, common to the Recollects and the Capuchins, which would particularly distinguish them from the Jesuits? This is a difficult question to answer, and it is not certain that specialists fully agree on it.[55] At the very least, it is sure that all the Friars Minor share a rather optimistic view of humanity, given the limits arising from an Augustinian perspective and the Catholic Reform's exaggerated view of humanity's guilt. More so than others, they were quickly attentive to the diversity of cultures, and they invited their missionaries to "adapt themselves."

The players and their stage. Old world Christendom

As the missionary fronts were expanding, the Capuchins were also very active in the fight against Protestantism in France. This was in conformity with a sort of unspoken tight-knit agreement between them and those most committed to the Catholic Reform in the Kingdom, torn apart by the wars of religion. The support that they received to establish their friaries and the role that the friars played in organizing elite groups of devout laity confirmed this tacit agreement.[56] The first major initiatives of the Capuchins took place on the borders of French territory and at the entry to Geneva, the "Protestant Rome." Around 1600, in the Duke of Savoy's states, friar Chérubin de Maurienne came up with an ambitious project called the "holy house of Thonon," which was to be a college, a seminary and the base camp for a group of missionaries who would go into the Chablais alps. In France itself, the Capuchins' apostolate gained momentum with the Edict of Nantes and the return of civil peace, as was evident in their frequent preaching of the Forty Hours. The core missionary activity among the Protestants was expressed in an elevated practice

54. Father Joseph of Paris, "the Éminence grise," succeeded in obtaining the title of prefect of all the Capuchin missions, contrary to the order's principle which wanted the prefecture to be granted to the superior of the province on which each mission depended.

55. Various works contributing to this debate were presented at the colloquium that gave rise to this book.

56. Of particular note in this respect is the role played by Father Hyacinthe of Paris in the foundation of the Compagnie de l'Exaltation de la Croix, also known as the Propagation of the Faith (John Mauzaize, *Le rôle et l'action*, II, pp. 1068–1073).

of the Eucharistic cult and an increase in preaching. These can again be traced to Joseph of Paris who, as provincial of Touraine, organized a solemn proclamation of Catholic truths at the Protestant synod of Poitou. The example was then followed in other provinces, such as Paris, where it was decided in 1620 to create a "flying camp that was able to move wherever the enemy was found."[57] The Capuchin missionaries received support for their apostolate of battling against Protestantism in Europe.[58] But far from limiting their activity to the mere "reduction" of heretics against the Church of Rome, they quickly added to this first objective the education of ignorant Catholics who were no less in danger of damnation than the deviants of the faith.

The Recollects' way of proceeding is not greatly different from that of the Capuchins. The Recollect missionaries, usually on behalf of the Congregation of *Propaganda Fide,* were present in several territories divided by tensions and confessional clashes, such as the Cévennes during the renewal of wars under Louis XIII, Pragelato, and the Val d'Aosta. Like the Capuchins, the Recollects also moved the controversies into the struggle against confessional minorities. The missions of the two Franciscan families, however, were also different in various ways. First of all, there were fewer Recollects involved in this apostolate, doubtlessly because their human resources were more limited. Also, perhaps since they were well established in the border regions, especially in the Alps, they maintained close relations with the army, were frequently garrison chaplains, and also accompanied the troops on their campaigns.[59] It seems, as well, that the Recollects' relations with the episcopacy were less conflictual than the Capuchins'. The Recollects did not hesitate to consider themselves as auxiliaries, while the Capuchins firmly defended their exemptions and pastoral freedoms. One of the most ardent Capuchin advocates, Yves de Paris, argued the friars' cause during the long conflict of the second quarter of the seventeenth century when they were opposed to the bishops.[60] The respective numbers of the two families can again provide an explanation for this difference in attitude, which undoubtedly originated in their difference regarding the hearing of lay people's confessions. The Capuchins refused in principle, while the Recollects ordinarily did hear

57. Bernard Dompnier, « Les missions des Capucins et leur empreinte sur la Réforme catholique en France », *Revue d'histoire de l'Église de France,* 70, 1984/2, pp. 127–147.

58. We must not forget that the Congregation of *Propaganda Fide* had received, at the time of its creation in 1622, the authority for the apostolate in the "heretical" countries. Finding it difficult to impose its authority in colonial empires because of the patronage system, it devoted its best efforts for several decades to Protestant Europe.

59. On these questions, Frédéric Meyer, *Pauvreté et assistance spirituelle,* pp. 139–141 and pp. 309–313.

60. Charles Chesneau, *Le père Yves de Paris et son temps. La querelle des évêques et des réguliers* (Paris, Veuve Denys Thierry, 1662), 531.

lay people's confessions as part of their apostolate. This created closer ties with bishops who alone were able to grant the power to exercise this ministry and who were always in search of good confessors.

A final remark should be made about the Franciscan mission presence in the French countryside. The mission apostolate took root in the 1640s with a growing number of participants from the new congregations of secular priests (Lazarists, Eudists) and from the old or newer orders (Dominicans, Discalced Augustinians, Maurists). The Capuchins and Recollects were among the first to commit themselves, but they did not receive support from their Observant brothers. Among the Friars Minor, the internal missions remained the monopoly of the most recent Reformed branches, as if they alone were able to take on the new challenges of the apostolate.

The missionary vocation of the Franciscans

The Recollects and Capuchins' Constitutions were not very explicit about apostolic activities. Both offered a commentary on chapter nine of the Rule about the behavior of preachers and the content of their message; but they did not specify what other activities could or should be carried out by the friars. We can note, however, in the Capuchins' Constitutions of 1536, that there was an attraction for foreign missions since they emphasized that the New World's natives were gentle and ready to receive the faith, unlike the Saracens whom the Rule of St. Francis mentioned.[61] Therefore, we must turn to other texts and to treatises particularly related to the "bishops' quarrels with religious" to understand what the mission was. These already mentioned conflicts arose when numerous bishops wanted better control, in their dioceses, of the religious and their pastoral activity. The conflict grew from 1625–1640 when the network of friaries had become particularly dense.

The Capuchin, Yves de Paris, defended the religious saying Franciscanism was essentially a missionary vocation. This was a position that he took up again a bit later in a work which explained that Saint Francis "wanted his children to carry the truths of the Gospel throughout the world and to continue the great work of converting humanity, which the first saintly Church leaders had begun."[62] Even more, by their lifestyle, the Franciscans imitated the apostles and Christ himself, "in abandoning the things of the world. . . , in their observance of a strict poverty . . . and in their fervent preaching."[63] The

61. *Constitutiones ordinis,* I, pp. 71–72. The typical Recollect documents that we have been able to consult do not mention this.

62. Yves de Paris, *Instructions religieuses tirées des annales et chroniques de l'ordre de saint François* (Paris, Veuve Denys Thierry, 1662), 531.

63. Yves de Paris, *Les heureux succez de la piété* (Paris, Veuve N. Buon, 1633), 605.

witness of this "apostolic life" strongly contributed to the effectiveness of the friars' ministry because it gave them "more authority in people's minds since they believed their eyes and accepted a truth proven as much by results and example as by reason."[64] As we can see, poverty thus served a double function: a way to personal perfection, and also a means to convince the public to whom the friars ministered.

The Capuchin's apostolic project made the friary a place of religious retreat, or rather of renewal between their two external efforts. Wherever the apostolate, the same dialectic was at work: to make the "cloister" a place of grace which was then dispensed in the "world." "The religious intoxicated by the sweetness of God's house was not jealous of others possessing this same bliss. According to the Psalmist, these marvels flowed from his mouth, and he could not stop from telling them."[65] The attraction that drew religious to the apostolate naturally extended to distant lands: "How could people consecrated to God be lights to the world, if they only illuminated a canton, a province, or a city and let so many peoples languish in the darkness of idolatry?"[66]

To these pages, which apply to all the Friars Minor, Yves de Paris added others more particularly devoted to the Capuchins whose origins were founded on this apostolate. Only circumstances would delay the development of their mission: "[The superiors] showed them that the first steps would be to reform the Order, to preach penance to people, and then to take the Catholic reform to the Infidels. . . , and this should not be dismissed, but the mission should take place at a time when it would be more successful."[67] For Yves de Paris, it was perfectly legitimate that the friars, faithful to a vocation inherited from their founder, be present in all areas of the apostolate, in Europe as well as among the populations needing to be evangelized. The actual practice sometimes pointed out the difficulty of harmonizing the mission with the ideals of religious life.

THE DANGER OF OUTWARD EXPANSION[68]

The Capuchins' Constitutions were aware that apostolic activities could give rise to neglecting and abandoning observance of the Rule. Their development on the subject of preachers always contained warnings about

64. Y. de Paris, *ibid*, 673–674.

65. Y. de Paris, *ibid*, 601.

66. Y. de Paris, *ibid*, 690.

67. Yves de Paris, *Instructions religieuses*, 535–536.

68. The formula is borrowed from Michel de Certeau, who writes about similar problems with the Jesuits in « La réforme de l'intérieur au temps d'Aquaviva, 1581–1615 », in *Les Jésuites. Spiritualité et activités. Jalons d'une histoire* (Paris, Beauchesne, 1974), 63.

possible deviation from the usual norms. The friars charged with a preaching ministry were thus reminded that they should deviate as little as possible from the obligations of fasting, of attendance at office, and especially of keeping poverty; in addition, a period of retreat was mandatory after a preaching mission. Although the Order seems to have taken all the necessary precautions to assure that the apostolate would not be in conflict with the Rule, some superiors demonstrated a strong mistrust of the usual types of activities, as was seen at the beginning of the seventeenth century in the missions to the Protestant countries.[69] Religious who were involved in the Alpine region made known their grievances to the Congregation of *Propaganda Fide* about their provincials who did not listen to their requests for reinforcement, did not recommend them to the prayers of the province's friaries, and even considered them to be gyrovagues trying to escape from communal life. Ignazio Bergamasco, a missionary in Valtellina during the 1620s, was so discouraged that he considered abandoning his apostolate to return "to the solitude of his friary," that is, to a quiet daily routine.

This division over missions was particularly noticeable at that time in the [Capuchin] Provinces of Genoa and Milan. In 1604 the provincial of Genoa, who had reservations about this apostolate, consulted Santi Tesauro, the Order's leading expert on interpreting the Rule. He gave a nuanced response saying that the purpose of missions was certainly good since it concerned increasing the honor of God and saving souls, but one should not overlook the risks that religious incurred by taking on this work. According to Santi Tesauro, "no one is obliged to put his personal salvation in danger, and one can even produce bad things while hoping to bring about good things."[70] If it were certain that the Rule could not be kept in a particular situation, the friars should not go on mission, even if it meant disobeying their superior's orders because only the Pope can dispense the Rule's obligations for a particular situation. Santi Tesauro's response along with other documents makes it possible to identify more clearly three of the main grievances on which the reluctance to undertake missions were based. The first had to do with dress, or more precisely with the need to wear winter shoes in certain mountainous regions. The second lay in the risk to chastity because the friars

69. On this internal contoversy, see Bernard Dompnier, « Tensions et conflits autour des missions chez les Capucins du XVIIe siècle », in *Religione, conflittualità et cultura. Il clero regolare nell'Europa d'antico regime,* ed. Massimo Carlo Giannini (Rome Bulzoni, 2006) [Cheiron. Materiali e strumenti di aggiornamento storiografico, 43–44], 159–184.

70. The full text of the response is reproduced in Costanzo Cargoni, *I Frati Cappuccini. Documenti e testimonianze del primo secolo,* III/2 (Perugia, EFL, 1991) 4315–4319 (here, p. 4315). The end of the quotation, in Latin ("Non sunt facienda mala ut veniant bona") corresponds to an adage common among jurists, taken from Saint Paul's Epistle to the Romans, 3, 8.

lacked their own residences. Finally, the ideal of poverty was damaged because it was impossible to beg in hostile territories and because the religious were obliged to build up reserves and to handle money, especially since they sometimes had to accept the functions of parish priests. During the first decades of the seventeenth century, in the provinces of northern Italy, this conflict was solved, either openly or tacitly, by various measures that came to be applied to the whole Order. A new type of "missionary friary" was created: it was exempted from the general rule of poverty; the friars employed in the apostolate were rigorously scrutinized; and there was a blurring of the specific characteristics required of the missionary which were codified and began to be assimilated into preaching.

These Italian disputes present another interesting aspect of the Capuchin's history, since they again make it possible to verify the countries' differences in understanding the Rule. In Italy there was an enduring reticence against missions, since, in addition to the reasons already mentioned, they were thought to disturb the friars' prayer life, particularly because they led to the ministry of hearing confessions. Additionally, although the needs of the Church might have made it necessary to preach in Protestant territory, the Italian friars were not allowed to preach in the entirely Catholic regions, that is to say in almost the entire peninsula. It was only in a letter written in 1676 that the Minister General formally approved *inter fideles* missions. The French approach, as revealed in Yves de Paris's treatises, did not bother with legalities and insisted on the apostolate's spiritual dimensions which were seen as producing a life of intense prayer and not as being an obstacle. Beyond expressing various sensibilities, these two conceptions reflected the tension between contemplative withdrawal and active apostolate which is at the heart of the Friars Minor's vocation, and particularly that of its reformed branches during the modern era, which was a time when desires and expectations were great in both camps. According to Yves of Paris's reasoning, the friar best suited for a fruitful apostolate was the one who preferred to devote himself to contemplation and was not spontaneously inclined to an apostolate. The intensity of his inner life made him particularly fit for external apostolates, and his acceptance of the work would be a sign that he renounced his own will, and it would lead to perfection.[71] The dialectic of "inner" and "outer"[72] was very complex. There was no evidence that the Recollects experienced this tension as intensely as the Capuchins. But their presence on missionary fronts suggests that some would have had discussions similar to those of the Capuchins.[73]

---

71. Yves de Paris, *Instructions religieuses,* 200.

72. Here again I use Michel de Certeau's terms to define the poles of the tension that he saw among the Jesuits.

73. Once again, we can only regret the lack of research on the Recollects.

Franciscan devotions

The history of worship always comprises two aspects in religious orders. On the one hand, the order's practices of worship identify it, bond the friars in their community, and shape the external image of order. On the other hand, in keeping ancient devotions and by disseminating new ones, the order recalls the religious family's role. We should realize, however, that innovation of devotions is a complex process. Attaining the objective of having a feast inscribed in the universal calendar and entering the proper office of the Roman breviary requires strong determination on the part of its promoters. The process usually begins with a devotion limited to a geographic region. The Congregation of Rites then approves it as a feast with its own office, and it is granted limited space in the calendar and its practice is restricted at first to one or more religious houses, or one or more provinces. Finally, it receives approval for larger territories, extending to one or more entire orders or to kingdoms. Throughout this process (which sometimes ends before the devotion attains universal acceptance), following others' procedures plays an important role, as is evident in the petitions addressed to the Congregation of Rites, which usually mention the favors already granted to other applicants. As can be imagined, religious orders have significant means, under the best conditions, to overcome various obstacles such as an important presence in Rome, the possibility of deciding in general chapter on the promotion of a cult by all the provinces, and the opportunity to send large numbers of supplications frequently, along with sovereigns' support of their devotional initiatives. . . . But it usually takes time for the full process to be completed.

During the Catholic Reformation, only devotions such as those of Saint Joseph, the Guardian Angels, the Sacred Heart, or the Poor Souls in Purgatory, which were deeply in accord with the Church's models of Christian life, were promoted quickly. In such cases, the devotion was advanced not by a single promoter but by several replicating one another, and Rome considered these requests with particular benevolence. Furthermore, it was also more difficult for Rome to limit each order's involvement in the growth of the devotion. Thus, it would be difficult to define exactly how much the success of the cult of Saint Joseph in the seventeenth century owes to the Franciscans, who are but one of its ardent promoters.

Mostly, during the modern era, the Friars Minor's worship and devotions corresponded to a heritage necessarily shared by all branches of the family. The unity of devotion was reflected in the almost complete fusion of the modern era's liturgical calendars: all the friars celebrated all the saints of the three Franciscan Orders, regardless of the particular habit worn by each of them.[74] The details of the Order's diverse composition were less important than the ways of sharing the devotion of certain saints with the laity, or the ways of accommodating a devotion (for example, for guilds where a saint's patronage is different from the Order's promulgation). The Capuchins and Recollects' locations seldom served as the base for lay associations. For these two families who claimed strict observance, the friary had to be preserved as a place of recollection or retreat, which led to limiting the laity's presence, even in the places devoted to worship. According to their Constitutions, only the Third Order and the Archconfraternity of the Cord of St. Francis were allowed in the Recollect churches.[75]

THE GREAT SUBJECTS OF DEVOTION[76]

The devotion to the Passion, which was rooted in Francis's own experience of the stigmata, obviously held a special place in the friars' devotion and invited them to *compassion*. In the modern era, the construction of calvaries or *Sacri Monti* had to be related expressions of this form of piety. The worship of Mary can also be linked to this spirituality, when it is addressed to Our Lady of Compassion, Pity, or the Seven Sorrows. Eucharistic devotion was a second bloc of piety for the friars, who greatly venerated the host. Saint Clare was traditionally represented with a monstrance in hand, and the Capuchins played a decisive role in the origins and dissemination of the Forty Hours devotion, which took place in uninterrupted exposure of the Blessed Sacrament. The Friars Minor showed a particular sensitivity to the Savior's humanity, which was reflected particularly in the worship given to the child Jesus.[77] Was it not Francis who is usually accredited with depicting the Nativity by means of the manger? The importance of this cult for the friars is also represented in the iconography of Saint Anthony of Padua receiving the Child

---

74. Thus the Capuchins' 1740 breviary contains the feasts of the saints of the three orders, plus that of a significant number of Blessed Franciscans. If we take into account that the main feasts were celebrated with an octave and that the most honored saints were entitled to a secondary feast during the year, we can easily understand why the Congregation of Rites was regularly concerned about the overload of the Friars Minor's sanctoral.

75. *General Statutes,* pp. 146–147 (for the Province of Paris): *Constitutiones et statuta,* p. 80 (for the Province of Lyon).

76. This is amply indicated in, Frédéric Meyer and Ludovic Viallet, *Le silence du cloître.* See also, Bernard Dompnier, « Ordres, diffusion des dévotions et sensibilités religieuses. L'exemple des Capucins en France (XVIIe et XVIIIe siècles) », *Dimensioni e problemi della ricerca storica,* 1994/2, 21–59, which is reiterated in Giulia Barone, « Un confronto di metodo. Le devozioni dell'età della Controrifoma. Riflessioni di una medievista », same work, 60–63.

77. For the modern era, see Fabienne Henryot, « Les Franciscains lorrains et la dévotion à l'Enfant Jésus », in Frédéric Meyer et Ludovic Viallet, *Le silence du cloître,* 379–394.

in his arms. In contrast to this veneration of Jesus' humanity, the worship of his Holy Name also held a prominent place. Bernardine of Siena brandished the IHS monogram during his apostolate, and we know that the friars were accustomed to repeat only the name, "Jesus," as a prayer.

These large pietistic tendencies, clearly affirmed by the Friars Minor, were also found in many other religious families, although the devotions were often nuanced or took on particular expressions. During the seventeenth century, Eucharistic worship was truly common to all Catholicism, devotion to the Holy Name of Jesus was also promoted by the Dominicans who believed they held a monopoly on confraternities holding this title, and piety towards the Christ child was also spread by Bérulle's oratory[78] or by the Carmelites. This fact is not really surprising: all the cults that have just been mentioned refer to central points of Christian doctrine and spirituality which flourished during the Catholic Reformation. The Friars Minor thus participated in a large pietistic movement, which was enforced by their preaching, their foundation of confraternities, and their publication of devotional booklets all of which resounded of their distinct spiritual tradition and history. Of course, all the devotions mentioned cannot be described as uniquely Franciscan. What was true concerning the worship of Christ also held good for Marian worship. Our Lady of Sorrows was venerated under various titles, some of which dated from the last centuries of the Middle Ages, such as Our Lady of Pity or Our Lady of Compassion. Many religious families, but especially the Servites, considered the cult of Our Lady of the Seven Sorrows specific to their order. It was a title that tended to impose itself in the seventeenth century; and the French discalced Augustinians, the Capuchins, and others used this title to express their devotion to our Lady's compassion. The piety surrounding the Immaculate Conception of Mary was most certainly but not exclusively promoted by the Franciscans. Its large role in the Order had more to do with theology than devotion. The Church's official recognition of the doctrine and the cult were triumphs for the promoters of the Immaculate Conception.

Old and new Franciscan Saints

It is perhaps in devotion to the saints of their Order that we see the true Franciscan qualities, although we know that Francis himself had expressed his

78. Translator's note: The Congregation of the Oratory of Jesus and Mary Immaculate, also known as the Bérullians or the Oratorians (and not to be confused with St. Philip Neri's Oratory) is a society of priests, founded by Pierre de Bérulle (later a Cardinal). It particularly promoted Jesus' humanity and exercised a large influence in the French school of spirituality in the 17th century. See Wikipedia: Pierre de Bérulle—https://en.wikipedia.org/wiki/ Pierre_de_B%C3%A9rulle

reservations about this type of demonstration. When friars were martyred in Morocco, Francis refused to allow them to be honored with a cult and insisted that "everyone should glory in his own passion, and not that of others."[79] After his death, there was a lively debate among his disciples about compiling his miracles which the Chapter of 1244 resolved. According to the oldest members of the Order, it was better to be interested in his life more than in his miracles. And the veneration of his remains, as well as the construction of a church to house them, also aroused many disagreements.[80]

This was no longer a concern during the modern era: not only was Francis's cult firmly established, but it was further increased by the development of a devotion specifically dedicated to his Stigmata. This was first promoted outside the Order's immediate sphere by a Roman confraternity in 1594. It then attained liturgical status by the creation of a secondary feast in 1668.[81] Similarly, medieval debates on the legitimacy of the worship of Franciscan saints were also forgotten. In the various religious families' imitating one another—that is to say, competing—to obtain new canonizations, the Franciscans were not slow to put forth the merits of the members who were most worthy of this honor. Beatifications followed one another at a relatively rapid pace during the first decades of the seventeenth century: Salvador of Horta (1606), Pascal Baylon (1618), Peter of Alcantara (1622), James of the Marches (1624). The following year, the Capuchins obtained the beatification of Felix of Cantalice.[82] But apart from the confirmation of Bernardin of Feltre's cult in 1654, this activity was interrupted until 1743, when Benedict the Moor (or of Palermo) was declared blessed. The Capuchins also had to wait until the eighteenth century to obtain new beati: Fidelis of Sigmaringen and Seraphim of Montegranaro in 1729, then Joseph of Leonissa in 1737 and Bernard of Corleone in 1768. As for canonizations, the papacy granted them even more sparingly. There are only three in the seventeenth century: Peter of Alcantara (1669) which let the Strict Observants have "their" saint; and in 1690, both the austere Observant John of Capistrano and the devotee of the Eucharist, Pascal Baylon.[83] Only two

---

79. Quoted by André Vauchez, *La sainteté en Occident aux derniers siècles du Moyen Âge d'après les procès de canonisation et les documents hagiographiques* (Rome, École française de Rome, 1988), 133–134.

80. André Vauchez, *La sainteté en Occident,* 134–135.

81. Alessandro Serra, *Culti e devozioni Delle confraternite romane in summer moderna* (doctoral thesis, Universities of Rome 3 and Clermont-Ferrand 2, 2010), 237–293.

82. In accordance with the part adopted for the whole of this article, the canonizations and beatifications taken into account concern only the various branches of the first Order of the Friars Minor.

83. Pope Leo XIII made him the patron of the Eucharist at the end of the nineteenth century.

additional saints were added to the Franciscan martyrology in the eighteenth century: James of the Marches (1726) and Joseph of Cupertino in 1767.[84] The Capuchins fared better with the canonizations of Felix of Cantalice (1712), Joseph of Leonissa and Fidelis of Sigmaringen (1746), and finally there was Seraphim of Montegranaro (1767). These are the saints and beati whose devotion had roots in the Middle Ages but who came to be included in the modern era's Franciscan sanctoral.[85] The reform of canonization procedures by Urban VIII, as seen in the sudden interruption of beatifications after 1625, established a much more rigorous screening process which prevented an increased number of saints and beati. Moreover, the papacy was careful not to favor one order over the others and was particularly careful to maintain an equal promotion of Francis and Dominic's holy sons. This attitude was even more noticeable in the inscription of feasts in the Roman calendar. During his reform of the breviary of 1568, Pius V had kept only two Franciscan saints (Francis and Bonaventure) and two Dominicans (Dominic and Thomas Aquinas). In 1586, the Friars Minor succeeded in having Anthony of Padua reintroduced, which was also the year that the Dominican, Peter Martyr, also found universal acceptance. Saint Hyacinth, a recently canonized Dominican friar, entered the Roman breviary in 1625, and then Bernardine of Siena in 1657. Finally, in 1670, each of the two Orders added a name to the list of saints honored by the whole Church: Peter of Alcantara from one, Raymond of Penafort from the other. The concern for parity was so scrupulous that it extended to determining the type of feasts. In 1586, Anthony of Padua and Peter Martyr were both reintroduced into the Roman calendar and thereafter their fate seemed to be inextricably linked: in 1602, both were demoted from a double to a semi-double rite; then again in 1670 both were promoted to a double rite. Suffice it to say that canonizations and approvals of feasts speak first and foremost of the papacy's strategy of fair distribution of honors among the most important religious families.

THE SPREAD OF DEVOTION TO THE ORDER'S SAINTS

Were the Franciscans trying to spread the devotion of their own saints among the faithful? The surest ways to try to answer this difficult question is to consider the presence of confraternities in their friaries. Even if the sources do not provide a complete count, the registers of the Roman Secretariat of Briefs indicate the writs of indulgences issued to confraternities and provide a

84. Joseph of Cupertino was beatified in 1753; he was a Conventual friar, whereas James of the Marches was Observant.

85. Religious orders are authorized to celebrate the cult of those who wore their habit and are beatified.

Anonymous, *Saint Pascal Baylon and Saint Peter of Alcantara,* seventeenth century. Oil on canvas, 3.50 × 1.80 m. Church of Saint-Jean-Baptiste, Bastia, Corsica.

useful and approximate record of the large number of recipients, and therefore of devotions. Although the data collected from them record several tens of thousands of confraternities located throughout the Catholic world, they remain very partial because the requests came almost exclusively from recently created associations, and not from older ones which were already endowed with indulgences. Moreover, not all the newly erected confraternities requested writs of indulgences.[86] A first survey, which covers the years 1653-1662, lists 2,500 writs in total. First Order Franciscan churches appeared only 173 times, and there was a very unequal distribution of writs according to the branches of the Order. The Observants obtained indulgences for 59 confraternities; the Conventuals for 57; the Recollects were presented with only 21 confraternities;

86. For the details of the collective survey carried out on this source and the information relating to religious orders, see Marie-Hélène Froeschlé-chopard and Françoise Hernandez, « Les dévotions des confréries, reflet de l'influence des ordres religieux? », *Dimensioni e problemi della ricerca storica,* 1994/2, 104–126. A significant number of confraternities, even new ones, do not ask for briefs of indulgences. This is the case especially for those of the Holy Rosary or the Holy Sacrament which are under the care of the Dominicans, since they are affiliated with the Roman friary of the Minerva; it is also the case for those confraternities aligned with a Roman archconfraternity.

and the Capuchins had only five.[87] In a way, this discrepancy was to be expected: the Capuchins, as has been said, did not want to make their churches to be places for lay devotions; the Observants and Conventuals traditionally welcomed confraternities. The Recollects' results were more surprising. Theoretically their requests should have been close to the Capuchins', but they were significantly greater, while the number of their houses was comparatively smaller than those of the other branches. The titles of these pious associations represented a multitude of cults which mostly corresponded to the Catholic Reformation's prominent devotions (Last Things, Guardian Angels, the Virgin) and, in the final analysis, they only granted a limited place to Franciscan saints. Only Anthony of Padua was really well represented with 44 confraternities dedicated to him among the Conventuals, 20 among the Observants, five among the Recollects and three among the Capuchins, all of which make up half of the pious associations linked to friaries. Saint Francis himself hardly appeared. He had no mention among the Conventuals and the Capuchins, four among the Observants, and one among the Recollects. As for the other saints, they were not associated with any confraternity. A few decades later, from 1691–1705,[88] Franciscan saints did not fare any better with confraternities found in friary churches, far from it. Anthony of Padua was still the most popular but with only 25 associations that took his name (14 among the Observants, four among the Conventuals, six among the Recollects, one among the Capuchins). Francis of Assisi seemed proportionally better represented than in the 1650s, with 14 confraternities, which were mainly Third Order fraternities. Other saints—recently canonized Pascal Baylon and John of Capistrano, Bernard of Siena, and Peter of Alcantara—appeared only sporadically with only one to three mentions.

One might suppose that the Franciscans would be more concerned about establishing the cult of their saints in parishes than in their own churches. Data from the 1650s would suggest an ambiguous conclusion. Admittedly, Anthony of Padua was honored by having 50 confraternities named after him and established outside the Friars Minor's churches, but the number [of churches] was lower than [confraternities] established for churches. As for Francis, only six confraternities outside Franciscan churches bear his name. Bernardine of Siena and Benedict the Moor (who was not yet beatified) each gave their name to a confraternity, but no other Franciscan saint appeared on the list. The examination of a third survey, covering the years 1721–1731 (2,500 briefs of indulgences), shows that it is probably necessary to consider the dynamics over a long period of time. Ten of the 15 confraternities of St.

87. In 31 cases, the writs do specify the branch in whose friary the confraternity had established itself.

88. This contains a total of 3,815 briefs of indulgences.

Jacques Callot. [The Japanese Martyrs], print, 15.9 × 11.1 cm, BnF.

Francis (or fraternities of the Third Order Secular) which requested and obtained indulgences during this period were in a friary church; on the other hand, 10 of the 17 confraternities of St. Anthony of Padua were located in a parish church. In other words, the cult of St. Francis remained a strong identifier [for the friars], while that of St. Anthony was widely adopted by the laity. This could tend to demonstrate that the efforts made over decades by the various components of the Order to popularize piety for Saint Francis, through the establishment of many confraternities in their own churches, bore fruit. Undoubtedly, Saint Anthony of Padua became the Franciscan saint par excellence for the faithful.

It would certainly be good to nuance this general approach to the spread of the Franciscan cult of the saints throughout various locations in the Catholic world. We will, however, present only one example—Mexico—chosen because it was a territory where the Friars Minor's expansion accompanied the implantation of Catholicism.[89] From the first decades of their presence, the friars actively spread the cults of Francis, Clare of Assisi, Anthony of Padua, and soon that of the creole, Philip of Jesus, who was born in Mexico City, martyred in Japan in 1597 and beatified in 1627. The more general

89. Pierre Ragon, *Les saints et les images du Mexique (XVIe–XVIIIe siècle)* (Paris, L'Harmattan, 2003).

devotions associated with the Friars Minor, such as the *Via Crucis,* were implanted during a second phase. In this new context which was very different from Christianity in the old country, it was first necessary to make the friars known and to distinguish them from the other orders. In Mexico, adapting the friars' cult of the saints to the expectations of the faithful was also a way to ensure the Franciscans' popularity. The friar-doorkeepers generally kept a cord (of Saint Francis?) to lend to pregnant women supposedly to guarantee a happy delivery.

The means of diffusing the devotions

Although the confraternities present a fragmentary picture of the devotions promoted by the Friars Minor, they do not provide information on the concrete means used to ensure their diffusion. This still largely unexplored field of research is immense; so, we will have to be content with providing several pointers, hoping that this will contribute to opening up this new field. The obvious means available to the friars were first of all word of mouth: preaching, instruction, and writing. The first, preaching, by definition has left few traces; on the other hand, the second, instruction, presents abundant works to analyze. The hagiographic collections of the Middle Ages left the public with the legends of the saints, which were revived and rewritten during the modern era.[90] With the invention of the printing press and with the example of sixteenth century Italian *Orazione*, small pamphlets of pious literature, a wider and wider dissemination of individual prayer and meditation was born. There followed many works of this genre which combined the story of a saint's life, a catalogue of attributed miracles, and prayers directed to the saint. The Franciscans were very involved in the production of this type of religious literature.

Pictures were also a chosen means for the propagation of cults. We obviously think first of painting which, thanks to Giotto's talent, made known Francis's deeds; and this led to a real revolution in religious iconography since prior to then artists had only portrayed ancient saints. Medieval and then modern altarpieces continued the tradition of representing Franciscan saints, sometimes in prayerful postures leading to veneration, or in edifying or instructional scenes. We should not forget sculpture or engraving, a term that includes both small portable carvings used as protective devotional supports, and high-quality iconographic series, which told the saint's life in a succession

90. In particular, we can consult the insightful article of Chaira Mercuri, « Raccolte agiografiche e osservanza fracescana » in *Europa sacra. Raccolte agiografiche e identità politiche in Europa fra Medioevo ed età moderna,* eds. Sofia Boesch Gajano et Raimondo Michetti (Rome, Carocci, 2002), 281–293.

of episodes.[91] Whatever the medium, the saints' images changed according to the times. We have already pointed out that Francis's iconography took on a very ascetic portrayal in the modern era. Iconography was not identical in all the branches of the Order, and, for this reason, it would be interesting to examine those aspects of the founder's life that each prefers.

During Francis's lifetime, "lauda" played an important role in promoting prayer.[92] Subsequently, the tradition of using easily memorized songs with simple melodies was retained by the Friars Minor. The Capuchin, Felix of Cantalice, went through the streets of Rome begging while singing short verses which he taught in the houses he visited. A witness for his canonization process reported that he would come to the gatherings of aristocratic women and say to them: "And now I want to teach you a beautiful song."[93] In the seventeenth century, the Capuchins, inspired by the example of the Roman oratory and the Jesuit Michel Coyssard, also used vernacular hymns during their missions.

Physical aids also help in the spread of cults. In the Middle Ages and in the modern era, the Friars Minor, like most of their contemporaries, also went hunting for saints' relics. Once the catacombs were opened at the end of the sixteenth century, trips to Rome for general chapters became an opportunity to get fragments from first-century saints' bodies. These were brought back to the friaries in various countries and offered for devotion. Increased collections of relics gave rise to the building of relic chapels in some churches of the Order. The same fervor extended to small objects of piety—Agnus Dei, rosaries, pictures, medals—which the friars generously distributed to the faithful of their apostolate, more so than did the members of many other orders. Félix of Cantalice, as his canonization process tells us, made "small crosses" (*crocette*) of wood during his spare time, which he then gave to the people he met. In some cases, indulgences which often had a protective value were attached to

---

91. See in particular Simonetta Prosperi Valenti Rodino, *L'imagine di un Francesco nella Controriforma. La diffuzione dell'iconografia francescana attarverso l'incisione* (Rome, Quasar, 1982).

92. Translator's note : *Lauda*, or *la laude* in French, were dramatic musical representations in verse of religious themes—e.g. of a biblical account, or a teaching. They arose in 14th century Italy, probably with Jacopone da Todi, o.f.m., who wrote many. One such is "Donna de paradiso" which recounts the interactions of Mary, the archangel Gabriel, Jesus, and a crowd. They were performed by confraternities, often in front of churches, and permitted the spectators' involvement, thus providing instruction and religious involvement. They differ from "Mystery Plays" by the addition of music. See Wikipedia, « Représentation sacrée », https://fr.wikipedia.org/wiki/Repr%C3%A9sentation_sacr%C3%A9e

93. « Or su ti volio imparare una bella canzone ». The life and apostolate of Felix of Cantalice are well known from various sources, including the edition of the acts of his beatification process: *Processus sixtinus fratris Felicis a Cantalice,* ed. Mariano d'Alatri (Rome, Institutum historicum OFM Cap., 1964).

these objects. In this practice can be seen the friars' full desire to respond to the faithful's expectations. These objects of devotion were certainly part of their daily experience to the point that, at the beginning of the seventeenth century, Capuchins' provincial chapters, on various occasions, had to prohibit their use as tokens when the friars dared to use them for card games.

Finally, the Friars Minor's history during the modern era is largely a continuation of that of the Middle Ages. We see the same tendency to interpret the Poverello of Assisi's message in various ways with the same lasting tension between the life of retreat from the outside world and the desire to follow Francis's calling people to conversion. The existence of diverse branches of the Franciscan family must be understood essentially as ways of finding a balance between these two poles. The uniqueness of the modern era may lie, ultimately and above all, in a recurrence of this fundamental tension. It arose both because of Christendom's increased mental prayer at the time of the Reforms and because of the opening of new and immense territories for apostolates. In the decades following the Council of Trent, the challenges of increased Protestantism and the demands of ascetical Catholicism also contributed to creating new types of Franciscan identities within the Strict Observance, whether by remaining in the Order, like the Recollects, or by detaching themselves institutionally, like the Capuchins. Finally, the characteristic of Franciscan history lies, perhaps, in the permanent questioning of solutions elaborated to resolve its two-fold and contradictorily original desire, which the Capuchin Yves of Paris summarized well:

> Our Father St. Francis established . . . in his Order a spirit of solitude but tempered it by both individual and public exercises that were directed to the glory of God, our salvation and that of our neighbor. He fashioned them on the example of Jesus Christ who gave his days entirely to healing, to preaching, to converting the peoples, and then to spending his nights in prayer on the mountain.[94]

In a way, the Order was no longer what it really had once been because the friars allowed themselves to be won over by the notion that they had attained a perfect balance. This seemed to be the case from the end of the seventeenth century throughout the entire Order, which then entered into a period of calm, without great internal conflicts, and without the emergence of new branches. At the very least, having been won over by the clericalization which profoundly marked Catholicism, Franciscan history changed its course, leaving behind the rich period of reforms that began around the beginning of 1400 and extended to the middle of the seventeenth century.

---

94. Yves of Paris, *Instructions religieuses,* 550.

The Recollects were among the most demanding participants in this quest for a Franciscanism that was detached from the world and committed to the apostolate. In the wake of the Spanish and Italian Strict Observance, they opted right from the beginning for a life of prayer and recollection. The Canadian adventure and their missions at home, however, also testify to their attention to the apostolic dimension of their vocation. This second aspect [of home missions] never knew the development it took on with their Capuchin brothers. Perhaps because of this, the Recollects' pastoral care seemed to change quickly to support for the secular clergy's style of care. Is this difference between the two reformed branches due only to the fact that the help to which the Capuchins (who were also more numerous) committed themselves continuously opened up vast fields of apostolates, of which the Recollects were deprived, or is it due to a specific and deliberate way of differentiating between the two demands? Only new research on these French Franciscans of the Strict Observance, still too little known, will make it possible to understand better their choices and their exact place in the panorama of Franciscan history.

Chapter 2

The Recollects in New France—Portraits and Pictures[1]

Paul-André Dubois and Dorothée Kaupp,
Laval University

So far, words have mostly substituted for the small number of iconic witnesses that would allow us to get a picture of the sons of Saint Francis in Canada. As it happened, descriptions of the first Recollects' moral features have replaced what the artist's brush has denied us. Only a few portraits of these early missionaries have come down to us. Three centuries ago, because of the exceptional success of his travel stories, Father Louis Hennepin[2] (1640–c. 1705) garnered a portrait which still allows us to see his penetrating gaze. Posterity demanded a face; Franciscan humility could not refuse it.

Whoever the painted subject might be, portraits are the Recollects' response to concerns about an individual's reputation as much as a legitimizing of his memory beyond the colony's boundaries. The recognition and affirmation of Canadian Recollects in France, or even in Europe, could not be better illustrated than by Father Joseph Denys (1657–1736), who once tried to promote, in Rome, the cause of the humble Canadian lay brother Didace Pelletier (1657–1699). Such desires for canonization, which are the beginning of the "true portrait" of friar Didace, take us to the level of the universal Church where hagiography cannot dispense with the real or imagined face of the person one hopes to see elevated one day. It is to this ambition and this necessity, that we owe what we know about the character of Didace Pelletier, this paragon of Franciscan

1. Translation of: Dubois, Paul-André and Dorothée Kaupp, « Les Récollets en Nouvelle-France : Portraits et tableaux » in Dubois, Paul-André, ed., *Les Récollets en Nouvelle-France : Traces et Mémoire*, Québec, QC, Les Presses de l'Université Laval, 2018; pp. 15–59.

2. On this character, see Catherine Broué's article in *Les Récollets en Nouvelle-France: Traces et Mémoires.* Québec, Presses de l'Université Laval, 2018, pp. 279–297.

humility on Canadian soil. At the local level, these portraits of Recollects speak to us less about the greatness of the Franciscan Order than of its roots in Canada.

Painting such a tableau from bits and of pieces of information, of unequal value, which is what these portraits are, is not without its difficulties. Relying on paintings as departure points in the narration forces us to yield a place to individuals who, objectively, are secondary actors in the Canadian history of the order. The approach is not without interest. The attention paid to the literary, symbolic, and ethnological aspects of a subject reestablish a once-well-known identity and give depth to the factual history which, following the British Conquest, normally ignored these details, considering them of little importance. The Recollects' history does not fundamentally change, but it is illuminated in a different way.

Placing these pictures in the text follows, as much as possible, the line of birth-maturity-decline that this religious order experienced in Canada. We did not want to deprive ourselves of adding "authentic" portraits of the Recollects. Some of these are old illustrations that allow the reader to approach the subject more closely; and some are later paintings that bring the reader into the era where these heroic figures become the historical and symbolic foundations of a society about which the clerical-nationalist French-Canadian elite dreamed. By their nature and their subjects, the seldom-seen portraits and paintings used in this article impose a structure on the narrative, perhaps even an unpredictable design to the story we intend to tell. Narrating the Franciscan Order's journey through this maze of obligatory stopovers is not easy. Therein lies the challenge of such an exercise; and there also, the reader may find some surprises.

From New Spain to New France: Finding Your Way

In sixteenth-century Spain, the ascetic spirit that had inspired the Alcantarine reform among the Franciscans remained essential to *discalced* spirituality; that is to say, to the Strict Observance. Whether in Italy or in France, this Franciscan reform retained a privileged relationship with the Spain of the Golden Age, if only through the hagiography that spread throughout the Order's houses. Paradoxically, the antagonistic relationship between the French and Spanish monarchs increased greatly during this period. Over the decades that the Recollects were established in France, the publication of the abridged and revised French version of Bartolomeo de Las Casas's *Brevisima relacion de la destruccion de las Indias* contributed greatly to darkening the reputation of Spain, which was seen to be increasingly jealous to extend its possessions and wealth. The distribution in France of Las Casas's classic under the title of *Histoire admirable des horribles insolences, cruauez, & tyrannies*

Anonymous. *The punishment of Native Americans for not having gone to church.* Ink and watercolor on paper, 30.1 × 20.5 [Samuel de Champlain], *Brief discours des choses plus remarquables que Samuel Champlain de Brouage a reconnue aux Indes occidentales* [1602?], John Carter Brown Library, Providence, R.I.

exercees par les Espagnoles es Indes Occidentales[3] and, a little later, the *Miroir de la cruelle, & horrible tyrannie Espagnole perpetrée aux Indes Occidentales*[4] perfectly illustrates this hostility to the Spanish crown. From the time of Francis I to Henry IV, everything distanced the two crowns politically. The traces of this loathing are evident in many writings, especially in the *Brief discours des choses les plus remarquables que Samuel Champlain de Brouage a reconneues aux Indes occidentalles.* Whatever the true authorship of this work, it must be noted that the anti-Spanish sentiment that motivated its author also condemned the violence perpetrated by the colonizers and missionaries, among whom were the Franciscans.[5] Also, it was in contradistinction to this

3. Bartolomeo de Las Casas, *Histoire admirable des horribles insolences, cruauez, & exerces par les Espagnoles es Ines Occidentales,* trad. Jacques de Miggrode, Genève, Gabriel Carrier, 1582.

4. Bartolomeo de Las Casas, *Le miroir de la tyrannie espagnole perpetree aux Indes occidentales,* Amsterdam, Ian Everts Cloppenburg, 1620.

5. *Bref discours des choses plus remarquables que Samuel Champlain de Brouage a reconneues aux Indes occidentalles : au voiage qu'il en a faict en icelles en l'année* [1599 à 1602], John Carter Brown Library, Codex Fr 1, 46 fol., fol 41v.

caricature of colonization and missionaries that the future French missionary activity would be defined, in theory at least.

At the time of the founding of Port Royal in Acadia and of Quebec a few years later, this mistrust remained strong. When the Jesuits arrived in Port Royal in 1611, the colonizers were strongly biased against the Society of Jesus which was so closely linked to the papacy and the Emperor of Spain. They had been banished from France in 1598 and readmitted to the kingdom four years later, after which they were only tolerated. The assassination of Henri IV in 1610, which some attributed to their clandestine plots, made them suspect again. In his *Histoire de la Nouvelle France,* Marc Lescarbot wrote of the Jesuits saying that the merchants of Dieppe "did not want them to receive them on board their ships bound for Acadia saying that the death of the King was too recent and that they did not want to provide them a dwelling that would be to the benefit of the Spaniards . . . but offering nevertheless to accept all other kinds of orders, Capuchins, Cordeliers, Recollects, etc."[6]

When they entered the colonial scene late in 1615, the Recollects found themselves caught in the middle of a curious paradox where their missionary traditions, shaped by their confreres in New Spain, were at odds with the prevailing anti-Spanish sentiment. It was from Spain, nevertheless, that the Strict Observance's apostolic spirit was derived. The *descazos* or discalced, by settling in the Spanish and Portuguese possessions, revived the Franciscan missionary spirit which had once led the disciples of St. Francis into non-Christian lands, stretching from the Holy Land and Africa to Asia and the East Indies. In sixteenth-century America, the first apostles of the West Indies laid the foundations of the Order in the New World, establishing Franciscan parishes called *doctrinas.* Seen in this light, it was not surprising that *Blessed Brother Martin of Valencia*, leader of the *twelve* Franciscan apostles in New Spain, appeared with St. Francis of Assisi on the frontispiece of the *Grand Voyage du pays des Hurons*, published in Paris in 1632. The Canadian mission was still too young to be able to dispense with evoking the Strict Observance's missionary glories which were needed to gain legitimacy. Caught between a rock and a hard place, the first Recollects navigated between their historical heritage and the necessary obedience to the monarch, because the Recollects were undeniably French subjects. In hindsight, everything indicated that the beginnings of the first Canadian foundation of the Strict Observance in Canada were marked as much by a willing reference to Iberian missionary models as by the need to endorse the French colonial ethic that no savage should be led to embrace Christianity other than "by every expression of tenderness."[7]

---

6. Marc Lescarbot, *Histoire de la Nouvelle France,* Paris, Perier, 1618, p. 664.

7. It is true that, to distance itself from rivals or to legitimize its position on the international political scene and to look good with the papacy, colonial France had opted

(Blessed Friar Martin de Valencia). Detail taken from the frontispiece of Gabriel Sagard Theodat's *Le Grand voyage du pays des Hurons,* Paris, Denis Moreau, 1632, BnF.

Driven by their own missionary traditions as well as the spirit of the early seventeenth-century Catholic Reformation, the Recollects of the Province of Saint Denys took on their apostolate with the naiveté and passion of beginners. The difficult transition from theory to practice or, more precisely, from reading about missionary activity to the reality on the ground forced them to review their plans and temper their zeal. Apart from the Amerindians who were located around Quebec, the emerging colony was practically empty. Admittedly, the agents of merchants from Malouin and Dieppe and the sailors who accompanied them occasionally expanded the number of Europeans at Quebec; but most of them were Huguenots and their presence contaminated the atmosphere of this colony more than it contributed to the rise of Christianity in Canada.[8] In this first period of the Recollects' adventure in

since the sixteenth century for an approach to colonization that openly opposed violence against Indians. In the Commission granted to Jacques Noël and Étienne Caron de la Jane on January 14th 1588, it was specified that the savages must be attracted "by every expression of tenderness" and that attempts must be made to "instruct them and bring them to the knowledge of God and the Christian faith." Samuel de Champlain, *Des Sauvages,* Montreal, Typed Edition, 1993, p. 210.

8. Paul-André Dubois, "Visages du christianisme en Nouvelle-France au temps de Champlain," in Miche from Waele and Martin Pâquet (dir.), *Québec, Champlain, le monde,* Québec, Les Presses de l'Université Laval, 2008, pp. 201–222.

New France, disputes abounded, and the mission bore little fruit. Despite their determined apostolic manner of preaching, the Recollects' presence served first and foremost the few French who resided around Champlain's "*Abitation*." This presence of religious men was essential both to administer the sacraments and to support the settlers spiritually and morally. Although the consecration of Canada to Saint Joseph, protector and provider of the Holy Family, in 1624, raised the hopes of this handful of French whose material survival depended on so few things, the friars' mission was still in embryonic form after being present nearly ten years.

Several factors explain this delay. The lack of resources in the first place. Then there is the fact that no coercion could be used to speed up the Amerindians' conversion, as had been seen in the Spanish territories. Finally, there was too rapid a turnover of missionary personnel. The "restlessness" that pushed these first eager apostles to see everything, to do everything, and on whom it fell to organize everything did not help in any way. The activities of the first four apostles of 1615, speak eloquently on this subject. Father Denys Jamet arrived at Quebec in 1615 and returned to France the following year; he returned to Quebec in 1620 and returned definitively to France two years later. Jean Dolbeau reached Tadoussac at the end of 1615 but returned to Quebec the following year. After spending two years in Quebec City, he returned definitively to France. In 1633, he was found at the Strict Observance's General Chapter in Toledo, Spain. Brother Pacifique Du Plessis spent three years in Trois-Rivières, then returned to France in 1618. The following year, he returned to Quebec, and died there. Undoubtedly, the relocation prize goes to Father Joseph Le Caron. From 1615 to 1629, this apostle stayed in Quebec five times, two times in Huronia, and three at Tadoussac. He crossed the Atlantic six times, not counting his definitive departure from Canada. Under these conditions, learning the native American languages remained a pious hope. As for the arrival of the Jesuits in 1625, which some might have thought would be an antidote to this flagrant lack of efficacy, they did not respond to the linguistic problem. They did, however, resolve the question of financing the Canadian mission. Since the Recollects, according to their rule, were unable to receive a bequest, they then relied on the Jesuits to take on this matter. As a religious society, the Jesuits could receive bequests and dispose of them according to the will of the benefactors and the needs that arose. The Marquis de Gamache's bequest to the Collège de Québec is a good example of this capability.[9] In 1636 Brother Sagard felt the need to explain to his readers the true reasons for the Jesuits' arrival in Québec, perhaps to diminish the importance of their coming. He

---

9. Lucien Campeau, *La première mission des Jésuites en Nouvelle-France (1611–1613) et Les commencements du Collège de Québec (1626–1670)*, Montréal, Éditions Bellarmin, 1972, 128 p.

wrote: "it was necessary for us to have the help of some religious to take care of so many peoples, to continue the conversion of savages, and to establish seminaries everywhere for the instruction of youth." And this solution, Sagard explained, was based on the practice that had prevailed until then in the East and West Indies where the Strict Observance had taken root.

A seminary was set up in 1620 in Quebec City. Some of the Amerindian boys who were educated there were sent to France, where, in the friaries of Saint-Denys Province, they were taught the French language and customs as well as reading and writing. Due to a lack of funds, staff, and the continued support of the children's parents, the seminary yielded few results. The institution was barely established on the banks of the Saint-Charles River before it was destroyed by the Kirke brothers who captured Quebec in 1629. The Recollects set sail again for France.

MISSIONARIES BY WRITING

Faced with the apparent failure of their apostolate—only a dozen conversions in fourteen years—the Recollects relied on writing, perhaps less to record their Canadian experience than to promote their return to Quebec. In the aftermath of the Treaty of Saint-Germain-en-Laye, which returned Canada to France, the time was undeniably ripe for those who wanted to make known their claims on North American territory. Samuel de Champlain's book, *Les Voyages de la Nouvelle France occidentale, dicte Canada,* the last expanded edition of which had just been published in Paris in 1632, clearly showed the importance of publishing their claims in the context of colonial rivalries between France and England.[10] The addition of the *Doctrine de Ledesme,* previously published in Rouen in 1630, to this edition of Champlain's travels was particularly harmful to the Recollects. The Jesuit translation by Jean de Brébeuf and Ennemond Massé, the Recollects' first Jesuit companions in Canada from 1625,[11] ignored any collaboration with them. It was not surprising, therefore, that Sagard in turn took care to add a dictionary of the Huron language at the end of his *Grand Voyage du pays des Hurons* de 1632.[12] Like his *Histoire du Canada,* published in Paris in 1636, this work depicts a missionary adventure that skillfully relegates the Jesuits to

10. Samuel de Champlain, *Les Voyages de la Nouvelle France occidentale, dicte Canada,* Paris, Collet, 1632.

11. *Doctrine chrestienne du R. P. Ledesme de la Compagnie de Jésus traduite en langage canadois pour la conversion des Habitans de ce pays. Par un Père de la mesme Compagnie,* Rouen, L'Allemant, 1630, 26 p.

12. Gabriel Sagard, *Le Grand Voyage du pays des Hurons* [...] *Avec un Dictionnaire de la langue huronne pour la commodité de ceux qui ont a voyager dans le pays, et n'ont l'intelligence d'icelle langue,* Paris, Moreau, 1632.

the rank of secondary actors while directing the spotlight on the Recollects' heroism.[13] Given this context, everything suggests that these first writings of Canadian Franciscans are attempts to establish symbolically their claim to a barely known territory. The written records left by the sons of St. Francis sought to compensate for their meager but real imprint left in New France.

With this editorial and political ploy, the Recollects reinterpreted reality and relativized it by associating it with the glorious experiences of the Order in New Spain. By putting their apostolate on a continental or even planetary scale, the French missionary adventure in Canada was no longer just a work in progress, waiting to be achieved. To speak today of the Recollects' missionary failure would err by being anachronistic. The men and women of the Catholic Reformation understood their participation in the God-given missionary apostolate quite differently. The Recollects' perspective was that personal sanctification took precedence over every other consideration and hardships were welcomed as an opportunity to purify intentions and to prove one's faith.

At the heart of this concept of holiness, martyrdom held a central place. The missionary literature of the time devoted many pages to the torments endured by the apostles of the modern era, in particular by the religious missionaries of the Strict Observance serving Portuguese and Spanish interests.[14] St. Peter the Baptist and his companions who were martyred in Japan stirred up the Recollects' desire for martyrdom, as St. Francis Xavier's example had with the Jesuits. Beatified in 1627, shortly before the French colony of Canada fell into the hands of the English, the martyrs of Nagasaki served as models of missionary sacrifice for the most ardent souls.[15] This Franciscan missionary gesture, in its attempts to establish historical coherence and an ordering of all past, present, and future events, based itself on providential logic.[16] By leaving for America with a firm resolve to profess Jesus

13. Gabriel Sagard, *Histoire du Canada et voyages que les frères Mineurs Recollects y ont faicts pour la conversion des Infideles* [...], Paris Claude Sonnius, 1636.

14. Luys Pineyro, *La nouvelle histoire du Japon divisée en cinq livres, ou il est traicté amplement de l'estat de sa Chrestienté, du progrès de la foy Catholique, des grandes persecutions qui y sont arrivées aux chrestiens, & des divers Martyres qu'un grand nombre, tant religieux que seculiers ont souffert soubs l'Empire de Cobusama, iusques à l'année mil six cens quinze,* Paris, Fouët, 1618, 879 p.

15. Nicolas Trigault, *Histoire des matyrs du Japon depuis 1612 jusqu'en 1620,* Paris, Cramoisy, 1624, 638 p.; Fulgence Férot, récollet, *Abrigé historique de la vie des saints et saintes, bienheureux et bienheureuses et autres pieux et célèbres personnages des trois ordres de Saint François,* Paris, Bastien, 1779, vol. 1, p. 77–82.

16. Barezzo Barezzi, *La quatriesme partie des chroniques des freres mineurs. Divisée en dix livres. En laquelle sont descrittes les vies admirables, les cruels martyrs, les merveilleux miracles* [...] *jusqu'à l'année présente 1609,* trad. R.P. F. I. Blancone, Paris, Veuve G. Chaupière, 1609. This was re-published in 1623 and 1627.

Philippe Dannoot, *Seraphic Saint Francis of the Atlantic—One world was not enough,* engraving from the *Abrégé des fruits acquis par l'ordre des Frères-Mineurs en quattres partie de l'univers,* Brussels, F. Vivien, 1652, BnF.

Christ, and even to shed one's blood as a witness of faith, every distress became grace. The crosses, sufferings, and trials encountered were presented as the seal of divine election and the promise of a fruitful apostolate. The difficulty of being heard by the Amerindians or the inability to communicate with them was patiently endured while waiting for better days. Moreover, the missionary hagiography of the time showed that Christianity's implantation could not be achieved without these virtues. Basing himself on the Order's own history, Sagard readily excused the first Recollects of New France by pointing out that "our fathers of the Indies, took thirteen or fourteen years before being able to convert the kingdom of Voxu; and they were nearly 38 years in Brazil before being able to do anything."[17]

Given the times and the location, the Recollects' situation seems less catastrophic than what historians too often like to point out. In the eyes of the known world, Canada was nothing more than one among many tesserae in the great mosaic of Franciscan missions carried out on a planetary scale by the provinces of the Strict Observance. There could be no better insight into this holistic view of Franciscan missionary territory and its extension into the

17. Gabriel Sagard, *Histoire du Canada,* 1866, vol. 1, p. 167.

north than in the allegorical work, *Abrégé des fruits acquis par l'ordre des Frères-Mineurs es quattres parties de l'univers.*[18] In it, four friars examine the earthly sphere and admire the extent of the Strict Observance's territory. Mexico, Peru, Brazil, and Canada appear in a whimsical representation that has nothing to do with chronology and historical realities. In the establishment of this Franciscan territory, because that is the point of this illustration, Canada was presented as the logical continuation of an apostolic community's struggles to expand ever further the limits of its domain.

The Return to Canada

The Province of Saint-Denys was not inactive between 1629 and the return of the Recollects in 1670. Requests to return to Canada were regularly made at court.[19] This long absence from the Canadian missions was much more a dormancy than an abdication. The plan to establish a mission in Madagascar in 1660 certainly reflected the desire to participate again in the overseas missionary scene. The Province of Saint-Denys, however, was struck with misfortune when the ship carrying their friars was attacked by three Algerian warships in [the waters off] northern Portugal. The friars who were to be missionaries returned to their home province. The project was

18. *Abrégé des fruits acquis par l'ordre des Frères-Mineurs es quattres parties de l'univers, nommément la conversion du Nouveau Monde, recueillies par un Père cordlier en Bruxelles,* Bruxelles, François Vivien, 1652, 171 p.

19. Caroline Galland, *Pour le service de Dieu, du Roi et du Bien public. L'apostolat des récollets en Nouvelle-France aux XVIIe et XVIIIe siècles,* thèse de doctorat, Université de Paris X-Nanterre, 2008, vol. 1, p. 182.

abandoned.[20] Despite this disappointment, the return to Canada was imminent. While some of the religious dealt directly with their project, others tried to convince influential people involved in the process of Canada's colonization. The Recollect Charles Rapine, author of a *Histoire générale de l'origine et progrez des Frères mineurs de saint François* published in Paris in 1631,[21] who came from an important family of Nevers, was one of the most significant figures involved in convincing the powers to be.

In 1667, Canada opened up. A contract dated March 11 of this year was signed between the Parisian Recollects' syndics and the notary, Romain Becquet, which allowed the religious to recover their former lands in the event of their return.[22] The crossing was organized. The departure date was set for July 15, 1669. The Recollects were once again filled with hope. The adventure was cut short: shipwreck, death, loss of their [land] titles at sea. The project was postponed to the following year.[23] In 1670, after an absence of nearly forty years, the Recollects finally set foot on the soil of this so greatly desired New France. The friary was in ruins and the Order's lands were occupied by others. The colony's spirit had changed. The colony's administrative reorganization had given a new shape to the country. The concept of mission had also evolved considerably due to the population's growth. The so-called missions to the "Savage," now largely controlled by the Society of Jesus, were practically closed to the Recollects. They were now left with obscure apostolic tasks.

In this respect, everything suggests that the Recollects' readmission to New France in 1670 echoed the colony's increasing militarization. The increase in the number of soldiers gave rise to new spiritual needs. Of the 1,300 men that Carignan's regiment brought to Quebec in the summer of 1665, 400 chose to remain there after the campaigns against the Iroquois. According to the principle of Roman colonization, where the *imperator* granted land to his veterans, the king did the same to the officers and soldiers who crossed the sea and fought for him. The growth of households composed of former soldiers and Filles du Roi led in turn to the development of new fronts of colonization

20. Frédéric Meyer, *Pauvreté et assistance spirituelle. Les Franciscains récollets de la province de Lyon aux XVIIe et XVIIIe siècles,* Saint-Étienne, Publication de l'université de Saint-Étienne, 1997, p. 314.

21. Charles Rapine, *Histoire générale de l'origine et progrez des Frères mineurs,* Paris, Sonnius, 1631, 775 p.

22. « Contrat conventionnel pour les RR PP. Recoletz touchant leur habitation au Canada, 11 mars 1667 » in Eugène Réveillaud, *Histoire chronologique de la Nouvelle-France. Depuis sa découverte en 1504 jusqu'en l'an 1632. Un panorama historique et chronologique de la Nouvelle-France. Publié d'après le manuscrit original de 11689, avec notes et appendice d'Eugène Réveillaud,* Paris, Fischbacher, 1888, p. 180–181.

23. Charles Le Clercq, *Premier Etablissement de la foy,* Paris, Amable Auroy, 1691, vol. 2, p. 87.

that called for the presence of an available and materially undemanding clergy. The Recollects met this profile. From this perspective, the return of the Recollects of Saint-Denys Province was far from uninteresting. From the state's perspective, their return to New France responded, we think, to their expectation that the French population would increase in the future. Thus, the favor enjoyed by the Recollects at Versailles should be reread through the perspective of the colony's revival and all the needs this entailed, especially in terms of the settlers' and soldiers' spiritual care.

When the Recollects set foot in Canada again, they were still moved by a missionary ideal. In this regard, the savage's evangelization remained a cherished objective for most religious who crossed the sea. In a strict sense, the Recollects' apostolic call would be realized only among the 900 or so Mi'kmaq of the Gaspé Peninsula, Chaleur Bay and Miramichi. Their mission in Restigouche was never contested until after the end of the French regime. Elsewhere in New France, the ministry, which took them to the colony's centers, only occasionally brought them into contact with the Amerindian populations. The French colonization of the territory, which increased during the last quarter of the seventeenth century, brought them into the new situation of rendering a demanding and useful service to the developing parishes and the outlying forts with the settlers' households. Whatever ministry they were given, all Recollects who crossed the Atlantic firmly believed that they were missionaries. Was it any less apostolic to hear the confessions of the garrison's soldiers and of the fishermen in seasonal settlements, people considered to be rough and rude, than to work for the Amerindians' salvation? Such was the prevailing thought among St. Francis's sons.

By solidly supporting the king as chaplains to the French troops in the Franco-Dutch war, the Recollects won the monarch's esteem and were granted the protection of his governor general in Canada. As such, Louis de Buade de Frontenac would always be the greatest supporter of the Recollects, whose syndic he became. In this way, the Recollects endorsed a political stance that inevitably aligned them with secular powers. The quarrel over the bell tower that broke out in May 1683 between the bishop and the guardian of the hospice of Quebec clearly exposed the Order's position and its manipulation by secular power. It all began in 1681, when having received land from the king for the construction of a hospice in Quebec City, the Recollects completed their construction by building a bell tower. The parish of Quebec, then united with the seminary, feared that [sounding] the chapel bell would draw people away from the parish. The Recollects, known as lenient confessors, were welcoming soldiers, sailors and inhabitants who willingly came to their confessionals more than to the parish or the Jesuits. In addition, the mass stipends paid to the Recollects resulted in a lost income for the parish of Notre-Dame de Québec. Bishop Laval, who opposed the public opening of this chapel, led the war against the friars. In 1684, the Recollects brought the case before the king. Even before the bell could be heard, the tower was knocked down. The parish and, in turn, the seminary temporarily won. The Jesuits had every interest in decreasing this ecclesiastical body's influence because it threatened to encroach on their apostolic territory and cause them to share the finances granted by the crown to the Society of Jesus in Canada.[24] Given this situation, the Recollects struggled to find their place in the city. Only under Bishop Laval's successor, Bishop de Saint-Vallier, was the difficulty somewhat resolved. The agreements reached between the new bishop and the Recollects show that there was now a spirit of cooperation. This was evident in 1692 when, in exchange for permission to establish a real friary in the upper town, the Recollects gave their Notre-Dame-des-Anges friary, located on the Saint-Charles River, to the bishop to be used as a General Hospital. An enduring peace was established, apart from some arguments about procedure which were typical of the *Ancien Régime.*

A PLACE IN HISTORY

The historical and geographical writings that were produced shortly after the Recollects' return to New France can really only be understood within the context of the Canadian literary landscape that already existed. The Jesuits' *relations,* written in the form of chronicles, had left a written record for the long period of 1632 to 1672. The missionary scene, still largely dominated by the Society of Jesus, seemed until then to have been occupied only by them. Even more eloquent [than these chronicles] was the Jesuit Paul Ragueneau's book entitled *Vie de la Mère Catherine de Saint-Augustin,* published in Paris in 1671. It was a symbolic proposal of a supernatural world order largely dominated by the Society of Jesus' great figures—Saint Ignatius, Saint Francis Xavier and Father de Brébeuf—who acted both as this nun's protectors and as judges of a misguided New France.[25] In 1677 and 1681, the *Vie* and the *Lettres de la vénérable Mère Marie de l'Incarnation* recounted Canada's apostolic history through the eyes of an exceptional woman.[26] In these works, the Recollects, those little-loved religious in a small colonial world, were ignored despite their

---

24. We find indirect echoes of this fear in a brief presented by Lamothe-Cadillac for the establishment of Detroit. Pierre Margry, *Découvertes et établissements des Français dans l'Ouest,* Paris, Maisonneuve, 1887, vol. 5, p. 163.

25. Paul Ragueneau, *Vie de la Mère Catherine de Saint-Augustin,* Paris, Lambert, 1671, 403 p.

26. Claude Martin, *La Vie de la Vénérable Mère de l'Incarnation,* Paris, Billaine, 1677, 757 p.: *Lettres de la vénérable Mère de l'Incarnation,* Paris, Billaine, 1681, 675 p.

Anonymous. *Portrait of Louis Hennepin,* 1694. Oil on canvas, 40.64 × 37.47 cm, St. Paul, Minnesota Historical Society.

preeminence as missionaries. Thus, the Recollect writings of the last quarter of the seventeenth century showed a clear desire to overcome this lacuna or, more precisely, to repair this injustice.

Profiting from a better situation and solid support, the Recollects started a writing campaign that was as much about a correction of history as it was about defending the prerogatives of the Order in New France. The Franciscan writings of that time expressed a firm desire to reinsert themselves, at all costs, in a Canadian history from which they had been removed. Their publication of *Premier Etablissement de la foy dans la Nouvelle France,* in Paris in 1691, which was duly dedicated to their eminent patron the Count de Frontenac, was much more than a chronicle about the Amerindians' early Christianization.[27] The subject of the book, in part attributed to the Recollect Valentin Le Roux, was so apologetic and polemical, that it was very difficult to see anything in it other than a collective manifesto for rewriting the framework of a Canadian history that for many appeared false and incomplete.

Father Chrestien Le Clercq, in his publication of *Nouvelle Relation de la Gaspésie,* aimed to establish the Recollect missionary presence with the

27. *Premier Etablissement de la foy dans la Nouvelle France,* Paris, Amable Auroy, 1691, 2 vol.

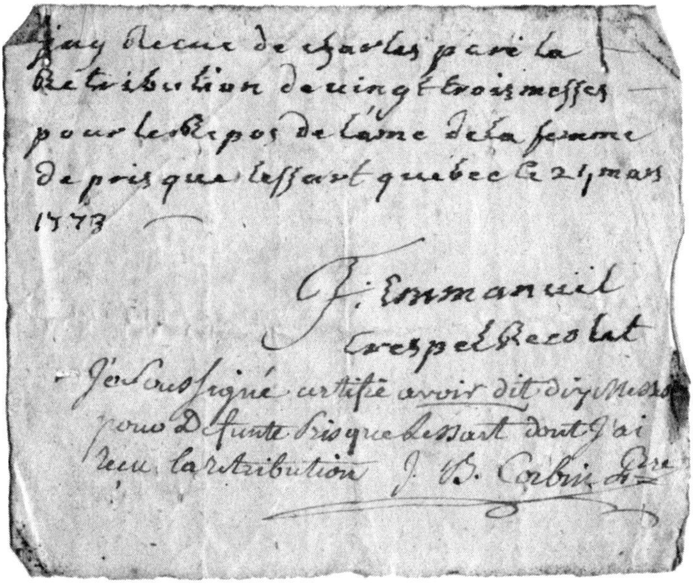
J'ay Recue de charles paré la Retribution de vingt trois messes pour le Repos de l'ame de la femme de prisque lessart quebec le 21 mars 1773

F. Emmanuel Crespel Recolet

Je soussigné certifie avoir dit dix Messes pour Defunte Prisque Lessart dont J'ai Reçu la retribution J. B. Corbin ptre

Emmanuel Crespel, *Receipt for 23 masses said for the repose of the soul of the wife of Prisque Lessard, March 24, 1773.* BAnQ, Fonds Famille Pouliot, p436, s999, p72.

Mi'kmaq of the Gulf of St. Lawrence.[28] Because the Parisian publishers respected the literary standards of the time and requested additional passages, this account is still today one of the most important sources for documenting the Mi'kmaq's traditional life. Regarding the Recollects' late seventeenth century writings, Louis Hennepin's must especially be noted, since they go well beyond the local disputes to become uncontested descriptions of the Mississippi and North American geography. Despite his questionable Franciscan identity and connections with the Franciscan Order, Hennepin remained the most famous Recollect of his time, as was indicated by the many editions of his *Voyages,* which were quickly translated into Italian, Dutch, German, English, and Spanish.[29] Hennepin's work outlived the polemics and, so to speak, New France itself. This probably explains why this Recollect who became famous throughout Europe had the privilege of being portrayed as a man of the world in those Protestant countries where, it should be pointed out, he was prohibited to wear a religious habit.

28. Chrestien Le Clercq, *Nouvelle Relation de la Gaspesie,* Paris, Auroy, 1691, 572 p.

29. Joseph Sabin, *A List of the Editions of the Works of Louis Hennepin and Alonso de Herrera*, New York, Sabin, 1876, 16 p.

One of the most vibrant decades for the Recollects of New France was the 1690s. The *Premier Etablissement de la foy dans la Nouvelle France,* which "sets the record straight," appeared in Paris in 1691, the year in which the [Quebec] hospice was erected as a friary. There, they preached, heard confessions, had public expositions of the Blessed Sacrament, and held funeral services. In short, they celebrated every service without being disturbed.[30] The Recollects were thriving. Enjoying the protection of the Governor General, they paid him tribute. In the pulpit, Frontenac was presented as a "St. Louis," he was described as a "zealous defender of the faith" and a "protector of the Church," not to mention the other glorious titles attributed to him. He was always addressed with deferential terms, such as "Monsignor" and "Excellency,"[31] to the great annoyance of the bishop and the seminary. These annoying Recollects, moreover, presented a real danger. In 1691, the Recollects attempted to attract theology students from Quebec's Grand Seminary, promising parents that their sons would be sent to France in the same year to continue their theology.[32] And then, there was the question of finances. Bishop Laval opposed the Recollects moving to the upper town, for fear that they would monopolize the alms badly needed by the Hôtel-Dieu and the parish. In her study of devotional practices in New France, Marie-Aimée Cliche counted 105 bequests made to the Recollects during the French Regime, which was the highest rate of donations made to any religious community by the Quebec government. These numerous bequests allowed the Recollects to pay various workers to complete the construction of their magnificent friary. Frontenac, who bequeathed them 1,500 pounds in his will, was among the donors. There were members of the Third Order, as well as influential and wealthy people, sometimes relatives of Canadians who made their profession in the Order. The son of Charles Aubert de La Chesnaye, the most important merchant in Quebec, bequeathed them 4,500 pounds in 1702. His maternal uncle, it should be noted, was none other than Father Joseph Denys, a prominent figure in the Order in Canada. This beautiful donation allowed the friars to complete the friary cloister. These are just two examples. From mass stipends alone, the Recollects collected 13,403 pounds, compared to the 9,970 pounds that the Notre-Dame de Québec parish collected during the same time. As a mendicant order, the Recollects received all sorts of donations in exchange for freely given ministry. Land was bequeathed to them.[33] Many faithful, moreover, wished to be buried in the

30. ASQ, Chapitre 160; Lettres M. no. 11, p. 3.

31. ASQ, Chapitre 160; no. 11, p. 3.

32. ASQ, Chapitre 160.

33. Odoric Jouve, *Le Frère Didace Pelletier, Récollet,* Québec, Couvent des SS. Stigmates, 1910, p. 245–259.

Jean-Baptiste Scotin, *The true portrait of the very Religious Didace Pelletier,* early seventeenth century. Ink on paper, Quebec City, Musée de la civilisation, Seminary of Quebec Collection.

chapel crypt more than any other place. Four governors were buried there: Frontenac, Callières, La Jonquière, Vaudreuil. Poverty and austerity only increased the prestige of the Recollects, who now were only lacking an unassuming saint suitable to the people's tastes.

In contrast to the figure of Hennepin is the incomparably more affable Didace Pelletier (1657–1699), a humble converse brother born in Sainte Anne du Petit Cap and a convincing embodiment of a Canadian Recollect. Didace Pelletier was a local image of Franciscan holiness according to the era's portrayal of saints. No wonder his superior of the time, Father Joseph Denys, proposed him as the artist's model for painting a likeness of Saint Pascal Baylon, whose canonization had taken place in October 1690. Everything suggests that Didace Pelletier was immortalized by the painter because of his outstanding virtues, which it was hoped would be brought to light after his death. The engraving that later came out of Jean-Baptiste Scotin's Parisian studio was the one that helped spread devotion to this Canadian religious. The text accompanying the engraving put forth the facts and attested to the power of this little Canadian's intercession: "A true portrait of very religious Friar Didace Pelletier, a Recollect friar, native of Sainte-Anne in Canada, who died in the odor of sanctity in the missions of New France, on February 21, 1699, at the age of 41 and after 20 years of religious life, whom God has honored with several miracles." Devotion to Didace Pelletier spread throughout the colony and even acquired a transatlantic dimension. Many travelers were thought to have confided in his protection during their return trip to France. At least that is what was suggested by four ex-votos representing Brother Didace Peletier which were still in Dieppe at the end of the nineteenth century. One of them, which we know only from an ancient photograph reproduced in the [original] article, showed a "Saint Didasse Peltier" who was canonized by popular piety. The face of our virtuous Recollect had been reworked and was covered over by that of a curly-haired child Jesus who, in many ways, evoked the Little King of Grace venerated at the Carmel of Beaune.[34] Despite its gauche reworking, this picture, which, judging from the hand gestures, was clearly inspired by Scotin's engraving, remains poignant. It illustrates above all how much the pictorial image was derived from oral and written glosses that preceded it, and how much in turn the image continued to contribute to the spread of prior attestations. Through the window that this portrait is, the intercessor "Didace Pelletier" could now be glimpsed, appropriated, chosen and called on by those who were about to cross the Atlantic.

The devotion to this holy Recollect is not the only one to have crossed the seas. Among the models of "exportable" virtues, there was also that of his contemporary, Father Simon Gérard de La Place (1657–1699), who died in the odor of sanctity among the Malecites of the Saint-Jean River in Acadia in 1699. The transference of his mortal remains to Quebec did not take place until 1705. The cadaver triumphantly entered Quebec City with an escort of 400 Amerindian allies. People ran to join them. A solemn funeral service was celebrated in the friary chapel. The powerful attended, with the governor general leading the way. Everyone asked for relics of the saint, notably pieces of his habit which remained intact despite having been in the ground for years. Father Simon's skull was placed in a reliquary that was installed in the church for the faithful's veneration. In 1710, after the increase of favors granted, Father Louis-Hyacinthe de la Place, the blood brother of Father Simon Gérard de la Place and a Recollect, devoted himself to writing the life of his blessed brother, recorded all the miracles attributed to him, and even drew his portrait.[35] For unknown reasons, the case was eventually dropped. The manuscript containing the life of the missionary to the Malecites and the details of the miracles attained through his intercession passed into oblivion. Obviously, Didace Pelletier was enough.

In Detroit, there was Constantin de Lhalle, who died accidentally in 1706 following a dispute of the Ottawa and Miamis tribes at Fort du Detroit. The

34. Odoric Jouve *et al.*, *Dictionnaire biographique des récollets missionnaires en Nouvelle-France*, Montréal, Éditions Bellarmin, 1996, p. 239–246.

35. *Ibid.*, pp. 239–246.

Anonymous, *Saint Didasse Peltier.* Ex-voto reproduced by Odoric Jouve in *Le Frère Didace Pelletier, Récollet,* 1910, p. 252.

body was moved from one church to another before ending up, in 1754, in yet a fifth church. The Recollect, Simple Bocquet, who was then parish priest in Detroit, stated that, in placing the remains of his late confrere under the high altar, they intended to grant him "a permanent tomb worthy of his merit and of the miracles that had been reported by several trustworthy people which were made by his intercession in favor of the whole parish."[36] Rightly or wrongly, Franciscan saintliness arose as much from the real virtues embodied by these friars as from the aura of holiness that surrounded these extraordinary men.

INSERTION INTO THE COLONY'S LIFE

It seems that, at the beginning of the eighteenth century, the Strict Observance still exercised a large influence on the people. Several seminarians were directed to the novitiate. Some were attracted to the regular life, such as Mathieu Amior who, when he had been turned away from the seminary, "vowed to become a Recollect," which he did in 1734, when he took the name of Friar Hyacinthe.[37] The inability to study, and to learn Latin in particular, prompted

36. *Ibid.,* pp. 269–273.

37. ASQ, Annales, année 1706, ms-2a, p. 35; Odoric Jouve, *Dictionnaire biographique,* p. 9–11.

many to move toward the Recollects' novitiate in Montreal, which seemed less demanding on these points. Among these students excluded from the seminary were some boys who had painful experiences. Raphaël Lecours entered the Petit Séminaire de Québec at the age of 10 in 1684. Unsuccessful in studies, he was sent to Île Jesus the following year to learn a trade, but instead he returned to his mother. A second attempt at the seminary in 1688–89 was no more successful. He was directed to the Recollects. In 1693 he took the habit at the Montreal friary and made his profession the following year under the name of Friar Alexis. On his return to Quebec, Friar Alexis succeeded in his studies of philosophy and theology and was finally ordained a priest in 1698.[38] Antoine de La Fresnay de Brusy followed a similar path. When he was dismissed from the Minor Seminary, he knocked on the door of the novitiate in Montreal. He took his vows there at the same time as Raphaël Lecours. Bishop Saint-Vallier was invited to the event, as was the Governor de Callières. The ceremony promised to be beautiful; however, everything went bad over a question of precedence between the bishop and the acting Governor General. The insulted bishop left the premises and placed an interdict on the Recollects' chapel in Montreal. The situation resolved itself.

Most Canadians who entered novitiate intending to go on to the priesthood had usually attended the Jesuit college for at least a few years and had completed some of their studies in the humanities. Some former seminarians at Québec who had been refused priestly ordination for various reasons, were also saved by the Recollects. Jean-Baptiste Le Neuf de la Vallière was one such person. He entered the Petit Séminaire in 1686 at the age of 14 on the recommendation of Bishop Saint-Vallier, who had recruited him in Acadia; but, the young Le Neuf de la Vallière was dismissed by the directors of the institution who "considered him unfit for the Church." His maternal uncle, Father Joseph Denys, welcomed him at Saint-Antoine friary in Quebec, where he finally made his profession in 1697 taking the name of Friar Bernardin.[39] Other seminarians thought of entering the Recollects but did not persevere.[40] Regarding studies, the Recollects were keen to offer their students in formation all the necessary tools to perfect their knowledge of the ecclesiastical sciences. This included a library, part of which was made up of Bishop Saint-Vallier's library, which they bought at a high price when he sold it to finance his general hospital.[41]

---

38. ASQ, Annales, année 1706, ms-2a, p. 13; O. Jouve, *Dictionnaire biographique,* p. 584–585.

39. ASQ, *Transcripta*, p. 6; O. Jouve, *Dictionnaire biographique,* p. 599–600.

40. ASQ, Annales, année 1706, ms-2a, p. 21: *Transcripta*, p. 11.

41. The annalist at Quebec's Hôpital Général wrote that Bishop Saint-Vallier "sold his Library of twelve thousand Books to the Recollect Fathers, although it was worth twice that much." Annales de l'Hôpital général de Québec, vol. 2, p. 22.

Among the laymen who came to the Recollects there were also unmarried men looking for a place to live. It seems, as well, that some boys had been sent to the Recollects by their parents as boarders.[42] There was the young Alfonse Tonty de Palludy who lived for a year in the friary before being admitted to their minor seminary in October 1699.[43] Since this was the third child of Alphonse Tonty de Paludy, the brother of Henri de Tonty, both of whom were close to Frontenac, the Recollects could do nothing but be accommodating. Other pious people took rooms in the friary to experience more fully a retired Christian life and to work out their salvation. In 1698, Brother Didace Pelletier's own father, Georges Pelletier, took a room as a boarder in the upper town's friary. He resided there until his death in 1708.

The upper town hospice was transformed into a friary in 1691, and it also occasionally welcomed older boys who were in transit from one place to another. Pierre Collas, a soldier and a fraster[44] in de Vaudreuil's company, stayed at the friary in 1701 as a layman and not a novice.[45] In the eighteenth century, this friary's very large dimensions with only a few friars residing there was an indication that the Recollects used it in many ways. Among the residents at one time was the son of a rowdy family, Claude Le Beau. Literally exiled to New France by his parents who were driven to desperation by his antics, the young Le Beau landed at Quebec in 1729 after a harrowing shipwreck along with the new bishop of Quebec, Mgr. Dosquet, and other clerics, including three Recollects among whom was the new Provincial Commissary for Canada, Father Donatien Dubois. Upon his arrival at Quebec, Le Beau was employed at the *Bureau du Castor* for six weeks during which time he stayed at the Recollects' friary as a boarder and under their supervision. Le Beau's relations with the friars seem to have been cordial. Moreover, it was thanks to Father Dubois that he obtained the position of first clerk of the King's Stores. About this Recollect, Le Beau would later write that he "was eternally indebted to him, as well as to several others of this

---

42. ASQ, Annales, année 1706, ms-2a, p. 25.

43. "The 8-year-old Alfonse Tonti entered [the minor seminary] on 15 October [1699] after having remained one year with the Reverend Recollect Fathers" ASQ, ASQ, Annales, année 1706, ms-2a, p. 27; René Jetté, *Dictionnaire généalogique des familles du Québec,* Montréal, Pes Presses de l'Université de Montréal, 1983, p. 1083.

44. Translator's note: Almost all military companies had a "frater" or "fraster" who was a soldier with some knowledge of first aid. Generally, he received a small supplement to his pay in addition to the usual soldier's salary.

45. Éva Guillorel, « De l'armée au séminaire : l'itinéraire et l'œuvre de Pierre Collas, migrant éphémère en Nouvelle-France, 1698–1703 », *Revue de Bibliothèque et Archives nationales du Québec,* 4, 2012, p. 20–31.

Landry after Liébault, *Portrait of R.F. Donatien du Bois, former provincial commissioner of the Missions in Canada*. Print, Liébault pinx., Flipart Sculp., 27 × 17.8 cm, BnF.

Order [including Joseph Denys], for all the benefits" received from them.[46] These residents certainly allowed the house to earn an income additional to their mass stipends, collections, bequests, and other donations, just as several other communities in Quebec did by receiving permanent boarders.[47]

The Recollects quickly became socially relevant to the colony, just as initially feared by Bishop Laval who foresaw that these religious would be too greatly esteemed by the secular power, weaken his authority, and create a loss of income for the parish. Not only were they lenient confessors sought out by the population to relieve their consciences, but they were pastors who could at will be easily moved from one parish or fort to another. Their presence in the forts was a win-win situation for everyone. From each 200-

46. Claude Le Beau, *Avantures du Sr. C. Le Beau,* Amsterdam, Herman Uytwerf, 1738, première partie, p. 71, 76, 311.

47. The Ursulines of Quebec also had "permanent" boarders at the Hôtel-Dieu and the General Hospital of Quebec. In our opinion, this is how we should understand the following entry in the register of seminary students: "Louis Jean Franquelin of France aged 23, in the care of M. le Comte de Frontenac, desiring to withdraw from the world was received at the Petit Séminaire on 28 April [1673]; he left on 30 Jan. 1676 to stay with the steward, Mr. Duchesnau." ASQ, Annales, année 1706, ms-2a, p. 4.

Religious of the Third Order of St. Francis of the Congregation of France without a mantle. Pierre Hélyot, *Histoire des Ordres monastiques, religieux et militaires,* Paris, J.-B. Coignard, 17141719, vol. VII, Part 5, p. 267.

pound grant given by the king to retain a Recollect in a fort, the Quebec friary received half.[48] As for the State, it commended itself for having such docile pastors at its service. These financially undemanding religious were perfectly in line with the reality of a developing colony. They were found in Percé, living among seasonal fishermen, and in Plaisance, Newfoundland, where three Recollects, including a converse brother, "had a small church, a small friary, a small garden and few donations."[49] This provisional service in forts and distant parishes would be the very essence of the ministry of 300 Recollects who worked in New France from 1670 to the Conquest. Between 1670 and 1760, nearly a third of them exercised this ministry as chaplains in frontier settlements in Acadia, Louisiana, in the *Pays d'en Haut*[50] and in Newfound-

48. *Voyage de Pehr Kalm au Canada en 1749,* annotated translation of his travel diary by Jacques Rousseau and Guy Béthune, Montreal, Tisseyre, 1977, p. 909.

49. Gédéon Nicolas de Voutron, *Voyages aux Amériques : Campagnes de 1696 aux Antilles et de 1706 à Plaisance et en Acadie,* Québec, Septentrion, 2010, p. 189.

50. Translator's note: The *Pays d'en Haut* should not be confused with the region popularly called by the same name and presently represented by the Federal electoral district of Pontiac (formerly Pontiac-Gatineau-Labelle). According to Wikipedia, it was: "a territory of New France covering the regions of North America located west of Montreal. The vast

land. Parish relief ministry and military chaplaincy were the Recollects' characteristic apostolates throughout the French Regime.

This accommodating Franciscan presence was evident in various places throughout the colony. From 1684 to 1690, two Third Order Regular priests, the Picpus Fathers or Penitents of Nazareth, carried out their ministry in Acadia, in Chedabouctou, among the seasonal fishermen.[51] Capuchins would settle in Louisiana. In short, the Franciscan Order with its many expressions ensured wherever possible an intimate ministry to the most humble. The parishes of Nouvelle-Beauce also had Recollects at their service.

Among these humble workers, Father Emmanuel Crespel was certainly the most prominent figure. He arrived in New France in 1724 and took up a path typical of the Recollects. He was ordained a priest by Bishop Saint-Vallier in 1726 in the chapel of the General Hospital of Québec. After that, he ministered in Sorel and the surrounding hamlets. In 1728, Crespel accompanied a French [military] detachment westward and visited Detroit. That same year he returned to Montreal only to leave again for Fort Niagara the following year. During this stay, he made another trip to Detroit. He returned to the friary in Quebec in 1733 and from there left for Fort Cataraquoui. Two years later, he was appointed to Fort Saint-Frédéric on Lake Champlain, where he lived in extreme poverty. He returned to Quebec in 1736 and returned to France the same year. Nothing distinguished Crespel from the other Recollects of New France: all of them were called to live in poverty. Mobility, adaptability, and proximity to humble people characterized these men whom the Church and the State move around, without worry, according to the needs of the moment.

It was the sinking of the ship on which Crespel sailed back to France that made him famous. His account of this shipwreck on Anticosti Island was published as a letter in French in Frankfurt in 1742, then republished in 1752. Meanwhile, in 1751, a German translation appeared. A French reissue was again published in 1757.[52] Crespel became a popular author, and his story of

---

territory included most of the Great Lakes region, . . . The *Pays d'en Haut* was established in 1610 and dependent upon the [French] colony of Canada until 1763, . . ." During the colonization period, this would refer to the Michigan-Wisconsin region, in the Ohio Valley, and down the Mississippi River system. Cf. https://en.wikipedia.org/wiki/Pays_d%27en_Haut

51. Michel Tériault, *Les instituts de vie consacrée au Canada depuis les débuts de la Nouvelle-France jusqu'à aujourd'hui : notes historiques et références,* Ottawa, Bibliothèque nationale du Canada, 1980, p. 82–83.

52. *Voiages du R.P. Emmanuel Crespel, dans le Canada et son naufrage en revenant en France : mis au jour par le Sr. Louis Crespel, son frère,* Francfort, Broennet, 1742, 135 p. The German translation appears under the title: *Des Ehrwürdigen Pater Emanuel Crespels merwürdige Reisen nach Canada,* Franckfurt und Leipzig, Bey Georg Peter Monath, 1751.

Attributed to Father Francis (Jean-Melchior Brekenmacher), *Father Emmanuel Crespel*, c. 1755. Oil on canvas, 81 × 64.6 cm, Québec, Musée national des beaux-arts du Québec, 1958. 187.

the shipwreck contributed significantly to the literature of his time. He returned to Quebec in 1750 as Provincial Commissary. From then on, he held various positions until his death in 1775. Relying on previous research, R. Bacon maintained that it was because Crespel saved the life of Dr. Jean-Baptiste Rieutord in 1760 that he was painted by his Recollect confrère François Brekenmacher. This assertion does not hold up. Not only would Brekenmacher have been at least 75 years old on that date, but, even more, there was no documentary evidence to support that he even returned to New France after having been guardian of the friary in Corbeil. It was essentially because of Crespel's renown as an author of an adventure story which he had the good fortune to survive that he became one of the Order's most sympathetic faces in the eighteenth century and for which he was immortalized by an artist before 1760.

The English translation appeared in 1707 under the title: *Travels in North America with a narrative of his shipwreck and extraordinary hardships and sufferings on the Island of Anticosti and an account of that island and of the shipwreck of his Majesty's ship Active and others*, London, Sampson Low, 1707, 187 p. In 1808, a third French edition of Crespel's work appeared at the Nouvelle Imprimerie.

The Poor among the Poor

During the capture of Fort Niagara in the summer of 1759, the Anglican pastor accompanying the British troops noted how much kind attention the resident Recollect paid to the Iroquois families who settled around the fort, even inviting them to attend celebrations "with great Ceremony and Parade."[53] This was not an exaggeration on his part, since it is corroborated by the Recollect, Emmanuel Crespel, who was stationed in the same place in 1729. Crespel had undertaken to learn the Iroquois language and even that of the Ottawa tribe, willing to jabber with them and to invite them to religious ceremonies. This interaction with unconverted Amerindians familiarized them with Christianity and gave them an appreciation for the Catholic faith. Noting how much this attention to the Amerindians had been beneficial to France, the Anglican pastor made this very timely reflection on English indifference to this matter: "This neglect will not give the Indians the most favorable impression of us."[54] Among the beautiful portraits of New France's Recollect missionaries, there is one which more than compensates for its iconographic failures by its power to evoke words. Father Michel Brûslé arrived in Canada in 1698 with Father Maxime Goyer[55] who became famous for his funeral oration at the funeral of the Comte de Frontenac. From 1705 and for the next seventeen years, Father Michel was a missionary to the Mi'kmaq of Restigouche in the Baie des Chaleurs. The testimony of an officer stationed in Louisbourg, Cape Breton, is worth quoting here:

> There was a band which came from eighty leagues away, from the Baie des Chaleurs along the Saint Laurent River, which was under the care of an apostolic missionary called Father Michel, a Recollect, who for 20 years lived with them, often ate raw meat like them, slept in the cold, and sometimes fasted for lack of provisions. He assured me that he had gone six years without eating bread. He could scarcely explain himself in French without mixing a little of this savage language. They honored

53. Charles Frederick Pascoe *Two Hundred Years of the S.P.G.: An historical account of the Society for the Propagation of the Gospel in foreign pats. 1701–1900.* London, Published by the Society's Office, 11901, vol. 1, p. 153; *Travels of R.P. Emanuel Crespel*, 1742, p. 23.

54. Charles Frederick Pascoe *Two Hundred Years of the S.P.G.*, Vol 1, p. 153.

55. Translator's note: According to the *Dictionary of Canadian Biography*, it was Father Olivier Goyer who preached at Frontenac's funeral: "In 1698 Goyer went to Canada as provincial commissioner and lived in Quebec. He was Governor Buade de Frontenac's confessor and was at his bedside until he breathed his last on 28 Nov. 1698. The funeral took place on 1 December, but the official service, presided over by Bishop Saint-Vallier, was not held until 19 December, at the Recollet convent. Father Goyer pronounced the funeral oration for the illustrious deceased before the highest ecclesiastical and civil dignitaries in Canada." Cf. http://www.biographi.ca/en/bio/goyer_olivier_2F.html

[Blessing of the crosses by Father Chrestien Le Clercq]. Illustration from Chrestien Le Clercq, *New Relation of Gaspesia,* Toronto, Champlain Society, 1910, separate folio.

> and respected him like their father. He returned with his troop after a month to the Baie des Chaleurs by land.[56]

Slight exaggerations aside, Chancels' testimony remains one of the most eloquent statements on Franciscan simplicity regarding the Recollects' life among the Amerindians. After only eleven years of ministry within this group of Amerindians (and not twenty as Chancels said), Brûlé literally gave himself to his flock by espousing their lives and their cause. He died in Montreal in 1724. If he was not the only Recollect of his time to work among the Amerindians, he is certainly the most perfect icon that the archives have kept to memory.

The year 1730 clearly indicates the Recollects' complete insertion into the urban landscape. Far from the jealousies of yesteryear, the friars had gained the authorities' respect and the people's affection. At the birth of the Dauphin, the Recollects presented a real picture of their unwavering loyalty to the French crown. The festivities began on September 18. In their large

56. Louis Chancels de Lagrange, « Voyage fait a l'Isle Royalle ou du Cap Breton en Canada. 1716 », in L.-A. Vigneras, « L'Isle Royale en 1716 », *Revue de l'histoire d'Amérique française,* 13(3), 1959, p. 431.

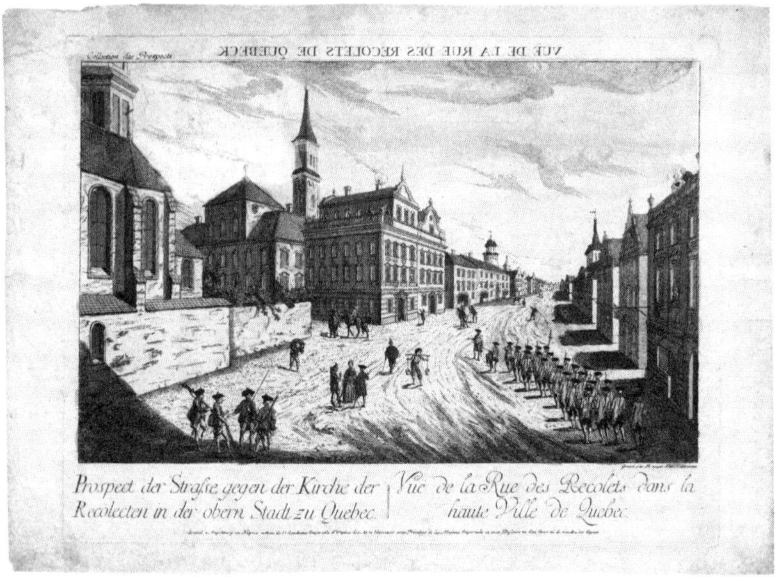

François-Xavier Habermann, *View from the Rue des Recolets in the upper town of Quebec,* c. 1775. Ink and water colour on laid papier, 36 × 49.7, Québec, Musée de la civilisation, Quebec Seminary Collection.

and beautiful church which, according to the Jesuit historian Charlevoix, "would do them honor at Versailles,"[57] "they sang a great mass with music, which the governor general, the intendant and all the nobility attended. At the end of Vespers, the Reverend Father F.-X. de La Haye, a friar of their Order, gave a speech on the occasion of the birth of my Lord the Dauphin which was universally applauded. A *Te Deum* was sung to music accompanied by the sound of artillery."[58] Soon after, the Provincial Commissary for Canada, Father Donatien Dubois, left Quebec, leaving behind a community that had carved out its niche in the colony's environmental structure.

Like the small towns of France where church spires and convents rise to the sky, the convents of Quebec City, Montreal and Trois-Rivières were now legitimately part of the urban landscape. The archives of the women's communities reveal that the Recollects were good neighbors and that they

---

57. François-Xavier de Charlevoix, *Histoire et description générale de la Nouvelle-France,* Paris, Rollin, 1744, vol. 5, p. 110.

58. Auguste Gosselin, *Québec en 1730; relation de ce qui s'est passé à Québec, en Canada, ville capitale de la Nouvelle-France, à l'occasion de la naissance de Mgr Le Dauphin,* Ottawa, Hope et fils, 1899, p. 8.

were on good relations with them. A Recollect said Mass for the Quebec Ursulines, for which he was given eight loaves of bread a month according to a mutually binding agreement. The ties were even stronger with the Ursulines of Trois-Rivières where the Recollects were the only pastors in the town. At Quebec's General Hospital, the friars served as chaplains and sometimes even as confessors. From then on, the Recollects' life was an organized conventual life and they provided services perfectly suited to the state's needs in New France. The easing of tensions corresponded to the fact that a significant part of the workforce was beginning to be made up of Canadians. The Recollects opened a novitiate in Quebec in 1677 to promote a lasting presence of the Order by encouraging local recruits. The majority of the 88 Canadians, however, who became Recollects, entered the Order of St. Francis during the first half of the eighteenth century.[59] Many of them came from prominent families, thus helping to insert the Franciscan reality even further into the social fabric of the colony. Unlike the Jesuits and Sulpicians, the Recollects opened their doors to Canadians.

In the eighteenth century, it seems that [the friars] were not too demanding concerning the intellectual ability of those they admitted. The Swedish traveler, Perh Kalm, conveyed the prejudices of Quebec's small ecclesiastical world when he wrote about the Recollects saying that "a monk of this kind often has no more understanding than an ox." Who is he talking about? Lay brothers? Possibly. According to this traveler, the Recollects' distaste for studies and their little learning would have been an accepted fact. There was a saying "to form a Recollect, you need a hatchet; to make a priest, you need a chisel; to produce a Jesuit, you need a paint brush."[60] It has to be granted, however, that the Recollects undertook architectural and artistic activity that did not entirely limit them to framing churches. There were distinguished painters and sculptors in the Order in Canada.

Far from the skilled Brother Luc, there were some architects and artists whose less well-known profiles also deserve attention. Among those, there was François Brekenmacher who would have been the most accomplished painter that the Order had in Canada in the eighteenth century, at least in theory. . . . In reality, nothing remains of his work, other than a few uncertain attributions. Brekenmacher was ordained a priest in Quebec's General Hospital chapel at the same time as Friar Augustin Quintal, and he carried out work commonly undertaken by the Order in the colony, namely parish ministry and chaplaincy. One thing is certain, in the aftermath of Montreal's Hôtel-Dieu fire in 1724, Brekenmacher, the architect and painter, designed and decorated the sisters' new church with the help of Father Juconde

59. Caroline Galland, *Pour le service de Dieu, du Roi et du Bien public,* p. 281–384.
60. *Voyage de Pehr Kalm,* p. 276, 319, 902, 903.

Drué.[61] Father Juconde designed the plans for Quebec's Saint-Antoine friary in 1693 and for Saint-Roch hermitage, where the General Hospital chaplains stayed so they could be closer to the poor and the sisters who ran the institution. It is thought that Friar Juconde popularized an architectural church model called "à la récollette" with a characteristic frontal bell tower soaring like an arrow into the sky. Drué's achievements were numerous and not exclusively limited to architecture. Odoric Jouve maintains that he was probably the person who painted the portrait of Saint Pascal Baylon in 1691 to which Brother Didace Pelletier lent his features.

Next from the Orders' group of artists in New France comes Father Augustin Quintal. He was born in Boucherville in 1683, entered the Recollects' novitiate in 1706, and took the name of Brother Augustin at his profession. Ordained a priest in 1713, he ministered to several parishes and helped Father Drué to decorate the friary church in Montreal. In Trois-Rivières, where he became parish priest, he redid the parish church and added to its liturgical furnishings with his own handiwork and by calling on other renowned Canadian craftsmen such as Noël Levasseur from whom he commissioned a tabernacle. By the way, two brothers of this famous sculptor from New France made profession with the Recollects in Quebec: Pierre-Marie [Levasseur] in 1717 and Jean-François two years later.

Perh Kalm's memories, recorded during his stay in Quebec City, attest to the Recollects' presence in the town's scene. Like other travelers, he praised the beauty of the large friary, its chapel overlooking the Place d'Armes, and its large, beautiful garden. Unlike the Jesuits, he noted that the Recollects participated in processions and appeared to be poor and prayerful.

The young friars went from house to house with a bag on their backs to beg for their needs: bread, meat, firewood, and other stuff. These collections annoyed those involved with the hospitals since they also needed these supplies, and this led to a mutual agreement between the people and the lay friars. The friars went, as necessary, to the houses of the rich and those living there to talk and eat and sometimes spend the night. After Montreal's fire at the Hôtel-Dieu in 1695, a Recollect friar on his way back to Quebec was given the task of bringing Frontenac a letter to announce the terrible news and to ask for his protection in these painful circumstances. Not too alarmed [by the situation], our Franciscan Hermes "took up a collection on the way back to his friary, going from house to house, which delayed him a lot and took him an entire month. . . ."[62]

They tirelessly continued their visits to the inhabitants in towns and villages along the St. Lawrence, barefoot in their clogs, wearing wool stockings

61. Marie Morin, *Histoire simple et véritable,* critical edition by Ghislaine Legendre, Montréal, Les Presses de l'Université de Montréal, 1979, p. 292–293.

62. Marie Morin, *Histoire simple et véritable,* p. 251.

James Pattison Cockburn, *Corpus Christi.* Watercolor on paper, 15.20 × 23.80 cm. Quebec, Ursulines of Quebec Monastic Collection.

in winter or shoes in the wilds, and, in their winter wanderings, using a kind of sled pulled by large mastiffs.[63] The many memories and anecdotes reported by Philippe Aubert de Gaspé in his *Mémoires* reveal lay friars who were close to the people and much less rigid than the Strict Observance's traditional representation would suggest. If the Recollects asked charity from the landholders and inhabitants who made such a fuss to take them in and feed them bread, meat and wine, they reciprocated this by welcoming into their friary the people from the country, who were not able to pay for a room at the inn when they visited the city, by keeping their horses in enclosures, by educating their children, and by seeing to their dead, until they were able to pay. A Canadian song collected by Aubert de Gaspé said: "I have a hundred reasons to love the Recollects: They are a good group of guys, who live with no pretense."[64] These "grey robes," a much-appreciated reality of the eighteenth century, ended up becoming legendary.

A nineteenth century legend features the Recollect Ambroise Rouillard. Born in Quebec in 1693, Louis-Joseph Rouillard joined the Recollects in 1718 and followed the usual path: profession in 1719 and priesthood in 1723. From then on, Father Ambroise exercised his ministry in the Bas-Saint-

63. Claude le Beau, *Avantures de Sr C. Le Beau,* première partie, p. 81.
64. Philippe Aubert de Gaspé, *Mémoires,* Ottawa, Desbarats, 1866, p. 55–84.

Laurent, between Ile-Verte and Rimouski. In the summer of 1768, while he was in Trois-Pistoles with Lord Rioux, the latter decided to have the friar's portrait painted. Once finished, the work was exhibited in the manor house and garnered the admiration of visitors who recognized Father Ambrose's features. Looking at his own portrait, the priest exclaimed, "I think I look like a drowned man." Leaving the lord's manor to go by sea to Rimouski, a storm arose around Bic, the boat capsized, and the Recollect was engulfed by the waves. One night, Brother Ambrose left the repose of the dead to return to the manor house to fulfill the promise once made to the lord to return a silver goblet that he had used out of deference to the lord of the seigneury but to the detriment of Lady Poverty.[65] Father Ambrose was remembered, everywhere he went, as a holy man. Furthermore, he assisted Toussaint Cartier, the hermit of Saint-Barnabé Island, in his last moments here on earth.[66] The two living legends met one another.

It is remarkable to note how much the Recollects' memory is frequently surrounded with gratitude in old parish monographs. In his history of the seigneury of Lauzon, J.-E. Roy asserted that the Recollects, who served it devotedly until the British Conquest, left a lasting memory among the people. One of them, Father Justinien Constantin, a Canadian born in Quebec in 1716, helped the settlers choose their land for seven years. In the lord's absence, he was in charge of preparing the concession contracts.[67] The opening of the road connecting the Chaudière River to the Etchemin River, in 1758, is also owed to Father Justinien. This road that crossed the thick forest of Sartigan became known as the Justinian Road.[68]

End of the French Regime

Virtually nothing is known about the social network on which the Recollects relied for a free workforce to maintain their friaries. Similarly, it is impossible to know whether the members of the Franciscan Third Order helped during the French Regime. Did the governor's guard occasionally lend a hand to the religious? That is possible. One thing is certain: Philippe Aubert de Gaspé reported in his *Mémoires* how much the Recollects, and particularly

65. Jean-Charles Taché, « Le gobelet d'argent du père Ambroise », *Le Bulletin des recherches historiques,* 4 (2), février 1898, p. 52–54.

66. Claude La Charité, « L'érémitisme en Nouvelle-France et la vocation singulière de Toussaint Cartier au XVIII siècle », *Études d'histoire religieuse,* 79 (2), 2013, p. 5–19.

67. Joseph-Edmond Roy, *Histoire de la seigneurie de Lauzon,* Lévis, Mercier & Cie, 1898, vol. 2, p. 201–202.

68. Part of the old Justinian Road now forms one of the sections of the current President Kennedy Road to Lévis.

[Association Diploma and spiritual affiliation given to Jean-Baptiste Perreault, merchant in Trois-Rivières, by Reverend Father Hyacinthe Berrier, provincial of the Recollects of the Province of Saint Denys in France], 1758. Leaf, 34.5 × 25.6 cm, Quebec, Museum of Civilisation, Fonds from the Quebec Seminary archives, Documents Faribault, no. 233.

the lay friars, were universally loved by the inhabitants of the countryside. They not only made abundant contributions, but also dutifully transported the friars during their wanderings from one parish to another, lodged them, and even went so far as to take turns to bring what was collected to Quebec City or Lévis, depending on the region that had been visited.[69] In the 1750s, there were about fifty Recollects in New France, more than three-quarters of whom were Canadian. The ties with relatives and friends were not only financially advantageous for the community, which in turn knew how to be generous. A certificate of affiliation—a kind of document assuring a union in prayer—was given in 1758 by the Recollects of Versailles to Jean-Baptiste Perreault, a merchant in Trois-Rivières, for all the good services rendered to the Recollects of this friary. It indicated how much care the friars took to maintain good relations with their benefactors and others who could be helpful to them, especially at a time when the misfortunes of war were about to befall Canada.[70]

69. Philippe Aubert de Gaspé, *Mémoires*, p. 61.

70. O. Jouve, *Dictionnaire*, p. 185.

The Recollects and the Conquest: Chronicle of a Death Foretold

Under British military rule (1760–1763), the Recollects were the smallest male [religious] community in the country. About fifteen French Recollects left Canada during this period, leaving behind about thirty Canadian friars whose fate became increasingly uncertain. The British authorities used a part of Quebec's Saint-Antoine friary, relatively undisturbed by bombs, as the official storage place for the public archives, while the chapel was requisitioned for Protestant worship two years later. Although the city's Recollects were forced to share their space with the English whose presence had an affect on what would become of them, the friars nevertheless continued to care for the parishes in the Laurentian Valley. The friaries of Montreal and Trois-Rivières remained unchanged. For the time being, the friars were tolerated by the occupiers. The penalty, however, came a few years later when the British Crown decided to dissolve male congregations. The Recollects were now prohibited from any recruitment, which was a medium-term objective aimed at hastening the disappearance of the Order. Ten years after the conquest, the Recollects, most of whom were old, were reduced to ten friars.

The Decree of Secularization

In the early 1780s Father Félix de Berey defied London by secretly reopening the novitiate in Quebec. Despite the firm ban on recruitment, he secretly welcomed twelve new Canadians. From 1784 onward, the Recollect community was joined by Felix Bossu and Bonaventure Deschenaux, candidates for the priesthood, as well as ten lay brothers—Louis Martinet called Bonami, Marc Coutant, Léonard Dumas, Antoine Fournier, Simon Fournier, Paul Fournier, François Giguère, Noël Proulx, Didace Tétrault and Friar Ambroise.[71] Although Governor Guy Carleton turned a blind eye to this illicit recruitment, Bishop Hubert, irritated by the Provincial's audacity, made the incident known to the Propaganda in Rome and then, for a first time, suggested the possibility of secularizing the new novices who had taken the habit.[72] These novices and temporarily professed friars infused a certain dynamism into what remained of the community of Saint-Antoine friary in Quebec. This state of grace, however, was only short-lived. Very quickly, the living relations between the young Recollects, mostly from modest families, and their elders, mainly from the bourgeoisie of the Ancien Régime, proved to be conflictual. The enthusiastic and imprudent young men criticized the

71. C. Galland, *Pour le service de Dieu, du Roi et du Bien public,* vol. 1, p. 292–301.

72. O. Jouve, *Dictionnaire,* p. 192–196.

Anonymous, *Portrait of Brother Louis Demers,* early nineteenth century. Oil on canvas, 82.3 × 65.8 cm, Québec, Museum of Civilisation, Seminary of Quebec Collection, 1991. 85.

impediments made to the *Rule* and were particularly virulent towards Fathers Félix de Berey and Louis Demers, the respective superiors of the friaries in Quebec and Montreal. In 1793, five of the twelve recruits sent a letter of complaint to the Bishop about Father de Berey. Whereas Father de Berey should have set an example, he willingly gave in to all kinds of worldly concerns to the detriment of observing the *Rule*. Moreover, they accused him of having deceived them by telling them that the recruitment ban, formerly pronounced by the British Government, had been lifted at the time of their entry into the novitiate and this, they argued, was done for the sole purpose of preserving his status as Provincial commissary.[73] Father de Berey responded by dismissing the five protesters from the friary at Quebec. They then found refuge in Montreal's friary. If Father de Berey's personality, as these young friars saw it, was at odds with the Franciscan ideal, the character of Father Louis Demers, guardian of the Montreal friary, did not create harmony among the members of his community. He was described by Father Pierre Denaut as a despot "who thinks he is a superior who cannot be replaced."[74] Father

73. *Ibid.*, p. 301.

74. Archives de la chancellerie l'Archevêché de Montréal, 901-001, 795-1.

Demers in turn came into conflict with the younger generation of Recollects. Just as they had done in Quebec, they objected to the relaxation and asked for a greater observance [of the Rule]. For Demers, these friars' rebellious spirit was incompatible with their religious vows.[75] Tension increased in the friary. Some claim that the troubles in Montreal were caused by the despotic attitude of Brother Alexis Demers, brother of Father Louis Demers.[76] It is very difficult to judge from our sources. Whether slanderous or real, these accusations reflect the community's disorder experienced in the last decades of the eighteenth century during a time of power struggles and conflicts of interest. The elders' transgression of the *Rule,* which was criticized by the young professed, was characteristic of the general relaxation of the Observants and Strict Observants in Franciscan provinces throughout the world in the middle of the eighteenth century. The decline in vocations and increased financial problems were a general situation in Order. In Canada, these last recruits' embodiment of the Franciscan ideal did not stop the community's disintegration. For better or for worse, the community survived until Bishop Hubert delivered the final blow by a decree of secularization in 1796. The lay brothers and priests had to live "according to the times" from then on, that is to say, outside the walls of the friary, while having the freedom to keep their religious vows individually and even to wear the Franciscan habit, which many of them did do.

Teaching or the Way of Salvation

The decree of secularization allowed the bishop to reestablish order in his diocese and to settle the thorny problem of the Recollects. In 1794 there were only a few aging friars left: Brother Demers, who remained in Montreal's friary until 1796 when the building was requisitioned by colonial authorities to establish lodgings for British troops. Friar Bernardin remained at Quebec with Father de Berey. In the same year, 1796, the Quebec friary was ravaged by a fire. Some secularized Recollects, such as the brothers Fournier and Dumas, gave up the habit and withdrew to their families. Most secularized religious became involved in primary education. The post-Conquest period saw a decline in the educational system established under the French regime, and the contribution of the secularized religious was welcomed. Brother Félix Bossu began teaching at the Petit Séminaire and then was appointed prefect and later director of studies. Friar Paul Fournier

75. O. Jouve, *Dictionnaire,* p. 276–281.

76. ASQ, Document Faribault No. 233. Jean-Baptiste Perreault was the brother of François-Joseph Perreault, Vicar General of the Bishop of Quebec at Trois-Rivières and the great-uncle of Joseph-François Perrault.

Anonymous. *Portrait of Brother Alexis Demers,* early nineteenth century. Oil on canvas, 80.9 × 64.9 cm, Québec, Museum of Civilization, Quebec Seminary, 1991.84.

was the director of some small parish schools in the Montreal area. Friar Louis Bonami, a colorful and endearing character, directed an elementary school in the Saint-Roch district of Quebec City for ten years which was attended by about sixty school-children. Friar Noël Proulx settled in Verchères where he became the factory's teacher. Brother Marc Coutant, meanwhile, worked as a watchmaker, but also became a schoolmaster at Sainte-Anne de la Pocatière and Saint-Thomas de Montmagny. At the turn of the nineteenth century, the former Recollect community redefined its identity and redirected its missionary apostolate towards the education of young children, particularly in the countryside and suburbs. Remarkably, most of these men still retained the title of Recollect and, upon their death, were buried in their Franciscan habit.

After the Recollects' secularization, the Order gradually disappeared from the Quebec landscape. In 1804, the government decided to raze the ruins of the Quebec friary and, a few years later, laid Holy Trinity cathedral's foundation stone, which was intended for the city's Anglican community. Louis Demers, the last Recollect priest, died in 1813, while Friar Marc Coutant died in 1849. The dissolution of the community was completed.

Joseph Légaré, *Friar Louis, Recollect,* c. 1830. Oil, gouache, paper glued on wood, 31.7 × 22.2 cm, Quebec. Museum of Civilization, Quebec Seminary.

The Quest for Memories

Ernest Gagnon told of a commonly believed legend where the Virgin Mary appeared on the battlefield in July 1758 to protect the royal troops and assure them of a victory. It is impossible to know whether these popular stories were inspired by the finding of the Recollects' banner or whether the stories preceded the relic's discovery in the nineteenth century. It is nevertheless undeniable that this flag entered the popular imagination by substantiating heaven's intervention in favor of France. The Recollect Louis Martinet, who was called Bonami, entered novitiate in Montreal in 1785. He is intimately linked to the preservation and "discovery" of this relic, which some say was brought back the day after the French victory by Father Félix de Berey, wo had it hung in the vault of the Recollects' church in Quebec City.[77]

77. According to Baillargé, he learned of the carillon flag's existence from "an old woman's diary" in the Recollect friary. Ernest Gagnon, however, claims never to have found any trace of this chronicle. Louis Gonzague de Baillargé kept the flag until his death in 1896. The Séminaire de Québec then acquired it. Furthermore, Father de Berey's presence at the Battle of Fort Carillon is uncertain. Cf. Ernest Gagnon, « Le drapeau de Carillon », *Revue canadienne,* Nouvelle série, 2 (3), 1882, p. 129–139; Georges-Frédéric Baillargé, *Louis de Gonzague de Baillargé, avocat, c.r., chevalier-commandeur de l'ordre de Saint-Grégoire le Grand,* Joliette, Bureaux de l'étudiant, du couvent et de la famille, 1891, p. 15.

In his old age, Brother Louis assured Louis de Gonzague Baillargé, a wealthy lawyer and philanthropist from Quebec, that the flag and some objects in the sacristy had escaped the flames of the Quebec friary fire in 1796. These remains from another era were faithfully preserved for more than fifty years in a chest. On his deathbed in 1848, Friar Bonami then entrusted the precious banner to Baillargé who unveiled it shortly after his departure.

Fifty years after the decree of secularization promulgated by Bishop Hubert, which sounded the death knell to the [Franciscan] community in Canada, and on the eve of its definitive extinction, the legend of the Carillon flag entrusted to Baillargé by Friar Louis assured the Recollects' history a place in French-Canada's destiny. Ten years after the failure of the 1837 rebellion, at a time when French-Canada was seeking to assert itself, the flag's discovery was providential. As a witness to the great deeds in the Canadian people's history, the object quickly became one of the symbols of French survival, which the bards of the time, Octave Crémazie foremost among them, sang through their poetry.[78] The last survivor of the Order, Friar Louis, was both the guardian and the promoter of a tradition that, if not historically indisputable, plunged New France into an idealized form of memorial practices surrounding the remembrance of the Recollects' past glories and the last figures of the Order, among whom was Father de Berey.

RESTORING THE RECOLLECTS' IMAGE

Nothing illustrates more the quest to remember the ancient Recollects than the little story that surrounds the portrait of Father Félix de Berey. It all began when the parish priest of Saint-Eustache, Father Jacques Paquin, decided to create a gallery containing portraits of his predecessors in the parish. Father de Berey had ministered there from 1769 to 1775. Since there was no portrait of the Recollect, Father Paquin decided to fill this lacuna by having a posthumous portrait painted. If history could be rewritten, so too could a face be recomposed. To do this, Father Paquin had the idea of bringing together some parish elders who had known the late Father de Berey. The artist Vital

78. The poem *The Carillon Flag* by the French-Canadian poet, Octave Crémazie, depicts a veteran of the Battle of Carillon who went to Versailles to ask the king for help, taking with him the battle flag, a witness of the French Canadians' heroism in the war against England. Rejected with contempt at Versailles, he returned home in great distress and breathed his last at Carillon where the standard was used to enshroud him. The poem personifies France's indifference the Conquest and glorifies the French Canadians' resistance. Cf. Henri Raymond Casgrain, *Œuvres complètes de Octave Crémazie,* Montréal, Beauchemin & Valois, 1882, p. 128–137.

Vital Durocher, *Portrait of Father Félix de Bércy,* 1841. Oil on canvas, 67.2 × 57 cm, Saint-Eustache, Saint-Eustache Parish Council, diocese of Montreal.

Durocher, a pupil of Antoine Plamondon,[79] was called upon to paint the portrait, and he made several sketches from memory of the Recollect's features. The painter then presented them to the elders who suggested various changes.

After several attempts, de Berey's face took shape in 1841. Everyone claimed to recognize him just as he was! De Berey's well executed portrait was hung among those of the other parish pastors and effaced the paradoxical past of the friar who had been the guardian and administrator of the Quebec friary which was then sadly transformed into a prison under the British regime.[80] The Recollects' history, expressed in portraits among which was one of an unremarkable friar, Félix de Berey, certainly deserves to be completed and reexamined both from before and after the event. The subject of "Recollect," even at a first tentative level, appears approachable only in light of religious, political and literary disputes that accounted for the creation of these paintings and their acceptance by future generations, which is what was suggested by a visit to this gallery.

79. David Karel, *Dictionnaire des artistes de langue française en Amérique du Nord,* Québec, Les Presses de l'université Laval, 1992, p. 272.

80. Édouard Lefebvre de Bellefeuille, « Le R.P. Félix Berey », *Revue canadienne*, 4, 1867, p. 366–367.

Anonymous. *Capuchin monk* [alleged portrait of Father Joseph Denys]. Oil on canvas, 80 × 67 cm, Québec, Collection of the Augustines' Monastery, Hôtel-Dieu de Québec.

On this same subject of searching for remembrances of the Recollects, we can place the "pseudo-portrait" of Father Joseph Denys, a painting preserved at Quebec's Hôtel-Dieu. This exceptional religious, if in fact he is exceptional, was the subject of a biography by Father Hugolin Lemay. During his research, he met with the Hôtel Dieu's archivist, who informed him in 1909 of an oil painting in the convent which depicted an absolutely unknown Franciscan who, she suspected, was Father Joseph Denys. Jacques Denys de la Ronde entered the novitiate at Quebec and made profession in 1678. His family had connections everywhere and was one of the most prominent of the time. He was well thought of by authorities and enterprising; he was present at the start of the missions in Percé, Plaisance, and D'Acadie, and at the construction of Montreal's and Trois-Rivières' friaries. He was also one of the witnesses of the construction of Quebec's great friary, where he ended his days in 1736. It is also to Father Joseph Denys that we owe the rise of devotion to Friar Didace, who was known by him personally at Percé and Trois-Rivières. To go through this remarkable friar's biography is to reread the entire history of the Recollects' second settlement from a Canadian perspective. Since the nursing sisters had once made their profession at Quebec's Hôtel-Dieu and had been associated with this friar, they were

Grégoire Huret, *Portrait of Anselme de Sainte-Marguerite.* Print, 14.5 × 9 cm, BnF.

persuaded that "this beautiful, gentle and noble figure" could only be that of Father Joseph Denys.[81]

The art historian G. Morisset had doubts about this portrait and stumbled by chance one day on an engraving that corresponded almost exactly to the painting. Thereafter, Morisset learned that the portrait in Hôtel-Dieu did not represent Father Joseph Denys, but rather Father Anselm de Sainte-Marguerite, prior of the convent of Notre-Dame-des-Victoires belonging to the Discalced Hermits of Saint-Augustin in Paris, otherwise known as the Petits-Pères.[82] Without anyone being able to say why, the mysterious portrait of Father Anselm ended up at the Hôtel-Dieu in Quebec City.[83] It should

81. Hugolin Lemay, *Le Père Joseph Denis, Premier Récollet Canadien, 1657–1736,* Québec, s.n., 1926, vol. 2, p. 189.

82. Edmond Lambert et Aimé Buirette, *Histoire de l'église Notre-Dame-des-Victoires,* Paris, Curot, 1872, p. 84. The engraving of Father Anselm de Sainte-Marguerite is mentioned in the work of Jacques le Long *Bibliothèque historique de la France,* Paris Herissant, 1775, vol. 4, p. 137; Gerard Morisset, *Les arts au Canada français. Peintres et Tableaux,* vol. 2, Québec, Éditions du Chevalet, 1937, p. 45–46.

83. The Capuchins wore beards as well as the penitent fathers of Nazareth who were also called the Picpus Fathers. Jean-Simon Renier, *Historique du couvent, du collège et de l'église des P. Récollets, à Verviers,* Verviers, Crouquet, 1862, p. 3–4.

also be noted that this bearded monk could not be Father Joseph Denys, because the Recollect clerics of that time did not wear beards.[84]

At the beginning of the twentieth century, when the Recollects' history was enthusiastically being written, this more or less conscious substitution of identity naturally came to the sisters, especially since the archivist was determined "to find a Canadian likeness for him."[85] When Father Hugolin Lemay published his life of Joseph Denys, he could not help but reproduce this pseudo-portrait in the second volume of his biography to make his hero even more real to his readers. The practice of finding a face was common in what could be called a legitimate quest to substantiate a recollection. Writing the history of New France was no exception. The proponents of the Canadian epic sought to put faces on their history's key players. At a time when the Franciscan Order was returning to French Canada, the Recollects' institutional history was too impersonal and nebulous and needed to be embodied in some inspiring faces.

REVIVING THE RECOLLECTS

The Third Order Secular Franciscans' enthusiasm in ultramontane French Canada as well as the difficulties that religious communities experienced to survive in republican Europe are the contexts that raised the idea of reestablishing the Franciscans in Canada at the end of the nineteenth century. Supported by Montreal's tertiaries, six Franciscans first moved into a dwelling [in the city] before founding a friary dedicated to Saint-Joseph, in 1906. The Franciscans had settled in Quebec City in 1900 and then in Trois-Rivières in 1903. The construction of a second friary in Montreal was undertaken in the 1920s; and they soon took on ministry to the Catholic populations of western Canada.[86] There were 59 Franciscans in Canada in 1903; 144 in 1909; and 135 in 1918. With its growth and extensive territory, the Canadian community was quickly established as a Commissariat in 1920, and then as a Province[87] dedicated to Saint Joseph, in 1927.[88]

---

84. Odoric Jouve, *Dictionnaire biographique*, p. 345, note 679. René Bacon mistakenly made this monk a Carmelite. He is a discalced Augustinian hermit from France.

85. Hugolin Lemay, *Le Père Joseph Denis,* vol. 2, p. 189.

86. Jean Hamlin, *Les Franciscains au Canada, 1890–1990,* Sillery Septentrion, 1990, p. 31–38 et *Les Franciscains du Canada (Les Frères mineurs). Leur histoire, leur vie,* Montréal, Revue du Tiers-Ordre et de la Terre-Sainte, 1915, p. 142–148.

87. A province is an ecclesiastical constituency that geographically groups a certain number of a congregation's houses under the responsibility of the same Provincial Minister, who is required, during a three-year period, to visit different houses. During his office, he presides over the definitory, a council, where the day-to-day affairs of the province are dealt with. Frédéric Meyer, *Pauvreté et assistance spirituelle,* p. 105–110.

88. Jean Hamelin, *Les Franciscains au Canada,* p. 25–40.

While settling and establishing themselves in the land that welcomed them, the Franciscans felt the need to justify and legitimize their presence in Canada by tracing it back to the first French Recollects, thus creating a historical continuum between those first friars and themselves. As a result, numerous works on the history of the Recollects in New France appeared, which were read mostly by the friars and members of the Third Order.

Father Désiré Petitnicolas, a Franciscan originally from Lorraine now established in Canada, was the author of an authoritative manual used by the Third Order. In 1892, he organized a retreat in the parish of Baie-Saint-Paul which was served by a Friar Minor who had founded a secular fraternity there at the beginning of the year.[89] A month later, the faithful expressed their gratitude to him in the *Revue du Tiers-Ordre*:

> The establishment of the Third Order Franciscans in our midst has reawakened our population to the ancient traditions of this parish. We happily remember that your Fathers, who did so much for our country, preceded the secular clergy, and even the Jesuits, in this land of New France. [. . .] Seeing the venerable Franciscan habit reappear in our church after an absence of more than a century and a half seemed to revive our ancestors who were, for a long time, the spiritual sons of your ancient Fathers.[90]

The establishment of the Third Order and the Franciscans was seen as a guarantee for the survival of French-Canadian culture and history. "Back to the roots" was the order of the day. Father Trudelle paid tribute to the Recollects of New France in his biography of Brother Louis Bonami, published in 1898, and called on French Canadians to express their gratitude for their former pastors.[91] The parishioners of Baie-Saint-Paul, for their part, assured Father Désiré that they had kept the faith and observed the moral teachings that the Recollects of the early eighteenth century had instilled in their ancestors.[92] The enduring Franciscan [saga] over such long absences enabled the transition from the old Recollects to the "new" Franciscans.[93] During the first half of the twentieth century and with the prevailing clerical nationalism, the Franciscans tried to reconstruct the patchy concept of Recollect presence in Canada by introducing some Franciscan figures into the pantheon of Canadian history. During the celebrations of Quebec City's

---

89. Ephrem Longpré, *The Secular Third Order of St. Francis of Assisi in Canada: Sketchesis historical,* Montréal Ménard, 1921, p. 101.

90. *Revue de Tiers-Ordre et de la Terre sainte,* 8e année, no. 3, 1er mars 1892, p. 92.

91. Charles Trudelle, *Le Frère Louis,* Lévis, 1898, 94 p.

92. *Revue de Tiers-Ordre et de la Terre sainte,* 8e année, no. 3, 1er mars 1892, p. 92.

93. *Revue de Tiers-Ordre et de la Terre sainte,* 8e année, no. 3, 1er mars 1892, p. 93.

tercentenary in 1908, Father Odoric Jouve was offended and complained that the Recollects were absent from any of the historical paintings that had been displayed, which thereafter brought about the Recollects' real restoration. It was from this date onward that the Franciscans became aware of the need to write their own history.[94] From then on, the Order's historians began to research and write the history of the Recollects in New France: first in the form of biographies or short historical notes; then, in the context of tercentenary celebrations of the [Catholic] faith, in various publications such as historical retrospectives, collections of legends, bibliographies, educational books and even an impressive souvenir volume.

The tercentenary celebrations, which took place in Quebec City in 1916 and culminated in erecting a monument to the faith on the Place d'Armes, provided the ground for the Franciscan's regaining their history. The erection of this monument, a commemorative event that expressed the French Canadian's national identity and faith, was also, through the Franciscans' predecessors being acknowledged, a symbolic form of their own reestablishment. This attention to celebrating the Recollects' history still resonated several decades later. Thus, by an astonishing tour de force, Archange Godbout, Hugolin Lemay and Odoric Jouve, to name but a few, revived the Recollect adventure and managed to transform the arrival of the Friars Minors (OFM) in the late nineteenth century into the third return of those who began the work. They were not the only ones to do so, because the [diocesan] clergy already smitten with this history was trying to put the spotlight back on some Recollects who were bound up with their local history.

In his 1898 monograph on the history of Sault-au-Récollet parish, Abbé Beaubien inserted a detailed account of the death of Recollect, Nicolas Viel, and added an illustration of this poor friar being thrown into the Rivière des Prairies' whirlpools by his executioners. Not satisfied with this depiction, he went on, in 1903, to have bronze statues made of Nicolas Viel and the convert, Ahuntsic, which he had installed in front of the parish church at Sault-au-Récollet.[95] The zealous parish priest then proposed to the bishop of Montreal a bold project of historical paintings to adorn the walls of his cathedral. His intention was clear: to build "a monument to mark the religious history of our homeland whose beginning had been accompanied by so many blessings."[96] The artist, Georges Delfosse, was entrusted with the realization

94. *Revue de Tiers-Ordre et de la Terre sainte,* 24e année, no. 10, octobre 1908, p. 496.

95. Charles-Philippe Beaubien, *Le Sault-au-Récollet : ses rapports avec le premier temps de la colonie,* Montréal Beauchemin & fils, 1898, 505 p.

96. Letter from Abbé Charles-Philippe Beaubien, Sault-au-Récollet, August 17, 1907, Archives of the Archdiocese of Montréal, 255.112, 907-2.

of this project.[97] He designed a series of seven historical paintings depicting the Jesuit martyrs of Huronia, Jeanne Mance, and other pioneers of the faith in Canada, including of course the Recollects. It would have been surprising if the principal backer of this project were not keen to see the heroes of his parish featured in this glorious assemblage. The paintings made by Delfosse in 1908 and 1909 are an example of artistic productions depicting the birth of French-Canadian civilization and heralding the future of Montreal which typically arose out of the commemorative fever surrounding Quebec's tercentenary celebrations.

One of the two paintings that Delfosse made of this subject depicts the first mass celebrated on the banks of the Rivière-des-Prairies in June 24, 1615—a mythical event that predated the saga of Ville-Marie by some twenty-five years. Against a backdrop of calm skies, Father Denys Jamet, assisted by Father Joseph Le Caron, offers the sacrifice of the Eucharistic. Behind the two Recollects stand Amerindians in postures dear to classical painting, as well as some French men—among whom is Champlain—kneeling in deep contemplation, sort of prefiguring the Christianity that would come to Montreal in the future.

The second painting, which depicts the martyrdom of the Recollect Nicolas Viel, evokes in its own way the supernatural foundation of the city of Montreal's church, which flourished and became powerful because, from its origins, it was watered with the blood of martyrs. Admired by the faithful who visit Montreal's cathedral, these large paintings allow a periodic return to the nation's history and, in this case, to two scenes from the Recollects' story. As a memorial, these paintings recounting the Recollects' deeds now recall a past whose values are intended to be a permanent and intrinsic part of the present society.

In addition to paintings, the illustrations accompanying Catholic children's literature and primary school textbooks also provided a modest place for the Recollects. In 1923, Marie-Claire Daveluy published a children's novel in which the names of Le Caron and Sagard were placed side by side with those of other key figures in the French colony. In the foreword to her young readers, Daveluy wrote: "I wanted to make known and familiarize you with the important personages from our ancestors. May your blond and brunette heads bow with love and pride before the noble and very often crucifying deeds of New France's heroes."[98] These Franciscan figures, who embodied the values of fidelity, dedication, and selflessness, remained an uncontested example for this society where the Church was involved in almost every aspect of life and where large families were working hard to build a country.

---

97. David Karel, *Dictionnaire des artiste*, p. 224–225.

98. Marie-Claire Daveluy, *Les aventures de Perrine et de Charlot*, Montréal Bibliothèque de l'Action française, 1923, 310 p.

Georges Delfosse, *First mass sung on the banks of the Rivière-des-Prairies by R.P. Denis Jamay*, 1908. Oil on canvas, 429.26 × 223.52 cm, Montreal, Marie-Reine-du-Monde Cathedral.

In the category of historical frescoes, there is the artist Guido Nincheri's painting of Father Joseph Le Caron consecrating Canada to Saint Joseph on March 19, 1624. It was envisioned to adorn the north wall of one of the transepts in the Sisters of St. Joseph of Saint-Vallier's chapel in Quebec City; and it is one of the most eloquent testimonies of the means by which the Recollects were reinserted into the nation's history. The details about the painting's conception are worth their weight in gold. Obviously unaware of the Canadian epic, Nincheri asked Abbé Brunet for some illustrations of the most important personages, and especially about their clothing, so that he might be inspired before putting them into the painting. Brunet had practically nothing to offer the artist, except a picture of Champlain and six photographs taken during Quebec's tercentenary pageant in 1908. He wasted no time to write the artist saying: "I think you will find some clothes from Champlain's time in the illustrated *Histoires du Canada* that are used in Montreal's schools, among others, that of Monseigneur Desrosiers' which is illustrated by Duquet."[99] It was unlikely that an artist of Nincheri's caliber

99. Letter from Father Eugène Brunet to Guido Nincheri, October 4, 1937. Archives of the Sisters of St. Joseph of St. Vallier, OR-01-177.

Georges Delfosse, *Nicolas Viel, first Recollect Canadian martyr, and the convert Ahuntsic,* 1909. Oil on canvas, 375.92 × 246.38 cm, Montreal, Marie-Reine-du-Monde Cathedral.

would be inspired by these illustrations; however, it was possible that he would be taken up with the spirit that was part of this iconographic crusade.[100] In this regard, it is worth recalling that the illustrator Jean-Baptiste Lagacé had designed a series of 36 historical paintings for use in elementary schools whose primary function was to complement Abbé Adélard Desrosiers and Camille Bertrand's Canadian history textbook then widely distributed in the schools of the Province of Quebec.[101] One of these paintings entitled "Champlain and the Recollects" depicted the arrival of the first four Recollects at Quebec in 1615. By 1923, Lagacé's series of paintings had already sold more than 3,000 copies.[102] The ideas that inspired the work which Nincheri planned for the chapel of the Sisters of St. Joseph of St. Vallier were closely linked to the historical representation characteristically presented in illustrated textbooks.

---

100. Adélard Desrosiers, *Petite histoire du Canada,* imagée par Georges-Henri Duquet, Québec, Garneau, 1933, 176 p. Adélard Desrosiers et Camille Bertrand, *Histoire du Canada,* Montréal, Beauchemin, 1919, 567 p.

101. Adélard Desrsiers et Camille Bertrand, *Histoire du Canada.* Three reprints appeared: the last two were published by Granger brothers in 1925 and in 1933.

102. Paul Aubin, *300 ans de manuels scolaires au Québec,* Québec, Les Presses de l'Université Laval, 2006, p. 50.

Many well-known images familiar to the French-Canadian population come from these [textbooks] and are now hopefully recognized in the historical paintings that adorn their sanctuaries.

Abbé Brunet responded on the artist's behalf to the comments and criticisms that Lagacé's preliminary watercolors were sent to the bookbinders before Nincheri's canvas was painted. Various changes, removals and additions were proposed so that the scene would approximate the seventeenth century reality while aligning itself with the day's characteristic values and ideals. Not only should the vault of the Recollects' primitive chapel be more pointed, but the stove that the artist had seen fit to add had to be removed. The statue of Saint Joseph should appear in its entirety; forget about shortening the altar steps. As head of the colony, Champlain should be gazing at St. Joseph. A Way of the Cross should appear on the walls, as well as a holy water font at the exit. The tassel at the end of the cord used for the Recollects' belts had to be removed. These are just a few examples of the corrections asked of the artist. In addition, Champlain's young wife had to have her shoulders covered with a coat, while Marie Rollet, Canada's first mother, had to be more prominent and alongside Louis Hébert, her husband, and their two children who, in fact, were no longer young children in 1624, since their daughter Guillemette Hébert was already married. But regardless of the chronological contortions, the Sisters of St. Joseph being mainly teachers thought it appropriate to have children in the composition. Similarly, Abbé Brunet considered that "two savage men and a savage woman with a child on her back would add a charming aspect to the scene."[103] They appear in the background. The Sisters of St. Joseph of St. Vallier's oral tradition still holds that members of the painter's family were used as models for the painting's key figures.

As portrayed by Nicheri, this endearing scene worthy of a Canadian history textbook and depicting the small colonial world of yesteryear was a reinterpretation of French-Canadian society in the 1940s. The Recollects' story reflected in this magnifying mirror was elevated to the level of a crusade in which the great colonial figures assured the French-Canadian people's providential destiny, according to the nationalist ideology then in vogue. The painting of Canada's consecration to St. Joseph arrived in Quebec City on May 24, 1940. A magnificent frame with carved maple leaves was then designed to highlight the canvas.[104]

---

103. Letter from Father Eugène Brunet to Guido Nincheri, November 18, 1937, Archives of the Sisters of St. Joseph of St. Vallier, OR-01-178.

104. Archives of the Sisters of Saint Joseph of Saint Vallier, Journal de communauté, 1939–42, p. 35.

Jean-Baptiste Legacé, *Champlain et the Recollects,* 1921. Illustration mounted on heavy cardboard, 50.8 × 91.44 cm, published in the *Tableaux d'histoire published by Desrosiers-Bertrand,* Montreal, Granger.

The Recollects Regain their Voice

The lectures, poems, and radio plays that were presented in 1942 recalled, or better celebrated, this history brought to the fore by French-Canadian nationalism. In 1942, Marie-Claire Daveluy, "an ardent patriot with a Franciscan soul,"[105] wrote plays for the 250th anniversary of the Recollects' arrival in Montreal which were performed on CKAC, that radio station "so popular in Quebec because it was Catholic and French-Canadian." For various reasons, the radio was abandoned in favor of afternoon talks where these plays were read. At every type of performance, these productions exalted the first Recollects, such as Joseph Le Caron, Irénée Piat, Gabriel Sagard, Joseph Denys, Charles Rapine, Didace Pelletier, Juconde Drué and others. Using a deliberately "good-natured" tone, Daveluy skillfully mixed factual history and twentieth century politico-religious sensibilities in the dialogues that she created and put in the mouth of these Recollects. Praise and humour

105. *Les Récollets et Montréal: huit manifestations commémorant le 250e anniversaire de l'établissement des Récollets à Ville-Marie, 1692–1942,* Montréal, Éditions Franciscaine, 1955, p. 17–32.

Guido Nincheri, *Consecration of Canada to Saint Joseph by Father Joseph Le Caron on March 1624,* 1940. Oil on canvas, 365.76 × 426.7s cm, Quebec, Sisters of St. Joseph of St. Vallier of Quebec. Photo credit Daniel Abel.

converged into a kind of nationalist creed that, if it was not always openly expressed, was powerfully felt by an audience already won over to the cause.

Eight historical festivals, which were organized by Marie-Claire Daveluy and took place from February 8 to June 20, 1942, appealed to the era's seasoned historians, such as the inevitable Abbé Lionel Groulx, Léo-Paul Desrosiers, Albert Tessier, Olivier Maurault and Gérard Morisset, to name a few. Songs and sometimes even poetry recitations about the Recollects were added to the events and conferences. Roger Brien, a poet from Nicolet, put his profoundly Catholic pen to the task and recounted Father Denys Jamet's first Mass which was celebrated at the Rivière des Prairies on June 24, 1615. Here are some lines from his poem entitled *Première Messe sur l'Île de Montréal*:

> On that beautiful June morning all afire
> with the blazing heart of God risen from the tomb,
> A great people was born in this new world.
> [. . .]
> And you Jamet, son of Francis of Assisi,
> Sublime Recollect, pure torch of the Church,
> You raised the host above these waves.
> You gave this world back to God. You dried its tears.

> You raised the Blood of God to snuff out Satan.
> Your deed will be a sign, a seal of love, for all times.
> [. . .].[106]

There was no shortage of academic lyrics to glorify these first symbolic acts whose somewhat exaggerated significance can only be appreciated in light of a society's dreams and hopes of regaining its identity and its native land. It would have been surprising if the evocative power of painting had not competed with history and literature and, in turn, appropriated to itself the heroes of the Canadian adventure. Inspired by the embellishments of historians and literary scholars, painters and sculptors visibly restored the Recollects' humanity, as we have seen. The beautiful radiant clean-shaven faces of Joseph Le Caron, Denys Jamet, Nicolas Viel and others, whose memories and ideals seemed worthy of being revived, were presented to ongoing generations of young Canadians. This multi-faceted artistic production was the visual counterpart to the historians and literary scholars' committed quest for a French Canada. Whether in paintings, statues, or literature, the Recollects' function was to lay the foundations of a history in progress and to perpetuate a patrimony and transform it into a legacy for future generations.

At the end of this overview of the Recollects' factual and cultural history, it is apparent that the figures encountered throughout this text have shown that we are on a path of human actions filled with turns and about-turns in changed locations and over time. Undeniably, this story is as much about real events as it is about those of past authors' understandings and their conviction of what was essential to hand on to us. Artists, in their turn, again presented these sons of St. Francis aesthetically but with the zeal that was characteristic of their time.

It must be admitted that today these historical and edifying paintings have been emptied of their emotional and ideological impact. Delfosse and Nincheri's friars with their fixed gaze are silent. Similarly, the bronze or stone Recollects that adorn public places leave most passers-by indifferent, serving instead as a perch for passing birds. The memory of the past that their solidity once glorified is fading, no longer supported by any social project. Once again, a page has been turned in the history of the Order of St. Francis in Canada. Although the Recollects' history in New France lacks documentation and is full of inaccuracies, it is not without interest for the twenty-first century researcher; quite the contrary. From a multidisciplinary perspective, there is a clear horizon where true and even embellished facts subtly dialogue with all kinds of silences, a little like the intertwining links of threads which create the delicate design of lace. This book is already a foretaste of what is possible.

---

106. *Les Récollets et Montréal,* p. 51–53.

CHAPTER 3

The Work of a Recollect: Recollects and Military Chaplaincy in New France, 1670-1760[1]

RÉNALD LESSARD, BIBLIOTHÈQUE ET ARCHIVES NATIONALES DU QUÉBEC

In 1725 a member of the congregation of Saint-Lazare in France, writing to the Secretary of State for the navy about how to secure New France against "English activities," had the following reflections:

> The Recollects must be urged to surrender the care of Trois-Rivières to the gentlemen of St. Sulpice or to the gentlemen of the Seminary in Quebec. [. . .] It is necessary to oblige the Sulpicians to take over the care of Detroit and Missilmakinak and those congregations that will be established thereafter in this new Government [Pay-d'en-Haut] and in Montreal. [. . .] It is necessary to leave the Recollects in all the posts where they are, but only as missionaries or chaplains of the forts and garrisons, and even to establish them in the forts that will be built thereafter and even in posts where it is not yet possible to establish parishes or priests. [. . .] I say the same thing about Jesuits who do not want to be parish priests, and who, I believe, will not want to be chaplains of the forts and garrisons, but who will gladly take charge of the missions to the savages [. . .] It is very important for the good of the colony to entrust these Iroquois missions to the Jesuits, and also to put them in charge of the Ouiatonons and other nations of the south, north and west, so they can instruct them in Christian truths and engage them in French interests. This should not impede the Jesuits and the Recollects from being able to settle in the colony's

1. Translation of: Rénald Lessard, « Un Métier de récollet : Les récollets et l'aumônerie militaire en Novelle-France 1670–1760 », in *Les Récollets en Nouvelle-France : Traces et Mémoire*, ed. Paul-André Dubois (Québec, QC, Les Presses de l'Université Laval, 2018), 151–171.

> towns and parishes and to carry out their functions there as they do in France [. . .][2]

These words recall, first of all, the three facets of the apostolate in New France: evangelization with Native Americans, military chaplaincy with soldiers, and pastoral ministry with settlers in convents and parishes. This author proposed to confine male religious communities to specific spheres: Native American missions to the Jesuits, parishes to the Sulpicians, and the functions of military chaplain and filling in where there was no parish priest, to the Recollects.

As part of the Order of St. Francis, the Franciscan Recollects, in imitation of Christ, tried to live a life of great poverty and evangelical simplicity. They were content with little and were at the service of the humble. Military chaplaincy suited them perfectly. C. Galland has clearly shown the importance of this aspect of their apostolate and its origins, but even if she located the places where the Recollect chaplains worked, she was not interested in providing an overall picture taking into account the number of soldiers and their distribution in the territory.[3]

To overcome this lacuna, we believe it is necessary to consider the importance of the number of military chaplains in New France. After establishing this, our article aims, more broadly, to examine the particular functions of military chaplains in order to get at what may have been the Recollects' work in New France. To do this, we will focus on the establishment of the military chaplaincy in New France, on the spiritual needs of the troops regarding their size and geographical distribution, on the involvement of the Recollects in military chaplaincy, and on a variety of situations depending on the presence or absence of a civilian population of European or aboriginal descent.

Recollect Military Chaplains: Their Numerical Importance

Based on the *Dictionnaire biographique des Récollets missionnaires en Nouvelle-France*, a masterful and fundamental work by Father Odoric Jouve and supplemented by the Franciscan Fathers Archange Godbout, Hervé Blais and René Bacon, Caroline Galland affirmed that 47% of the Recollects had, at one

---

2. Recollections of a priest from the Congregation of Saint-Lazare (Jean Bobé?) in « Ce qu'il faut faire pour mettre la Colonie en sureté contre les Entreprises des Anglois », [1725], Archives nationale d'outre-Mer (ANOM), fonds des Colonies, sous-série C11A, vol 47, f. 511–512v.

3. Caroline Galland, *Pour la gloire de Dieu et du Roi. Les récollets en Nouvelle-France aux XVIIe et XVIIIe siècles,* Paris, Les Éditions du Cerf, 2012, p. 331. 385.

time or another, fulfilled the function of chaplain to the king's troops.[4] According to this author, 164 Recollects out of a total number of 344 were military chaplains. However, 344 represents all the Recollects who lived on Canadian soil and, in fact, not all Recollects could become chaplains. Only those ordained priests, that is, those who can administer the sacraments, were fit to serve as chaplains. It is therefore fitting that Father René Bacon, also retaining the number of 164 Recollect chaplains, put this in relation to the presence of 267 Recollect priests. "This means that about 3 out of 5 Recollect priests devoted themselves, for greater or shorter times, and more or less often, to the military apostolate. This is considerable."[5] We share this view regarding the importance of military chaplaincy. However, we must clarify here that affixing the epithet military chaplain to a Recollect poses a problem of definitions. Are we to consider all Recollects who administered sacraments to military personnel to be military chaplains? Several Recollects would have thus held several offices, mainly in Acadia, on Île Royale, and on Île Saint-Jean. They could be entrusted with a congregation in a parish where civilians and soldiers lived together. In Trois-Rivières, a garrison town, the parish was continuously under the rule of a Recollect between 1693 and 1773. A Recollect friary was established there in 1693. Should each of the priests of Trois-Rivières be considered a military chaplain? Was this the case for Father Bernardin de Gannes de Falaise, the first Acadian Recollect to have acceded to the presbyterate in 1729, who collaborated in serving the parish of Trois-Rivières between November 1732 and December 1733? Was this same priest the chaplain when he stayed a few months at Fort Saint-Frédéric? Even though a population was just beginning to settle there, the establishment was primarily military. Some Recollects were the king's chaplain with remunerations attached to the office. The lack of archives, however, does not allow us to know precisely all these appointments.

Relying, as did C. Galland and Father René Bacon, on the masterful *Dictionnaire biographique des Récollets missionnaires en Nouvelle-France*, we returned to the calculations, and excluded the Recollects who were not priests and who did not practice in New France between 1670 and 1760.[6]

---

4. Odoric Jouve et *al.*, *Dictionnaire biographique des Récollets missionnaires en Nouvelle-France,* Montréal, Bellarmin, 1996. 903 p.; Caroline Galland, *Pour la gloire de Dieu et du Roi,* p. 339.

5. Père René Bacon, *Présence et Apostolat des Récollets en Nouvelle-France et au Canada (1615–1645, 1670–1813)*. Unpublished text of a conference given in Trois-Rivières on May 7 and in Montreal on June 19, 2015. Our thanks to the author for sharing this text with us.

6. The Recollects devoted themselves instead to the evangelisation of the Native Americans between 1615 and 1629. The military presence in New France was at this time

R. P. BERNARDIN DEGANNE-FALAISE, Récollet.

R. P. Bernardin Deganne-Falaise, Récollet. J. Trudelle, *Les jubilés et les églises* [...] *de Québec,* Québec, Le Soleil, 1901, p. 186.

That left 227 individuals. We found 82 Recollects presented in the documents at least once as chaplains and 12 others strongly indicated as having been, which represents 41% of the Recollect priests. This would be a minimum, since data on their presence in forts is incomplete. Moreover, the situation on Ile Royale, where the Recollects also served the parishes and the Brothers of Charity who took care of the King's Hospital, is often poorly documented.

The Slow Establishment of Military Chaplaincy in New France (1665–1691)

The royal power first used the Recollects as chaplains to its troops during the siege of La Rochelle in 1628. The career of Father Henri Le Roy, future Provincial Commissioner of the Recollect mission in New France, is a good illustration of the evolution of military chaplaincy in France. In 1670, he with 19 other Recollects was put in charge of chaplaincy at the military camp in Saint-Sébastien, near Saint-Germain-en-Laye, where 30,000 soldiers were gathered; two years later he took part in the Dutch campaign as chaplain to

very limited. On the historiography relating to the Recollects in New France, see Dorothy Kaupp, « 'Nos premiers missionnaires'. L'histoire des Récollets dans les ouvrages franciscains au Canada, XIX–XX siècles », *Études d'histoire relieuse,* vol. 75, 2009, p. 25–38.

the troops.[7] It is really from this war that the Recollects began regularly to follow the royal troops.

In New France, the Recollects were first present from 1615 to 1629, then they returned to France following the capture of Quebec by the Kirke brothers. Their action at that time was essentially devoted to the evangelization of the Native Americans. Despite much opposition, especially by the Jesuits', their return was desired by the king, and they returned to Quebec in 1670.

During their absence from the colony, the Jesuits mainly assumed the military chaplaincy. The Carignan-Salières regiment, with its 1,300 soldiers and officers who landed in 1665, had its own chaplain: Father Jean-Baptiste Dubois d'Esgriseilles.[8] The Jesuit fathers Charles Albanel and Pierre Raffeix, as well as the Sulpician François Dollier de Casson (1666–1667) accompanied these soldiers on the expeditions of 1666 and 1667. The number of soldiers decreased rapidly from 1668. That year, peace returned: 412 soldiers settled in the colony, 300 soldiers including officers were grouped in four companies of 75 men each to ensure the defense of Canada; the rest of the soldiers returned to Europe in 1668.[9] The following year there were 23 garrisons in Fort Quebec, one company of soldiers in Trois-Rivières, and another in Montreal. Six new companies of 50 men each, including one for Acadia, arrived in Canada in 1670. However, these soldiers were dismissed in 1671.

It was in this context of weak military manpower that the Recollects landed. Their mandate was not clearly associated with military chaplaincy. The civil authorities saw their presence as a counterweight to the Jesuit's and Bishop Laval's power.[10] The support of the king and governor of New France was, in this context, essential. The royal instructions given to Frontenac in 1672 confirmed this privileged link with the French state:

---

7. Jacques Valois, « Le Roy, Henri », dans *Dictionnairc biographiqc du Canada,* vol 2. Université Laval / University of Toronto, 2003, searched March 20, 2016, http://www.biographi.ca/fr/bio/le_roy_henri_2F.hrml.

8. Jean-Baptiste Dubois d'Esgriseilles, chaplain of the Carignan Regiment, landed in Québec on August 19, 1665 with the Marquis de Salières. He was in Montreal on Christmas day 1665, then in Quebec on August 19, 1666, where he began preaching to the Jesuits. In autumn, he took part in the expedition against the Agniers. It is not clear what became of him afterwards. In May 1671, he appeared in Trois-Rivières. André Vachon, « Dubois de Cocreaumont et de Saint-Maurice, Jean-Baptiste » in *Dictionnaire biographique du Canada,* vol 1, consulted March 2016, http://www.biograpi.ca/frébio/dubois_de_cocreaumont_et_de_saint_maurice_jean_baptiste_1Fhrml.

9. « Estat en abrégé du nombre des familles ... », 1668, ANOM, Fonds des Colonies, série B, vol. 1, f. 110r et v.

10. Caroline Gallant, *Pour la gloire de Dieu et du Roi,* p. 139–175.

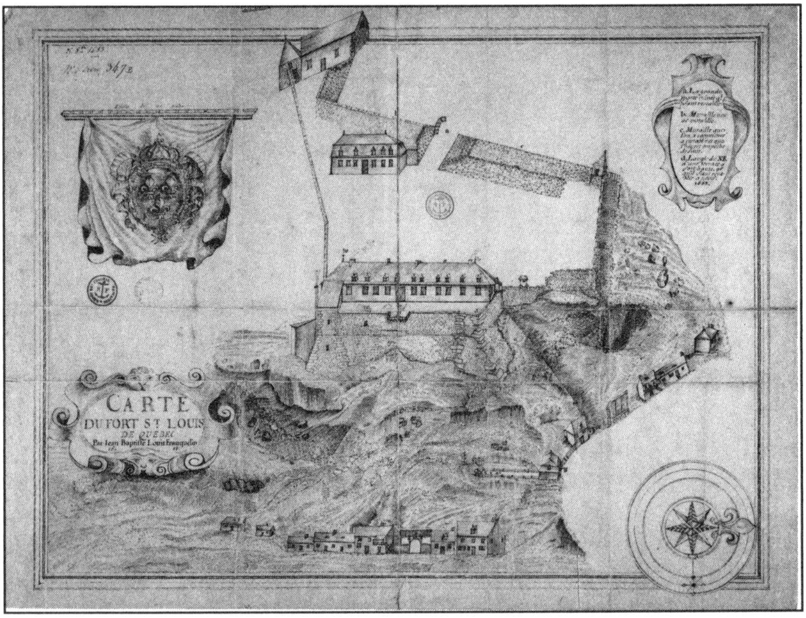

Jean-Baptiste-Louis Franquelin, *Map of Fort St-Louis in Quebec City,* 1683. Pen drawing on canvas paper, 49.3 × 66.2 cm, Archives nationales d'outre-Mer (ANOM), Dépôt des fortifications des colonies, n° 247B.

> The colony of Montreal, situated above that of Quebec, receiving much relief and consolation from the ecclesiastics of the Seminary of Saint-Sulpice who are established there, it will be necessary that the Sire de Frontenac give them all the protection that he is able, just as for the Recollect Fathers who have settled in that same town of Quebec, these two ecclesiastical bodies ought to be supported to balance the authority that the Jesuit Fathers accumulated to the prejudice of that of His Majesty.[11]

Frontenac, governor of New France from 1672 to 1682 and again from 1689 to 1698, quickly took up the Recollects' cause and even became their syndic general, imitating his predecessor Courcelles. In his letter of April 28, 1677, the king reiterated his position in favour of the Recollects: "As far as the Recollect Fathers are concerned, I am sending two of them to Canada

11. « Mémoire du roi pour servir d'instruction au sieur comte de Frontenac, que sa majesté a choisy pour gouverneur et lieutenant général pour sa majesté en Canada », 7 avril 1672, published in *Rapport de l'archiviste de la province de Québec pour 1926–1927,* tome 7, Québec, L.-Amable Proulx, 1927, p. 6.

this year, and I hope that you will always continue to give your protection to these religious so that they carry out their duties properly."[12]

At that time, the role of military chaplain was highly symbolic for the Recollects, since it associated them with the governor and the king. On the other hand, this was relatively marginal[13] in regard to the energy invested. It is true that the Recollects were few in number. It was not until 1692 that the Recollect brothers and priests permanently exceeded 20 individuals. The military numbers were just as small and would remain so until 1683: about 77 soldiers in 1672, of which a maximum of twenty were at the Château Saint-Louis, the Governor's residence. The census of 1681 tells us precisely that the "Governor's residence housed twenty-five people. The garrison held twenty-one soldiers."

In 1681 the Recollects, having returned to Canada in 1670 and living at the friary of Notre-Dame-des-Anges, three kilometers from the city, wanted to have a hospice in town "to go to when it was dark or when inclement weather surprised them while undertaking their institute's work." They made several arguments in favor of this establishment. Exercising their function as military chaplains and the desire to get closer to the governor are at the heart of their concerns:

> 7° We are the regular chaplains of the fort, of the garrison and of the Governor which it will always be necessary to care for now and hereafter, and which, according to the course of events in this country, will never agree with the endless conspiracy in this country which in the same way is opposed to our establishment. In order to relieve ourselves of this impediment to our duties, Providence could not carry us more advantageously than to the place which we have received this year from the king's liberality, which is located near the fort, with only the place of arms in between.[14]

The Recollects had obtained from the king on May 28, 1681 a "useless" place in the service of the king "situated in the upper town of Quebec right

12. « Lettre du roi au gouverneur de Frontenac, 28 avril 1677 », published in *Rapport de l'archiviste de la province de Québec pour 1926–1927,* tome 7, Québec, L.-Amable Proulx, 1927, p. 91.

13. André Lafontaine, *Recensement annoté de la Nouvelle-France 1681,* Sherbrooke, s.é., réédition de 1995, p. 1.

14. « Eclaircissement nécessaire pour l'establissement d'un hospice que Sa Majesté nous a accordé dans la haute ville de Quebek » (Copy of an unsigned memorandum that had to have been written by one of the Recollect fathers at Notre-Dame-des-Anges to the superiors of the Order in France) [1681] published in *Histoire chronologique de la Nouvelle France au Canada depuis sa découverte (Mil cinq cents quatre) jusques en l'an mil six cents trente deux / par le Père Sixte Le Tac, Récollet : publiée pour la première fois d'après le manuscrit original de 1689* [...] par Eug. Réveillaud, Paris, Fischbacher, 1888, p. 202.

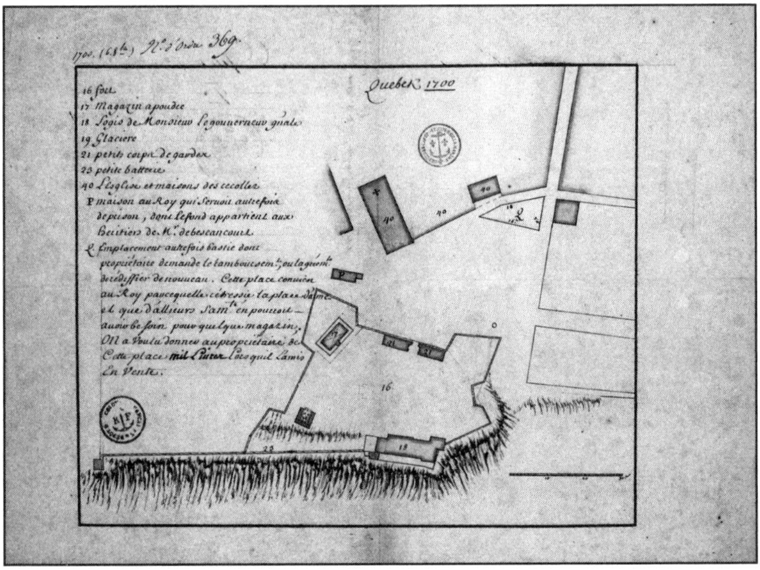

Jean Bochart de Champigny and Louis-Hector de Callières, *Map of Quebec,* 1700. Pen drawing on paper, 31.3 × 41.5 cm, ANOM, Dépôt des fortifications des colonies, n° 369C.

in front of the Senechaussée" strategically located near the Château Saint-Louis.[15] From 1692, after a few years of open conflict with the bishop and the Jesuits, their friary was established.

When reinforcements arrived in 1683, the links between Recollects and soldiers were limited to the Château Saint-Louis at Quebec and to Fort Cataracoui, which later became Fort Frontenac, as well as to Fort Niagara. From 1673 to 1685, the Recollects served the newly established Fort Cataracoui but they were soon ousted by the Jesuits. During their stay there, the Recollects had a threefold role: to act as military chaplains to the fort's soldiers, to serve the French families established in the vicinity, and to participate in the evangelization of the Iroquois who had settled nearby. The number of soldiers, however, remained limited: the review carried out in 1677

15. « Concession par le Roi aux Révérends Pères Récollets d'une place sise en la Haute-Ville de Québec où était la Sénéchausée pour y élever un hospice pour s'y retirer lorsque la nuit et le mauvais temps les surprennent dans les fonctions de leur institut puisque leur maison est éloignée d'une demi-lieue de la ville de Québec », 28 mai 1681, Bibliothèque et Archives nationales du Québec à Québec (BAnQ Québec), TP1, S36, P180, *Registre des insinuations du Conseil supérieur de Québec établi en Canada par l'Édit du Roi Louis XIV de mois d'avril 1663* (28 décembre 1628 au 1er mai 1682), volume A, f. 90v.

reported the presence of only one sergeant and a maximum of twelve soldiers.[16] A statement of expenses from the same period lists a sergeant, a surgeon, a lieutenant and 11 soldiers.[17] A sign that the presence of the Recollects seemed to be related to their desire to ensure the conversion of the Native Americans rather than to their role as chaplains, [is apparent in] the 1678 letter of confirmation from the king to the Recollects in the settlements at Fort Frontenac and Île Percée. It emphasizes that "we [the king] know perfectly the zeal these religious have for converting the 'savages' and for giving our subjects, living in this same country, all the spiritual help they need."[18] There is no allusion to military chaplaincy, even if the raison d'être of the Franciscan presence at Fort Frontenac is stated in the document. In 1679–1680, Father Méliton Watteau served Fort Niagara, but it was short-lived, since the fort was destroyed by fire and abandoned. Apart from the Château Saint-Louis, at Quebec, Frontenac and Niagara, we can only attribute a limited place for military chaplaincy. A few dozen soldiers were served across Canada; which is not many.

THE DEVELOPMENT OF MILITARY CHAPLAINCY (1692–1760)

From 1683, due to the resumption of hostilities with the Iroquois and soon with the English, the actual number of soldiers and non-commissioned officers grew rapidly and reached 1,418 in 1688; fell back to 698 in 1708; stabilized at around 800 after the Treaty of Utrecht, between 1713 and 1749; rose to 1,500 in 1750; and reached a peak of 6,288 in 1757 (see Table 1). In times of war, one must take into account the movement of troops and the

16. « Extrait de la Reveue faite au fort de Frontenac par Monseigneur le Gouverneur » 7 septembre 1677, published in Pierre Margry, *Découvertes et établissement des Français dans l'ouest et dans le Sud de l'Amérique septentrionale 1614–1698. Mémoires et documents inédits,* Première partie : *Voyages des Français sur les Grands lacs et découverte de l'Ohio et du Mississipi (1614–1684),* Paris, Maisonneuve et Cie, 1879, p. 296–298.

17. « Estat de la dépense faite par M. de la Salle, gouverneur du fort de Frontenac [...] y compris le payement et la nourriture des officiers, soldats et travailleurs dudit fort », no date, published in Pierre Margry, *Découvertes et établissement des Français,* Première partie, p. 294. The sergeant's pay is 300 pounds, the surgeon's 300 pounds, a lieutenant's 600 pounds and 11 soldiers at 150 pounds each.

18. « Confirmation par le Roi de l'établissement des Révérends Pères Récollets au fort Frontenac et à l'île Percée », 12 mai 1678, BAnQ Québec, TP1, S36, P152, *Registre des insinuations du Conseil supérieur de Québec établi en Canada par l'Édit du Roi Louis XIV de mois d'avril 1663* (28 décembre 1628 au 1er mai 1682), volume A, f. 78–78v. (Consulted at the on-line site of the Bibliothèque et Archives nationales du Québec (BAnQ)).

TABLE 1
CHAPLAINS AND MILITARY PERSONNEL IN NEW FRANCE[a]

	Recollects		Soldiers and non-commissioned officers (theoretical (T) or real (R) numbers)[b]		
	Brothers or priests[c]	Identified Chaplains	Canada	Acadia and Île Royale	Newfoundland
1670	6	0	250 (T)	50 (T)	
1672	9	0	77 (T)		
1687	17	0	1400 (T)	60 (T)	25 (T)
1688	19	1	1418 (R), 1750 (T)	90 (T)	
1697	30	2	1260 (R)		
1698	33	3	1400 (T)	129 (R)	
1699	35	2	840 (T), 1400 (T)		138 (R)
1702	32	3	912 (R)		
1705	36	3		184 (T)	
1708	31	3	698 (R)		
1722	42	1	768 (R), 812 (T)	300 (T)	0
1739	73	11	840 (T)		0
1741	77	7	840 (T)		0
1750	59	10	1500 (R et T)		0
1754	71	8	1500 (T)	1117 (R)	0
1757	68	4	6288 (R)	2080 (R)	0

[a] Data on military personnel comes from Marcel Fournier, Jean-Yves Bronze, Suzanne Galaise, Luc Lépine, Renald Lessard and Micheline Perreault, *Combattre pour la France en Amérique. Les soldats de la guerre de Sept Ans en Nouvelle-France 1755–1760,* Montréal, Société généalogique canadienne-française, 2009, 6262 p.; René Chartrand, *Le patrimoine militaire canadien. D'hier à aujourd'hui, Tome 1 (100–1754),* Montréal, *Art Global,* 1993; Gilles Duprès, *Immigration et colonisation militaire en Nouvelle-France 1716–1748,* Paris, Maîtrise d'histoire, Université Paris IV Sorbonne, 1994; Renald Lessard, « Le corps des Volontaires-Étrangers : une contribution importante à la défense de la Nouvelle-France », in Laurent Veyssière and Bertrand Fonck (dir.), *La guerre de Sept Ans en Nouvelle-France,* Paris, Paris-Sorbonne, 2011, p. 243–267; Rénald Lessard, « Les soldats des compagnies franches de la Marine au Canada et à l'île Royale : le prix de la défaite (1750–1763) », in Bertrand Fonck and Laurent Veyssire (dir.), *La fin de la Nouvelle-France,* Paris, Armand Coin, 2013; Boris Lesueur, *Les troupes coloniales sous l'ancien Régime,* Thèse de doctorat (Histoire), Université de Tours, 1992; *Extrait du rôle des sergents, caporaux, anspessades et soldats entretenus en la Nouvelle-France suivant a revue qui en a été faite le 1er octobre 1702* [1702], ANOM, Fonds des Colonies, sous-série D2C, vol. 47; *Revue des compagnies de Marine qui tiennent garnison en Canada,* 31 octobre 1708, ANOM, Fonds des Colonies, sous-série C11A, vol 44, f. 272; *Extrait Général des Reveües des Compagnies Entretenües en la Nouvelle France faites par Le Controleur de la marine en ce port, à Montreal par Le Commissaire ordinaire aud. Lieu et aux Trois Rivières par Le Major des Troupes, pendant La présente année 1750. Fait a quebec Le 2e Novembre 1750, ANOM, Fonds des Colonies sous-série D2C, vol. 48, f. 129r;* Extrait général de revue des compagnies entretenues à l'île Royale la

Table 1 notes continued at top of next page

Table 1 notes continued

présente année suivant les postes où elles sont en garnison è compter du 1 novembre 1753, 1er octobre 1754, ANOM. Sous-série D2C, vol. 48, f. [246]; *État actuel des troupes entretenues par sa majesté en Canada suivant la revue du 6 octobre 1754, 2 novembre 1754,* ANOM, Fonds des Colonies, sous-série D2C, vol 48, f. [247]; *Lettre de Vaudreuil de Cavagnial au ministre de la Marine,* 29 octobre 1757, Fonds des Colonies, sous-série C11A, vol. 102, f. 142–143; *État de la situation des Troupes d'infanterie françoise servant au Canada, et des changement qu'il y a eu dans chaque bataillon depuis le 1re Novembre 1756 jusqu'au 1er Octobre 1757 et Extrait General de Revüe des Compagnies Entretenues à l'isle Royale, Le premier Octobre 1757 Suivant les postes ou elles sont en Garnison, faitte par nous Ecrivain ord.re de la marine faisant les fonctions de Commissaire des Trouppes, 1er octobre 1757,* Service historique de la Défense, sous-série A1, vol. 3457, pièces 153 et 162.

[b] Real numbers may vary considerably from theoretical numbers.

[c] Caroline Galland, *Pour la gloire de Dieu et du Roi, p. 470.*

many "war parties" that were undertaken. A chaplain accompanied the most important expeditions. In peacetime, soldiers lived in city garrisons and forts.

Spiritual needs increased in proportion to the increase in troops and their dispersion throughout the territory. Priests were needed in forts and on major military expeditions to provide spiritual comfort to the entire troop, and this included the celebration of religious festivals and masses, the organization of evening and morning prayers, the administration of the sacraments, assistance to the sick and dying, and, finally, religious instruction and conversion of Protestants. Many soldiers were young; it may be supposed that they required more accompaniment and support than the presence of a chaplain on site was likely to provide. A study of the "great recruit" of 1750, in regard to the age of the 396 known individuals reveals the following: 70% were between 16 and 25 years old, 13 individuals were under the regulatory age of 16, and 18 others were over 40 years old.

The recourse to Recollects imposed itself naturally and their role as military chaplains in Canada was officially recognized by the Royal Letters Patent of 1692:

> Louis, by the grace of God, etc. Our friend & faithful Counsellor, the Bishop of Quebec, made known to us in Council, that, having a convent of religious Recollects of the Order of St Francis, he would arrange that a part of the said religious be sent to various places of New France, the isle of Newfoundland & other places of North America, & especially to Montreal, Plaisance, & the isle of St-Pierre. The inhabitants of these places would draw from these religious all the spiritual help that could be expected from their zeal & piety; & [these religious] would apply themselves to focusing more and more on their missions & other functions to assure their establishments in the said places. For these

> reasons, we have allowed and allow these same Recollects to keep their establishment as much in the said town of Quebec as in Villemarie or Montreal, Plaisance, the isle of Saint-Pierre & in any other place where they are deemed necessary, provided that it be by the agreement & consent of the Governor & our Lieutenant General of the said country & of the inhabitants of the places where they wish to settle. In all these places, they will serve as chaplains for our troops & even do the curial functions when the bishop deems it necessary & gives them the power, [and] wants them to receive as alms the salaries intended by our State for the chaplains of our same troops. As we have already amortized, we also amortize, by these present [letters] signed by our hand, the costs of the churches, housing & enclosures of the established convents & those which may be established hereafter so that they not be bound to pay us, or to pay succeeding kings any finances, rights of amortization, or other indemnities which we have already given to them and remit to them by these present letters. So given as a command to our friends, etc. for such is our pleasure, etc. Given at Versailles, in the month of March in the year of grace one thousand six hundred and ninety-two, and the forty-ninth of our reign. Signed: Louis, & on the folded side, King: Signed Phelypeaux & sealed, etc.[19]

This document concluded 22 years of debate, often bitter, on the relevance of the Recollects' presence in New France and guaranteed their settlements and possessions. Indeed, the material property owned by religious congregations—including the Jesuits, Sulpicians, Recollects, or hospitals—thus escaped the rules of transfer at death and therefore the royalties associated with it. In compensation, those who owned these assets had to pay depreciation duties to the king and were subject to various obligations and rights. The payment of depreciation guaranteed the transfer of ownership. In order to avoid having to pay indemnities and having their properties or the income derived therefrom disputed, the Recollects obtained, on 9 May 1677 and 13 May 1678, letters patent of amortization for the land where their convent at Notre-Dame-des-Anges at Quebec was located. They had them registered with the Sovereign Conseil of Quebec on December 5, 1678.[20] Through these

19. Collated copy of the « Lettres patentes en cire verte d'etablissement du Roy pour Montréal, îsle de Terre Neuve et autres lieux de Canada pour les Recollets », mars 1692, published in *Histoire chronologique de la Nouvelle-France ou Canada depuis sa découverte (Mil cinq cents quatre) jusques en l'an mil six cents trente deux / par le Père Sixte Le Tac, Récollet : publiée pour la première fois d'après le manuscrit original de 1689* [...] par Eug. Réveillaud, Paris, Fischbacher, 1888, p. 240–241.

20. « Arrêt d'enregistrement des lettres patentes du Roi, concernant un amortissement de 106 arpents de terre en faveur des Pères Récollets établis au couvent Notre-Dame-des-Anges à Québec, le 9 mai 1677 », insinué le 5 décembre 1678. Bibliothèque et Archives

TABLE 2
SOLDIERS AND CHAPLAINS ON ÎLE ROYALE AND ÎLE SAINT-JEAN

Soldiers and Navy troops (île Royale and île Saint-Jean) September 30th 1754[a]		Documented presence of a Recollect claiming to be a king's chaplain[b]
At Louisbourg	837	(1725–1745, 1749–1754) Fathers Isidore Caulet and Luc Cottin in 1754
At Port-Toulouse	39	(1731–1733, 1736)
At la batterie royale	41	(1734–1745, 1749–1750)
At Port-Dauphin	42	(1717, 1730, 1753–1754) Father Hyacinthe Lefebvre in 1754
At l'île St. Jean (Port-Lajoie)	42	(1723–1741, 1749–1758) Father Gratien Raoul, chaplain to the soldiers and parish priest of Port-Lajoie in 1754
In Acadia	35	
Total	1036	

[a] *Extrait général de revue des compagnies entretenus à l'île Royale la présente année suivant les postes où elles sont en garnison à compter du 1er novembre 1753,* 1er octobre 1754, ANOM, Fonds des Colonies, sous-série D2C, vol. 48, f. [246].

[b] If only the presence of a Recollect were taken into account, the regular presence of a Franciscan would be even stronger.

documents, the Recollects obtained confirmation for possession of their properties and for exemption from duties and royalties to the king. In 1692, they obtained the same favors for their new acquisitions. To justify these privileges, the king recognized the importance of their role and specified that the Recollects would serve as chaplains for the king's troops and that they could exercise curial functions in the places designated by the local bishop.

This role as military chaplains for the Recollects grew in importance as New France expanded geographically. To the east of the colony, as shown in Table 2, the presence of military chaplains is regularly attested at Plaisance (Newfoundland) as early as 1689, if not before, and later at Louisbourg, which replaced the latter after the signing of the Treaty of Utrecht in 1713, as well as at Port-Dauphin, Port-Toulouse and Port-Lajoie.

It is from the end of the seventeenth century and the beginning of the following century that we can date the presence of Recollect military chaplains

nationales du Québec, TP1, S28, P2167, Registre no 3 des arrêts, jugements et délibérations du Conseil souverain de la Nouvelle-France (11 janvier 1677 au 23 décembre 1680), f. 75–75v.

TABLE 3
ATTESTED PRESENCE OF A RECOLLECT CLAIMING TO BE A CHAPLAIN TO THE KING

Forts	Region
Fort Cataraccoui (later became Fort Frontenac) (1673–1686, 1703–1706, 1714, 1733–1746, 1750, 1752)	Great Lakes
Fort Niagara (1679–1680, 1729–1732, 1738–1739, 1741–1743, 1754–1755)	Great Lakes
Détroit (1701–1715, 1719–1760)	Great Lakes
Fort Bourbon (1704–1706)	Hudson Bay
Fort Saint-Frédéric (1732–1758)	Richelieu and Lake Champlain
Presqu'île and Rivière au Bœuf (1753) Ohio valley	South of the Great Lakes and in the
Fort Duquesne (1753–1756) Ohio valley	South of the Great Lakes and in the
Fort Carillon (1756, 1758–1760)	Richelieu and Lake Champlain
Fort Saint-Jean (1758–1759)	Richelieu and Lake Champlain
Camp de Beauport (1759)	St. Lawrence valley
Fort Jacques-Cartier (1759–1760)	St. Lawrence valley
Fort de l'île aux Noix (1760)	Richelieu and Lake Champlain
Fort Lévis (1760)	St. Lawrence valley

in Acadia, along the Saint John River (Fort Naxouat) and at Port-Royal. It should be noted that Fort Naxouat, also called Saint-Joseph, was then, for a time, the capital of Acadia, despite its short existence (1691–1700).

The westward expansion and affirmation of the French military presence in the Great Lakes region resulted in the establishment of forts: Detroit (1701), Frontenac (abandoned in 1689, reoccupied in 1702) and Niagara (abandoned in 1688 and rebuilt in 1726). The militarization of the Richelieu-Lake Champlain axis, initially centered on Fort Chambly (1665), gradually moved to Lake Champlain: Fort Saint-Frédéric (1727), Fort Saint-Jean (1748), Fort Carillon (1756) and Fort de l'île aux Noix (1759). Following the taking possession of the Ohio Valley in 1753, construction began on a series of forts of varying sizes: Fort de la Rivière au Bœuf (1753), Fort Presqu'Île (1753), Fort Machault (1754) and Fort Duquesne (1754). The presence of Recollect military chaplains followed suit, as shown in table 3.

To understand how the State provided for the spiritual needs of its military, it is interesting to look at the Swedish traveler Pehr Kalm. In 1749, while visiting Canada, he aptly noted:

> The king always places in each fortress of a garrison of forty men one of these monks [Recollects] as chaplain, he receives free food, lodging, various services that are necessary to him and, in addition, a salary of 200 pounds per year. He sends half of this to the community in Montreal or Quebec and uses the other half for his needs.[21]

Kalm's statements are corroborated by Recollect presences reported following the distribution of soldiers and non-commissioned officers on the territory for the month of November 1750, as illustrated in Table 4. The Recollects were found in forts with more than 40 men on duty, except Chédaik (Shediac) where Abbé Le Loutre served the Acadian and aboriginal population. It should be noted that in Detroit, there was a population of Europeans and a garrison totaling about 500 people which was served by a Recollect, and nearby aboriginal villages under the direction of a Jesuit.

In the eighteenth century, the Recollects, alone or accompanied by Jesuits, participated in militia expeditions: troops going to Chagoumigon (1723), an expedition against the Renards (1728), an expedition against the Chicachas (1739–1740) and a war party of French and "Savages," commanded by François-Pierre de Rigaud de Vaudreuil (1747). In 1742 the chaplains of the forts of Chambly, Frontenac, Saint-Frédéric and Niagra, all Recollects, earned annual salaries of 200 pounds.[22] Pehr Kalm's statements are thus validated. It should be noted that the Recollect missionaries in Miramich and Restigouche received 400 pounds during the same time.

BEING A MILITARY CHAPLAIN: THE CANADIAN LIFE OF FATHER EMMANUEL DE CRESPEL (1724–1736)

Rarely are there testimonies or accounts from Recollect military chaplains. The 1796 fire at the Recollect friary in Quebec and the loss of their archives are responsible for this situation. In the eighteenth century, no Recollect published a major account of the Franciscans' work in New France. There was no Sagard or Sixte le Tac, as in the previous century. Father Emmanuel Crespel is an exception. His notoriety did not lie in his activities as chaplain

21. Pehr Kalm, *Voyage de Pehr Kalm au Canada en 1749*, Montréal, Pierre Tisseyre, 1977, f. 902.

22. *Bordereau des recettes et dépenses faites par le sieur Tachereau, commis en ce pays de Messieurs les trésoriers généreaux de la Marine, pendant l'année 1742* [...] 12 octobre 1743, ANOM, Fonds des Colonies, sous-série C11A, vol. 79, f. 363r; 430r.

Exterior view of the « house with machicolations », Fort Niagara, Youngstown, New York, c. 1725, Gaspard-Joseph Chaussegros de Léry. Photo by Rénald Lessard.

or parish priest but rather in the tragic sinking of his ship off Anticosti Island on his return to France in 1736. His account of his first visit to Canada, however, eloquently illustrates the importance of military chaplaincy for the Recollects.[23]

Born at Douai, Flanders, on March 13, 1703, he sailed for Quebec in 1724, completed his training there, and in March 1726 was ordained priest. Various mandates followed: parish priest at Sorel (1726–1728), participation as military chaplain in the expedition organized against the Renards, a Native American nation living west of Lake Michigan (1728), service as military chaplain at Forts Niagara (1729–1733), Frontenac (1733–1735) and Saint-Frédéric (1735–1736), and, finally, care of the parish at Soulanges (1737–1738). This means that he spent most of his apostolate during his first stay in Canada serving as a military chaplain. It is exceptional. Crespel informs us that a military chaplain's mandate is generally three years: "When my three years of residence in Niagara expired, I was relieved; that's the custom."

This story portrays Crespel as a true disciple of St. Francis: attentive to humans and the world around him, curious, eager to discover and understand the other, especially by learning the language of the Native Americans, and

23. Odoric Jouve *et al., Dictionnaire biographique des Récollets missionnaires en Nouvelle-France,* Montréal, Bellarmin, 1996, p. 148–162; Emmanuel Crespel, *Voiages de R.P. Emmanuel Crespel, dans le Canada et son naufrage en revenant en France. Mis au jour par le Sr Louis Crespel son Frére,* Francfort sur le Meyn, 1747, p. 3–35.

TABLE 4
DISTRIBUTION OF THE 1500 SOLDIERS PRESENT IN CANADA IN NOVEMBER 1750[a]

Garrison towns (909):
Québec (648)
Trois-Rivières (202)
Montréal (650)
Soldiers seconded to the various posts (591):
Chédaik (110) and with de Vergor[b] (29)
Detroit (68) R
Fort Frederick (50) R
Niagara (50) R
Fort Frontenac (40) R
Chambly (25)
Fort Saint-Jean (25)
Saint John River (20)
Miamis (34)
Ouiatanons (27)
Laprairie (20); Lake of Two Mountains (12);Sault-Saint-Louis (25)
Michilimakinac and Sault Ste. Marie (16)
La Baie and aux Sioux (10); mer de l'Ouest (10);La Présentation (12)
Belle Rivière (5); Nipigon (1); Michipicoton (1); Chaouamigon (1)

[a] *Extrait Général des Reveües des Compagnies Entreteneües en la Nouvelle France faites par le Controleur de la marine en ce port, à Montreal par Le Commissaire ordinaire aud. Lieu et aux Trois Rivières par Le Major des Troupes, pendant La présente année 1750. Fait a quebec Le 2[e] Novembre 1750,* ANOM, Fonds des Colonies, sous-série D2C, vol. 48, f. 129r.

[b] In mid-September 1750, Vergor was dispatched aboard the brigantine *Saint-François* to escort the schooner *Aimable Jeanne*, which was carrying ammunition and supplies from Quebec to a small French post on the Saint John River (New Brunswick). Early on the morning of October 16th, about ten leagues west of Cape Sable (Nova Scotia), the French ships were overtaken by a British sloop commanded by Captain John Rous. Despite the inferiority of his arms, Vergor engaged in combat which allowed the *Aimable Jeanne* to reach the Saint John River. The fighting continued for most of the day, after which, with only 7 able-bodied men out of 50 and with the *St. Francis* without a mast and taking on water, Vergor was forced to yield. Bernard Pothier, « Du Pont du Chambon de Vergor, Louis », in DBC (1771–1800), vol. IV, 1980, p. 268–271.

concerned about human suffering. Of the friary in Quebec, he notes: "If there is nothing superfluous, at least one does not lack the necessities; and, what is no small pleasure, one receives news of one's native land, and finds people with whom one can converse." Speaking of his colleague Bonaventure Léonard [Liénard], chaplain in Detroit, he notes with pride and envy that his apostolate is a success and that he lives simply, dividing his time between the dutiful fulfillment of his tasks and keeping busy with the things of the countryside: a happy and fulfilled life.

Anonymous, *Père Emmanuel Crespel.* Estampe, collection Centre d'archives de Québec, BAnQ, P10000, S4, D83, PC120.

> He was a man a little older than I and very commendable for the successes of his apostolic work. His house was pleasant and agreeable, it was, so to speak, his workplace and an abode of virtue. He spent his time, which was not taken up by the duties of his office, with study and the occupations of the countryside. He had some books, and the choice of them gave an idea of his good character and the breadth of his knowledge. The language of the land was quite familiar to him, and the ease with which he spoke it endeared him to several savages who spoke with him about all kinds of subjects, and chiefly about religion. Affability attracts confidence, and no one deserved it more than this religious. He had extended these good relations with some of the inhabitants of Detroit to the point of teaching them the French language. [. . .] Throughout the time that I remained with this religious, I found every day new reasons to envy a life like his. In a word, he was happy, as men should be, without being embarrassed by their happiness.[24]

After his shipwreck, Father Crespel occupied the parish in Soulanges, then returned to France in 1738 as chaplain aboard the king's ship. In France, he served for some years as "Chaplain in the French Army, commanded by the

24. Emmanuel Crespel, *Voiages by R.P. Emmanuel Crespel*, pp. 23–2k4.

Marshal de Maillebois." In 1750 he returned to Canada as Provincial Commissioner and died at Quebec on April 29, 1775.

GENERAL PORTRAIT OF THE RECOLLECTS SERVING AS MILITARY CHAPLAINS

We have based our analysis, it should be recalled, on the group of 82 Recollects mentioned, in the documents, as chaplains at least once, and on the other 12 for whom there are strong indications that they exercised this function. One quarter of them were Canadians, which corresponds to the number of Canadian-born Recollects. Several priests had recently been ordained or had recently arrived in Canada at the time of being appointed to this position, but this was not the beginning of most Recollects' careers: a quarter of the chaplains had just arrived in Canada and half of them stayed for fewer than five years.

Being a military chaplain was therefore part of the Recollects' normal course. Indeed, we see that between two and three out of five Recollect priests became chaplains, at one time or another, but few spent more than three years in the same assignment—which seems to be in accordance with the rule. It was even rarer for them to have more than one assignment as a military chaplain. The Recollects stationed at Île Royale seemed to be more connected than the others to military chaplaincy, but the available sources do not permit an identification of their apostolate's daily routine.

We can say that being a military chaplain was a lesser part of the Recollects' ministry. In 1739, in Canada, 11 out of 73 Recollects (of whom about 55 were priests) were chaplains. In 1750, for the same territory, 10 out of 59 Recollects (more than half of whom were priests) were chaplains. It is true that this indicates a minimum number of chaplains. It can be estimated, however, that the number of forts with at least 40 soldiers is also limited, as well as the number of soldiers stationed outside the cities of Quebec, Trois-Rivières, Montreal and Louisbourg. In sum, military chaplaincy represents a significant, but small, part of Franciscan life in Canada. The importance of chaplaincy is symbolic: it testifies to the link between the French Crown and the Recollects, a link officially recognized in the letters patent of 1692.

The diversity of the places served by the Recollects testifies to an assortment of situations in which they intervened as military chaplains. They are found in cities with large civilian and military populations (Quebec City, Trois-Rivières, Montreal and Louisbourg). Except perhaps for the Fortress of Louisbourg, the chaplain's role is not clearly defined. Moreover, there do not seem to be assignments specifically connected to the role of military chaplain, another sign of the variable importance given it by the authorities. Military and civilians worked side by side in the campaigns around Forts Chambly,

Saint-Jean and Saint-Frédéric. In Chambly, the expenses for the king's chaplain disappeared in 1743[25] with the development of the parish. An aboriginal presence is observed around Forts Niagara and Frontenac, but they were not major mission sites, at least in the eighteenth century. Detroit was a special case. It was a settlement with a substantial aboriginal presence, a major trading center for the fur trade, and a military establishment: Detroit asserted itself as the true capital of the Great Lakes. Recollects and Jesuits shared tasks in this region, each in his sphere of activity: Jesuits in the missions, Recollects in the garrison and the parish. There is no assignment recorded in 1742 for the Recollects in Detroit. Here as elsewhere, the Recollects often combined several functions, among which chaplaincy varied according to the place and circumstances.

In their service of the little ones, the Recollects functioned in New France as military chaplains in the same way that they acted as parish priests or missionaries to the civilian population, particularly in colonized areas or outlying places. We can point out several similarities between the better-known qualities attributed to the Recollects and those demanded of a military officer. The Recollect adapted. He asked little. The case of Father Bonaventure Carpentier, Recollect, dated September 28, 1766, best confirms these qualities: "I think I am obliged to warn you that the mission [that] Bonaventure [serves] cannot support a missionary: the income from the said mission may be up to 150 pounds; it requires a fairly large supplement to maintain a priest [in the mission], unless he wants to do the job of a Recollect."[26]

Annex

Emmanuel Crespel, *Voiages du R.P. Emmanuel Crespel, dans le Canada et son naufrage en revenant en France.* Mis au jour par le Sr Louis Crespel son Frére, Francfort sur le Meyn, 1747, 3–35. Extracts:

1724, May 1. "I left [Paris] the first of May to go to La Rochelle, where I arrived on the eighteenth of the same month: I did not stay there long, for after having provided myself with what was necessary for the crossing, I embarked on the King's ship, Camel [. . .]"

1724, July 24. "The twenty-fourth of July, the day we set sail [. . .]"

1724, October 8. "After two and a half months of fairly smooth navigation, we arrived at Québec: I remained there until 1726 [. . .]"

25. Caroline Galland, *Pour la gloire de Dieu et du Roi,* p. 343–344.

26. Letter published in Odoric Jouve *et al., Dictionnaire biographique des Récollets missionnaires en Nouvelle-France,* p. 85.

1726, March 17. "On the seventeen of March of the year of my departure from Quebec, Monsieur de la Croix de St. Valier, the Bishop of that city, conferred the priesthood on me, [. . .]"

1726, October 1. "[. . .] and after a little while, he gave me a mission or congregation at Sorel, located south of the St. Lawrence River, between the towns of Trois-Rivieres and Montreal."

1728. "I was taken from my congregation, where I had been for two years, to be made chaplain of a group of four hundred French, which Monsieur le Marquis de Beauharnois had joined to eight or nine hundred savages of numerous tribes: there were chiefly Iroquois, Hurons, Népissings and Outaoüacs, whom the priest, Monsieur Péset (François-Michel Pellet), and the Jesuit, Father de la Bertonnière (Jacques-David Quentin de la Bretonnière), served as chaplains. These troops, commanded by Monsieur de Lignerie, were commissioned to go and destroy a tribe called the Renards, whose principal dwelling was about four hundred and fifty leagues away from Montreal."

1728, June 5. "We left on the fifth of June . . ."

1728, August 1. "We stayed for a while [at MichiliMakinac] to repair what had been damaged by the portages and rapids. I blessed two flags and buried some soldiers there who had been taken from us by fatigue or disease."

1728, August 10. "On the tenth of August, we left from Michillima-Kinac and were at Lake Michigan [. . .]"

1728, August 17. "On the seventeenth, around noon, we stopped until the evening, in order to arrive during the night at the Poste de la Baye. We wanted to surprise the enemies, who we knew to be the Saquis and their allies whose village is near Fort St. Francis. We set out in darkness and, at midnight, arrived at the entrance to the Renard River, where our Fort is built."

1728, August 24. "On the twenty-fourth of August, we arrived at the Puant' village, well disposed to destroy the inhabitants that we would find there, but their flight had been precipitated by our arrival, and we could only burn their huts and destroy their corn, which serves as their main food [. . .]"

1728, September 28. "[. . .] I arrived there [Montreal] on the twenty-eighth of September, and did not leave until Spring, to obey the order given to me to go to Quebec."

1729. "I no sooner arrived in this city, than our Commissioner assigned me to the position at Niagara, which is a new establishment, with a fortress situated at the entrance of a beautiful river which bears the same name, and which is famous for Niagara Falls, to the south of Lake Ontario and six leagues from our fort."

1729, June. "I then took the road for Montreal, and from there I went to Frontenac, or Catarakouy, which is a fort built at the entrance of Lake Ontario [. . .]"

1729, July 22. "We set sail on the twenty-second day of July, and arrived at our post [Niagara] on the morning of the twenty-seventh [. . .]"

1729, July 27. ". . . Fever soon set in on the pleasures we enjoyed at Niagara and inconvenienced us until the onset of autumn. [. . .] We did not receive our provisions until the first day of May. Since St. Martin's Day, the lack of wine prevented me from celebrating Mass; as soon as the boat arrived, I celebrated Easter for the whole garrison, and I left for Detroit, at the request of a religious of my Order who was a missionary there [Father Bonaventure Léonard] [...] I arrived at Detroit seventeen days after my departure. The religious whom I went to visit received me in a manner which perfectly demonstrates the pleasure which we ordinarily feel when we find one of our countrymen in a distant country. Add to this that we were of the same Order, and that the same motive had taken us from our homeland. [. . .] He was a man a little older than I and very commendable for the successes of his apostolic work. His house was pleasant and agreeable, it was, so to speak, his workplace and an abode of virtue. He spent his time, which was not taken up by the duties of his office, with study and the occupations of the countryside. He had some books, and the choice of them gave an idea of his good character and the breadth of his knowledge. The language of the land was quite familiar to him, and the ease with which he spoke it endeared him to several savages who spoke with him about all kinds of subjects, and chiefly about religion. Affability attracts confidence, and no one deserved it more than this religious. He had extended these good relations with some of the inhabitants of Detroit to the point of teaching them the French language. [. . .] Throughout the time that I remained with this religious, I found every day new reasons to envy a life like his. In a word, he was happy, as men should be, without being embarrassed by their happiness. After accomplishing what attracted me to Detroit, I took the road again to Niagara, where I stayed for another two years; I learned during this time enough of the Iroquois and the Outaoüacs languages to converse with them [. . .]"

1732–1733. "When my three years of residence in Niagara expired, I was relieved; that's the custom; and I spent the winter at the friary in Quebec. It was a great satisfaction for me to spend this difficult season there; if there is nothing superfluous, at least one does not lack the necessities; and, what is no small pleasure, one receives news of one's native land, and finds people with whom one can converse."

1733, July. "The chaplain of Fort Frontenac or Catarakoüy fell ill at the beginning of Spring, and our Commissioner assigned me to take his place."

1735, spring. "I stayed there only two years: I was called back to Montreal, and a bit later I was sent to Pointe à la Chevelure, on Lake Champlain. [. . .] The fort we have in this place is called St. Frederick [. . .]"

1735, November 17. "I arrived [at Fort St. Frederick] on November 17, 1735. The season, which began to be demanding, increased our exhaustion along the way: it was one of the most difficult I have had in Canada, [. . .] The building where we were put was not yet finished, we were only poorly protected from the rain, and the walls, which were twelve foot thick, had only been completed a few days before; added to that was the inconveniences of the snow and rain. Many of our soldiers came down with scurvy, and our eyes were so bothered that we feared losing our way without help. We were no better fed than we were housed. [. . .] Our building was completed as soon as the season permitted, but we preferred to camp during the summer rather than stay there any longer; yet we were not any more comfortable, since fever overtook us, and no one could enjoy the pleasurable countryside. This state, I confess, had begun to weigh heavily on me, when, about the month of August, I receive an obedience from my Provincial to return to France."

1736, September 21. "The Religious whom our Commissioner sent to relieve me was from our Province, and was named Pierre Verquaillé; he arrived on the twenty-first of September 1736 at St. Frederick's, and I left the same day at four or five o'clock in the evening."

1736, September to November. "[. . .] I stayed a while in Quebec waiting for an opportunity to return to France. Two arose at the same time: the first was on the King's ship, the Heros, which I did not take; the other was offered by the Sire de Fréneuse, a Canadian, and our connection brought me to accept his offer, and I could not refuse the invitation to serve as his chaplain."

1736, November 3. "We weighed anchor and set sail on the third of November, with several other ships, and anchored all together at Trou-St.-Patrice, three leagues from Québec."

CHAPTER FOUR

The Récollets at Louisbourg[1]

A.J.B. JOHNSTON, PARCS CANADA

Between the bookend dates of 1713 and 1758, the French colony of Île Royale (as Cape Breton Island was called at the time) was home to the following religious personnel: about fifty Franciscans—mostly Récollets de Bretagne but also a fair number of Récollets de Saint-Denis; at least thirty-eight Brothers of Charity of St. John of God, who operated the 100-bed King's Hospital; a dozen Sisters of the Congregation of Notre-Dame, who came not from France but from Canada and whose focus was female education; and seven missionaries dedicated to the spiritual well-being and military usefulness of the Atlantic region's Mi'kmaq and Maliseet. My focus in this paper is on the Récollets from Brittany, but let us recall that both they and the Récollets de Saint-Denis had the same responsibilities: to look after all aspects of parish life in the different communities on the island and to serve as military chaplains where there were garrisons.[2]

The first Franciscans to arrive in the colony were two friars of the Récollets de Saint-Denis (Dominique de la Marche and Jean Capistran) who came from Canada to be part of the initial settlement group in 1713. (La Marche signed the *prise de possession* on September 2, 1713.) The following year, the first Récollets from the Province de Bretagne arrived, coming from Placentia, Newfoundland, whose French population had already mostly relocated to the

1. Johnston, A.J.B., "The Récollets at Louisbourg," in Dubois, Paul-André, ed., *Les Récollets en Nouvelle-France : Traces et Mémoire*, Québec, QC, Les Presses de l'Université Laval, 2018; pp. 139–50.

2. With one exception, the totals for the number of religious come from the appendices at the end of A.J.B. Johnston, *Religion in Life at Louisbourg, 1713–1758* (Montréal & Kingston, McGill-Queen's University Press, 1984), p. 155–160. The figure for the number of missionaries who served the Mi'kmaq on Cape Breton Island between 1713 and 1758 comes from the list on p. 134 of A.J.B. Johnston, *Storied Shores: St. Peter's, Isle Madame and Chapel Island in the 17th and 18th Centuries* (Sydney, Cape Breton University Press, 2003).

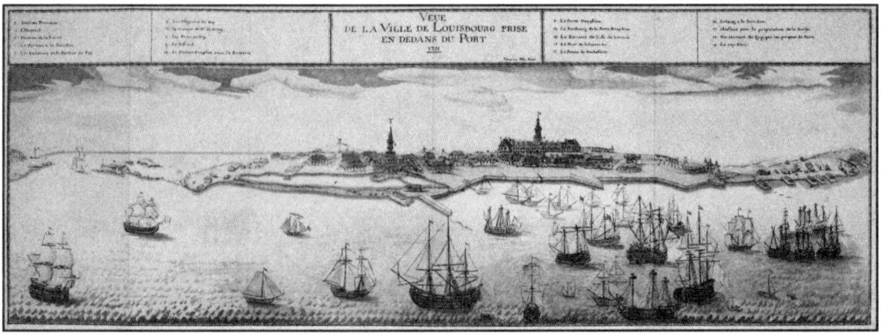

Verrier, the son, *Entry into the city of Louisbourg from inside the port, 1731.* Pen and watercolor, BNF. Department of Maps and Plans.

new colony of Île Royale. Gratien Raoul is the only one of that group whose name was recorded.[3]

France's minister of the Marine at the time, the comte de Pontchartrain, articulated his thinking on why he wanted two groups of Franciscan friars involved in the founding of the new colony. He was expecting Île Royale to attract settlers from both Acadia and Newfoundland, a twin migration caused by the loss of those two regions to Great Britain according to the terms of the Treaty of Utrecht. The minister observed that the colonists relocating from Newfoundland were served by the Brittany Récollects while those in Acadia were familiar with the Paris group. He reasoned that it would be more appealing for the relocating of French colonists if they were to have contact with the same religious figures with which they were already familiar. It was to be an interim arrangement. The senior royal officials in the colony were to determine which of the two Récollect provinces would in the longer term be "the most suitable and agreeable to the inhabitants." The Bishop of Québec, however, held the Récollets de Bretagne in low regard in comparison with those of the Province of Saint-Denis. So it was with reluctance that Bishop Saint-Vallier accepted the arrangement the minister of the Marine proposed.[4]

The system of double representation persisted for nearly twenty years. The Récollets de Bretagne served the parishioners of Louisbourg and the nearby smaller communities while the Récollets de Saint-Denis were located in the other two settlements where there were soldiers and a few royal officials, Port-Dauphin (Englishtown) and Port-Toulouse (St. Peter's). The arrangement ended in 1731

3. R.P. Hugolin [Stanislas Lemay], « Les Récollets de la province de Saint-Denis et ceux de la Province de Bretagne à l'Île Royale de 1713 à 1731 », *Mémoires de la Société royale du Canada*, Sec. 1, 3e série, 25 (1931), p. 77–113.

4. Johnston, *Religion in Life*, p. 23–25.

when those of Saint-Denis withdrew and the spiritual life of the entire island became the responsibility of the Récollects from Brittany. Royal officials reasoned that not many Acadians had migrated to Île Royale and that the colonists of the island preferred the Brittany group. That was not a surprise, because a significant proportion of the colonial population was originally from Brittany or nearby Normandy or the west coast of France. Like Brittany, Île Royale had a definite orientation to the sea and the Récollets de Bretagne appeared to fit in better with the colonists in their maritime occupations and recreational habits.[5]

Louisbourg was by far the largest and most important centre on Île Royale. It was also the community for which the most complete records exist. In over four decades at Louisbourg, the Récollets de Bretagne handled over 2,200 baptisms, 565 marriages, and nearly 1,200 burials in the town. (The records for some years have not survived).[6]

Those numbers reveal not only the size of the Louisbourg community but also how many religious "events" there were in the community on a daily or weekly basis. We do not, however, have data to tell us how many parishioners attended Mass, made confessions, performed penances, conducted routine household prayers, took part in or watched religious processions, observed times of fasting and abstinence, went to vesper services and attended or performed other religious obligations. In addition to the entries in the parish records, our ideas on religious life in the fortified town and seaport come from occasional mentions of personnel or of accounts of incidents in the official correspondence of the governor and *commissaire-ordonnateur*, from the extensive court records and from a selection of letters written by the Brittany Récollects.[7] Here is a short extract from a letter a Récollet named Michel-Ange Le Duff sent to his superior in Brittany in 1727:

> I took the liberty of explaining to Your Reverence the infirmity with which God has been afflicting me since I have been in the colony, and which I can only ascribe to the fatigues I have endured in the ice and snow and to the wretched food we have here, since throughout the year we are obliged to eat no flesh, and fresh meat is rare and very expensive. All these fatigues have so altered my health and exhausted my strength that I now find myself suffering from a very considerable hernia.[8]

---

5. Johnston, *Religion in Life*, p. 46. For a discussion of the origins of the people of Louisbourg, see A.M.B. Johnston, *Control and Order in French Colonial Louisbourg, 1713–1758* (East Lansing, Michigan State University Press, 2001), p. 42–46.

6. There is a fairly detailed analysis of what can be discerned from the Louisbourg parish records and other sources in Chapter 5 of Johnston, *Religion in Life*, p. 109–150.

7. Archives départementales du ministère, Quimper, 23H14. Papiers affaires commerciales, papiers des Récollets.

8. Archives départementales du ministère, Quimper, 23H14. Lettres des Récollets, pièce 17, Le Duff à Dirop, 3 novembre 1727.

Clearly, at least some of the religious order found the living conditions on Cape Breton Island to be a difficult test.

It is likely that there is no place on the planet that is ever completely "typical," yet even so, French colonial Louisbourg was by any standard a distinctly unusual place for the Récollets to find themselves in. I shall elaborate in a moment but first it is important to acknowledge that there was on the island colony, as there was everywhere in France and its colonies, the usual Gallican Church partnership between the officials of the monarchical state and the Roman Catholic clergy. A verse summed up the relationship, as it was ideally conceived:

> Mariage de bon devis
> De l'Église et des fleurs de lis
> Si l'un ou l'autre partira
> Chacun d'eux si s'en partira.[9]

More prosaically, historian Guy Fégault succinctly summarised the partnership in this way: "The men of State are Catholics, the men of the Church are servants of the King."[10]

The ideal of having the Roman Catholic faith be of central importance in people's lives at Louisbourg was expressed symbolically. The military engineer who established the initial town grid located the emplacement for the town's parish church right in the middle of the rectilinear layout facing the waterfront. It was a strong statement. Or rather, it would have been, had any church ever been erected on that spot. Though there was a plan for the church, only the foundations were ever built.

From the perspective of the royal officials, the Récollets were valued because they inculcated morality, ensured social cohesiveness and encouraged loyalty to the king and in general deference to authority.[11] Nothing at Louisbourg illustrated the close ties between church and state better than the lavish expenditures made by royal officials each year for the late August Feast of Saint-Louis (the 13th century Louis IX, the former king who at the time was France's patron saint).[12]

---

9. Quoted in Joseph LeClerc, « Le Roi de France, Fils Ainé de l'Église », *Études*, 214 (1933), p. 24.

10. Guy Frégault, *Le XVIIIe siècle canadien : études,* Montréal, Éditions HMH, 1968, p. 148.

11. One highly influential study of the overall place and role of the church in New France has been Cornelius J. Jaenen, *The role of the Church in New France,* Toronto, McGraw-Hill Ryerson, 1976.

12. Johnston, *Religion in Life*, p. 14; also of interest might be A.J.B. Johnston, "In the Name of the King: the monarchical atmosphere of French Colonial Louisbourg, 1713–1758," in Colin Coates (ed.), *Majesty in Canada. Essays on the Role of Royalty,* Toronto, Dundurn Press, 2006.

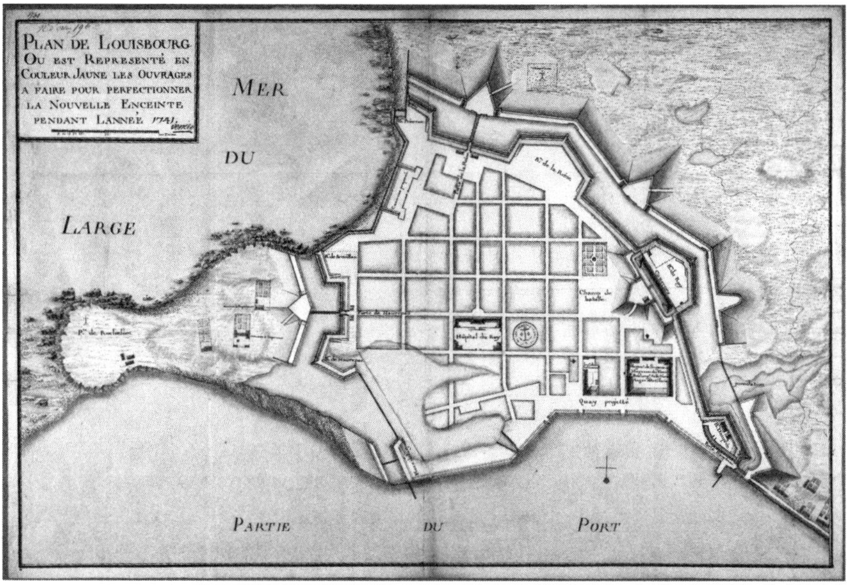

Etienne Verrier, *Plan de Louisbourg*, 1741. Watercolor, pen drawing on paper, 55.5 × 83.3 cm, Archives nationale d'outre-mer (ANOM), Dépôt des fortifications des colonies, no. 196B.

Yet as already hinted at, on Île Royale the state-religion partnership differed from how it operated in contemporary France and Canada. At Louisbourg it was a decidedly uneven relationship. Both the Récollets and the Frères de la Charité de Saint-Jean de Dieu depended on royal officials for their existence in the colony, with their salaries coming out of one royal budget or another. (The Congrégation de Notre-Dame differed in this respect, in that they came on their own and generally struggled without a royal salary or subsidy.) Moreover, though the church calendar was deeply imbued in everyone's mind—it was how each year unfolded to mark people's time and lives—there were many ways in which the administration and the populace on Île Royale did not manifest the customary devotional attitudes and sentiments expected for the period.

Let us begin with nomenclature, which on Île Royale was anything but evolutionary. Where in Canada religious place names and street names were common, on Île Royale they were not. Ports on Cape Breton Island that *for a century* had been known to French mariners as Saint-Pierre and Sainte-Anne were *renamed* after 1713 as Port-Toulouse and Port-Dauphin. The initial name proposed for Louisbourg in the fall of 1713 was Port-Saint-Louis, a reference to the sainted Louis IX. That suggestion was overruled in France in favour of the name we all know, Louisbourg, in reference to the aging Louis XIV. Similarly, at Louisbourg the one and only religious name used was for a short street called rue Saint-Louis. This was in contrast to Québec, Montréal and Détroit where saints' names were often used for streets and bastions. In yet another tilt toward a secular-dominated society, at Louisbourg there was no clerical representation on the Conseil Supérieur, as there was at Québec (for the bishop). The only voices heard in Louisbourg's administration were those of the military and merchants. Both visually and in fact, the fleur de lys and not the cross dominated Louisbourg.

The ordinary colonists appear to have picked up on the secular trend set by the administration. Despite the size and stature of the seaport and fortified town—which grew quickly from a few hundred to several thousand—the parishioners of Notre-Dame-des-Ange, the parish at Louisbourg, refused to contribute toward the construction of a *bona fide* parish church. They argued that it should *not* be they who paid for a church but the king—as he paid for so much else erected at Louisbourg. Rather than build a church, the parishioners opted to use first the Récollets' chapel in Block 3 and then the military chapel in the barracks as interim parish churches.

The parsimoniousness of the Louisbourgeois similarly came to the fore when attempts were made to compel the parishioners to pay a tithe (*dime*) similar in value to that paid by their counterparts in Canada (The tithe in Canada was 1/26; half what was normally required in France.) Again, the fishing population and merchants objected. They claimed they were not in a secure financial position to make such a contribution. Long-serving colonial governor Saint-Ovide observed that "there is perhaps only Isle Royale in the world which does not pay the tithe to its priests."

There was one attempt to introduce secular priests into the town, but the parishioners rejected the idea, preferring instead to have the Récollets de Bretagne whose salaries were paid for by the king.

A few other noteworthy details about Louisbourg: the town was neither entirely French nor monolithically Roman Catholic. The town's permanent population, until 1745, included up to 150 soldiers of the Karrer Regiment, all of whom were Swiss or German and many of whom were Protestant. There were several hundred Basques who worked in the fishery and lived primarily on properties outside the walls and around the harbour. Their language was beyond the comprehension of most of the French, including the local priests. In addition, there were several dozen Irish Catholics in the town and smaller numbers of English, some of whom were Protestant. A number made appearances in the parish records as converts to Roman Catholicism. The town was also home at any one time to dozens of people of African origin. Most were slaves but a few were freed individuals with their own trades. Representatives of the Mi'gmaq and Maliseet visited from time to time.

I am not trying to make the case that French colonial Louisbourg was just like today's cosmopolitan and secular society, because it was not. I do, however, think a case could be made that it was an early precursor of sorts, for the reasons cited above. For the Récollets and other religious in the town, who were used to a more devotional atmosphere, serving at Louisbourg had to have been a somewhat intriguing if not puzzling experience.

Thus far my focus has been on the general state of things in the colony where the Récollets served. I would like to turn now from the general to the particular, by offering brief portraits of a few of the Récollets de Bretagne who came to live and work on Île Royale.[13]

Isidore Caulet first came to Louisbourg in 1723, and was frequently identified as a military chaplain over the next thirty years. In 1752, he was sent to the adjacent colony of Île Saint-Jean, where he served at its administrative centre of Port-La-Joye. His stay on that island was short, because he came back to Louisbourg and was named interim *cure*, a position he filled until he died in 1754. His nearly thirty years' service in the colony made him by far the longest serving Franciscan in the history of Île Royale.

Bénin Le Dorz was in Louisbourg for only three years, 1724–1727, but they were extremely eventful. Le Dorz had a drinking problem, or so it was alleged in reports that reached the Bishop of Québec. Perhaps the people of Louisbourg, with all its drinking establishments, liked the man's willingness to drink with them? What Bishop Saint-Vallier heard was that the Récollet who was Louisbourg's *curé*, the superior of the local Récollects and the bishop's vicar general was known occasionally "to become intoxicated and in that state to dance and do other excessive things." Bishop Saint-Vallier summoned Le Dorz to Québec where he was reprimanded. Maybe continued drinking was the cause, or maybe it was something else, but Le Dorz further drew the ire of Bishop Sain-Vallier when he solemnized "three indefensible marriages." The bishop sent his vicar general to Louisburg hoping that the parish would be taken away not only from Le Dorz, but from the Franciscans entirely. The bishop wanted Notre-Dame-des-Anges entrusted instead to secular priests. The bishop's envoy, Abbé Fornel, stood up at the end of high mass and announced that Bénin Le Dorz was immediately suspended and Isidore Caulet appointed in his place. Caulet, however, refused. The matter was referred to the officials in the Marine ministry in France for a resolution.

---

13. R.P. Hugolin [Stanislas Lemay], « Table nominale des Récollets de Bretagne, missionnaires et aumôniers dans l'Île Royale (1713–1759) », *Mémoires de la Société royale du Canada,* Sec. 1, 3e série, 25 (1931), p. 81–100. For biographies of the Récollets who served in all of New France (and later Québec), see Odoric-Marie Jouve *et al, Dictionnaire biographique des récollets missionnaire en Nouvelle-France 1615–1645, 1670–1849* (Montréal, Bellarmin, 1996).

The solution, worked out between the royal officials and the provincial of the Récollets de Bretagne, was to recall Le Dorz to France and to send a new priest from Brittany to take over as *curé*, superior and vicar general. Thus ended the one and only attempt to introduce secular priests at Louisbourg.[14]

Michel-Ange Le Duff, whose letter we quoted earlier in this paper, was the Récollet named to replace Le Dorz. Le Duff had previously served as a missionary in the small outport of La Baleine, and then come into Louisbourg to be one of the garrison's military chaplains. He was much more deferential to the bishop than Le Dorz had been, but as shown above he greatly disliked the cool, damp climate and occasional shortages of food. It was not long before the provincial of the Récollets de Bretagne, Saturnin Dirop, recalled Michel-Ange Le Duff to France.

Eager to render the parish at Louisbourg more stable after the period of controversy with Le Dorz and then uncertainty with Le Duff, the provincial of the Récollets de Bretagne named Zacharie Caradec as the new *curé* at Louisbourg in 1728. Caradec had already shown himself to be energetic and high-principled,[15] and that was exactly what he was in the colony. He took his responsibilities as seriously as anyone could and was named by Bishop Saint-Vallier as vicar general for Île Royale. Caradec carried out inspections no other Récollet did before or after, or if they did, they left no trace in the documents.

Alas, Caradec apparently had a bit too much energy and too many reforming ideas. First, he annoyed the ship captains at Louisbourg when he tried to do away with an old tradition they enjoyed. Caradec proposed four new churchwardens rather than the ship captains who had occupied those positions for decades, going back to the earlier colony in Plaisance. Next, because of the absence of any tithe, Caradec tried to introduce a tax on fishing crews, with the revenue to go to the parish. When that idea caused an uproar, the Récollet *curé* asked the royal officials to imprison a few individuals as an example for others. The anger and resistance of the Louisbourgeois deepened. The local royal officials referred the matter to the minister of the Marine, who replied that since there was no compulsory tithe, the clergy could only use persuasion, not force, to convince people to contribute to the church. The provincial helped calm the situation by recalling the overly innovative Caradec back to France in 1734.

The very next year there was a suggestion Caradec should return to Louisbourg. That's because the Récollet's energy and reforming ways had

---

14. Jacques Valois, biography of Bénin Le Dorz in vol. 2 of the *Dictionary of Canadian Biography,* Johnston, *Religion in Life,* p. 38–41.

15. For more details on Caradec than are found in the next few paragraphs please see A.J.B. Johnston, « Deux Récollets de l'Île Royale », dans *Chroniques et Documents,* vol. 37, no. 1, Janvier 1984.

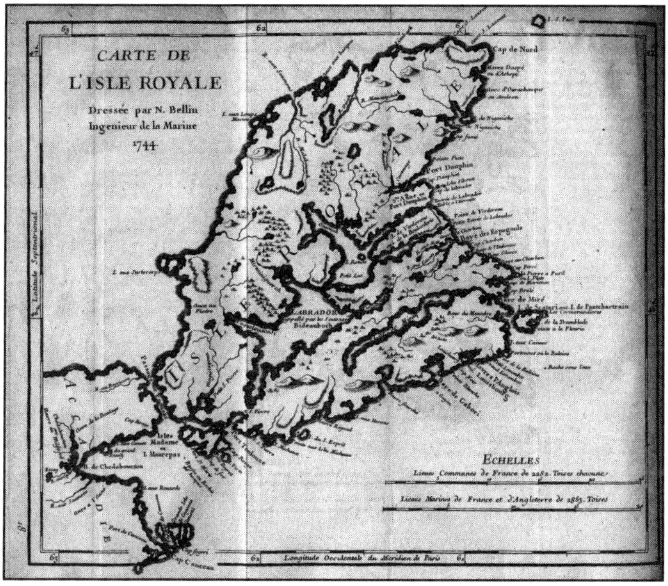

Map of Isle Royale, taken from Pierre-François-Xavier de Charlevois. *Histoire et description générale de la Nouvelle France,* Paris, Nyon, 1744, vol. 2, p. 384–385.

won him some admirers, including Governor Saint-Ovide, the missionary to the Mi'kmaq, Abbé Pierre Maillard, and the comte de Maurepas himself. Caradec's return, however, was blocked by *commissaire-ordonnateur* Le Normant, who described the Récollet as stubborn and unpopular. In 1737, however, the minister of the Marine did authorize Caradec's return. It was not long before those who opposed him began to voice their complaints, about what Le Normant described as Caradec's "vindictive" ways. In the summer of 1739, after two more years of turbulence, Zacharie Caradec was ordered back to Brittany. He would not return to Île Royale again.

The final Récollet I wish to profile is Athanase Guégot.[16] According to the available documentation, he first arrived on Île Royale in 1732. Yet his name rarely appears in the parish records because Zacharie Caradec was then officiating at most baptisms, marriages and funerals. From 1733 to 1736, Guégot was in the sister colony of Île Saint-Jean (today's Prince Edward Island). Back to Île Royale, he served first in a small outport before, in 1737, coming once again to Louisbourg. There he would remain until 1745 when a combined force of New England provincial soldiers and ships along with a

16. Athanase Guégot is the second of the two Récollets whose career on Île Royale is summarized in Johnston, « Deux Récollets de l'Île Royale », 1984.

flotilla of British naval ships captured the French stronghold and forcibly removed virtually the entire population of the colony to France.

In 1739, with Caradec's departure, Guégot became the *commissaire* of the local Récollets and for a short period the vicar-general of the Bishop of Québec. The latter title was taken away from him and given to Abbé Pierre Maillard in 1740. By 1742, Guégot and the other Récollets on Île Royale were complaining to their provincial and to royal officials in the colony and in France that Maillard was meddling unnecessarily in the affairs and causing them to lose face in front of their parishioners. Moreover, Guégot alleged, because of that meddling, Maillard was neglecting some of his duties with regard to being a missionary to the Mi'kmaq. The comte de Maurepeas was shocked to hear such a charge, and threatened Maillard with being recalled to France. Bishop Pontrbiand and the Abbé de l'Isle-Dieu spoke strongly against such a move, and came up with a compromise. Athanase Guégot and Pierre Maillard would share the functions of being the bishop's vicar-general. The solution seems to have worked.

Guégot and other Récollets came back to Île Royale in 1749, after the return of the colony to France by the Treaty of Aix-la-Chapelle (1748). Once again he became the *commissaire* and superior. It was not long, however, before some severe criticisms of Guégot and the Récollets began to surface. The complaints came mostly from Abbé de l'Isle-Dieu in France. Since the Bishop of Québec's vicar-general overseas had never been to Île Royale, it is almost certain that he was getting his information from Abbé Pierre Maillard, who was in the colony. Isle-Dieu wanted to see the Récollets removed from the colony, and affirmed: "six prêtres séculiers feraient plus d'ouvrage que neuf Récollets." Writing specifically of Guégot, the Abbé de l'Isle-Dieu described him as "une espèce qui n'a ny talent ny parole, et peut être aussi peu de bonne volonté et de zèle pour son ministère."[17] The commandant of Île Royale, the comte de Raymond, was also in favour of taking the parish at Louisbourg away from the Récollets. His assessment was that the Récollets led unregulated lives and were too ignorant.[18]

The provincial of the Récollets de Bretagne could not ignore the pressure, and gave orders for Guégot to return to France. Before Athanase Guégot could make that trip, however, he died at Louisbourg in February 1752. He had been in poor health ever since his return to the colony, a reality that undoubtedly created the situation of which the critics of the Récollets complained.

---

17. *Rapport de l'Archiviste de la Province du Québec* (1935-36), p. 310–313; p. 313–315.

18. Archives de la Guerre, Archives du Service historique de l'Armée, Série A1, Reg. 3393, pièce 38, janvier 1752.

To close this paper I would like to say a few words relating to the conference theme of "Traces et mémoire." How well is what the Récollets de Bretagne experienced and accomplished at French colonial Louisbourg remembered today? The short answer is that it is not especially well remembered, unless one is inclined to read an academic article or book.

Beginning in the late 19th century, and continuing for several decades in the 20th century, a variety of groups came to Louisbourg to raise monuments and memorials in memory of those who had been a part of that site's history in the 18th century. Both the Sœurs de la Congregation de Notre-Dame and the Frères de la Charité de Saint-Jean de Dieu erected monuments to their predecessors. No one, however, put up a memorial to the Récollets de Bretagne. Presumably that is because that branch of the Franciscan order had been dissolved by Pope Leo XIII in 1897 and there was no one within the Ordre des Frère Mineurs who saw the need for any such remembrance of what the Récollets had experienced and achieved. In the decades that followed, once the reconstruction of the Fortress of Louisbourg came along, the vogue for raising monuments declined. The new approach was "living history," a term that described people in costume carrying out activities in period settings.

As it turned out, the one-fifth portion of Louisbourg selected in the 1960s for reconstruction excluded by the narrowest of margins the Récollet property in Block 3. The front of the block, facing the waterfront, was rebuilt, but not the back half, which is where the presbytery and the chapel had stood. This decision was taken for a combination of aesthetic and financial reasons, not out of any conscious decision to exclude the Récollets. The buildings along the quay completed the "look" of the 18th century waterfront; those on the back of Block 3 were judged to be unnecessary to achieve the three-dimensional effect of walking through a French colonial town. As for communicating aspects of 18th century parish life, the thinking in the 1960s and 1970s was that the Fortress had enough to tell that story in the chapel that served as the town's parish church.

The Chapelle Saint-Louis within the King's Bastion barracks did indeed serve as Louisbourg's parish church for many years. Because it was a crucial part of the largest and most important building at Louisbourg, it was rebuilt by Parks Canada and furnished according to period descriptions. So too, two small rooms just off the chapel, the sacristy and the chaplain's room. Generally speaking, visitors are simply presented with the atmosphere of the chapel and adjacent rooms and left largely to their own devices to grasp the significance of religion in people's lives. Sometimes there might be a costumed animator in or near to the chapel to share some stories, but that is not always the case. More commonly, visitors gain an impression of the décor and furnishing of the period, but not a great deal about the many storylines associated with the Récollets and the parishioners, unless it is a special interest tour.

In an attempt to convey at least the basics about the story of the Récollets at Louisbourg Parks Canada recently introduced a ground interpretation panel in the space that, back in the 18th century, had been reserved for the town's un-built parish church. It provides a few basics about the religious order and its travails at Louisbourg. For more than that, one still has to resort to the old-fashioned way of reading articles or a book.

CHAPTER FIVE

Historical Overview

JEAN HAMELIN[1]

I. A LATE RESTORATION—1860–1890

In the mid-nineteenth century, the French-Canadian episcopacy emerged victorious from the battle which pitted it against both the Anglophone and Francophone secular liberal elites. This battle was for control of public education, welfare assistance and, more generally, the very organization of society. The victory was won in stages. The failure of the uprisings of 1837–1838 delayed the Patriots' plan to bring about a secular and democratic society, and it decimated their leaders. This left the field free to the Catholic hierarchy's activity. At the same time, the fortunate political alliances between Louis-Hippolyte Lafontaine, Augustin-Norbert Morin and the former Patriot Party brought the episcopacy, little by little, into the structures of political power. The episcopacy came to have a freedom to act which it had not known even under the French regime. While in other countries the temporal power of the Church was being battered, here on the shores of the St. Lawrence, a type of Christianity was being established where the Church had the upper hand on the control of social welfare and operation of social mechanisms—the family, the school, the parish.

Ignace Bourget, named coadjutor of Monsignor Jean-Jacques Lartigue in 1837, then Bishop of Montréal in 1840, was the architect of this victory. He is the executor of his predecessor's legacy. Monsignor Lartigue had given him an Ultramontane vision of the Church which saw it as a perfect society independent of civil powers; and he had left Bourget with a desire both to emancipate and to affirm the policies of this Church. He began a program of action centered on the formation of clerics, the supervision of the faithful, the instruction of the working classes, the relief of the needy, and the censoring of ideas. It was an ambitious program which required hiring many laborers

1. Hamelin, Jean, « Survol Historique », in Hamelin, Jean (dir.), *Les Franciscains au Canada, 1890–1990*, Sillery, QC, Septentrion, 1990; pp. 13–95.

to work in the vineyard of the Lord. The classical colleges, set up in the first half of the 19th century, provided Monsignor Bourget with the priests he needed for the pastoral and parochial supervision of the faithful. But for social works, he had to rely on religious communities; and he had them come from France—the Oblates of Mary Immaculate in 1841; the Jesuits and the Sisters of the Sacred Heart of Jesus in 1842; the Clerics of Saint Viator and the Congregation of the Holy Cross in 1847. Strangely, Monsignor Bourget did not appeal to the Order of Friars Minor.

1. The Tertiaries' Expectations

There is something surprizing in this absence. The Recollects, a former branch of the Order of Friars Minor, founded in 1209 by Saint Francis of Assisi, had been the first missionaries of the country. There had been at least 380 in New France and Acadia, who had exercised their ministry in the missions, in 117 parishes and 20 military posts. At the time of Canada's transfer to England, about 45 remained of which at least twenty were of Canadian origin. The British Government, which considered communities of men as parasites, had banned them from recruiting members. In the fall of 1796, after the fire of the Recollects' friary and church in Quebec, Monsignor Jean-François Hubert reduced ten young Recollects who had entered the Order "illegally" after 1784 to the secular state "with permission to keep the religious habit." In accord with their wish and their charism, the four still-living priests continued to exercise their ministry and then died one by one. Louis Demers, the last priest, died in Montreal on September 2, 1813, and Marc Coutant, the last brother, died in Montmagny on September 15, 1849. Their remaining goods were divvied out. In Trois-Rivières, the Anglican community used their buildings. In Montreal, the Sulpicians, who became owners of their chapel after Father Demers' death, demolished it in 1867. In the mid-19th century, there remained little material traces of the Recollects' apostolate, but their remembrance lived on in the collective memory of the people. And the spirit of St. Francis still animated the hearts of some isolated tertiaries.

Outside Canada, the Observant Franciscans—which included the Recollects in France, the Reformed in Italy, the Alcantarans in Spain—had similar experiences. The 1768 Chapter of Valencia in Spain, which brought together 77,000 delegates from 167 provinces, marked a summit in the history of the Order. Due to the religious persecution in various countries, the Order was in decline. Entire provinces had been ruined in Spain, Poland and Russia. In Italy and Mexico, persecution was rife. Nonetheless, in some countries, provinces were coming back to life. This is the case in France where Father Joseph Aréso, an Observant from Spanish Navarre, tried to reintroduce to the Order "all the primitive purity of its founder." He founded a fraternity at

Saint-Palais in the Diocese of Bayonne in 1851. Then other foundations followed; so much so that in 1860 the Province of Saint Louis, also known as the Province of Aquitaine, was erected and brought together 5 convents and 58 religious. In Provence, under the guidance of Father Benignus of Valbonne, another province was on the way to being formed. But the French Observants were still not very numerous, and their restoration was done with rigorous austerity and outmoded forms of spirituality which were out of keeping with the new spiritual trends directed to action. While the Dominican Father Henri Lacordaire's restoration was inspired both by the tradition of his Order, particularly the Parisian traditions, and by the new currents of spirituality, Joseph Aréso, to the contrary, drew inspiration from the Cistercians. He resurrected a rigidly structured conventual life that was not very open to the needs of the changing modern world. He was concerned about training apostolic men, but he neglected their doctrinal formation. It was natural therefore that Monsignor Bourget should turn to the services of the new religious congregations to carry out his apostolic program. They were more open to the world, and more numerous and resolutely action oriented.

A fortuitous event, however, brought Monsignor Bourget to renew his ties with the Franciscan family. On June 8, 1862, he was in Rome to attend the canonization of the 26 Martyrs of Japan: 3 Jesuits, 6 Franciscans and 17 tertiaries all of whom died on February 5, 1597. Monsignor Bourget, whose great pastoral concern was to oversee the faithful, was amazed both by the Third Order's ability to bring about a holiness and by the regenerative influence that tertiaries, who were striving to live the evangelical beatitudes as laity within the world, could have in Montreal's parishes. He obtained an indult from Rome which allowed him to establish the Third Order of the various religious orders in his diocese. He published this on December 8, 1862, and subsequently encouraged his priests to introduce the Third Order of St. Francis in their parishes. The Third Order was not entirely unknown to the faithful. The Recollects had established the Third order in Quebec City and Trois-Rivières around 1670, and then in Montreal in 1694. This Third Order began to decline with the Recollects' dispersal and with the absence of directors from the secular clergy who wanted to keep it going. By 1860 there was only a small number of tertiaries, called "isolated tertiaries" scattered around in parishes.

Under the impulse of Monsignor Bourget, the Third Order restarted slowly. In his diocese, he entrusted their leadership to the Sulpicians. They established the Fraternity of St. Elisabeth in May 1863, then St. Francis in 1866. Father Cyrille Beaudry, a Cleric of Saint Viator, established one at the Seminary of Joliette in 1865 and the parish priest, Léon Provancher, established another in his parish in Portneuf in 1866. Monsignor Louis-François Laflèche erected two in his diocese of Trois-Rivières in 1876 and in 1877.

According to Monsignor Bourget the tertiaries longed for Friars Minor to animate their spiritual life—especially the Recollects. Some began to demand a restoration of the Order of Friars Minor in Canada. This is the case of Léon Provancher, himself a tertiary since 1864, who begged the General of the Order of the Friars Minor, in Rome, to send Franciscans to Canada. These demands became more frequent and more insistent. Monsignor Bouget thought it would be good to intervene by means of Telesphore Harel, then a cleric studying in Rome. On January 25, 1875, he entrusted him with the task "to make loud and clear the first overtures" to the General of the Order. Monsignor Bourget placed his hopes in the Province of Saint Joseph of Belgium, which had fifteen houses and more than 300 religious. The General asked for time. Montreal's tertiaries then committed themselves to paying the costs that the Order would incur in the first year. To no avail. The General replied in the fall of 1875 that he did not believe the time had come to proceed with a restoration of the Order in Canada, even if he would be "very happy to see a house of Recollects based in Montreal." The tertiaries, nevertheless, did not give up. Bishop Louis-Zéphirin Moreau, recently appointed Bishop of Saint-Hyacinthe and himself a tertiary, as well as François-Xavier Lantier, a merchant and rector of the Fraternity of Saint-François, put on the pressure: one with the General of the Order in 1876; the other with the Provincial of the Belgian province, Father Bernard Van Loo, in 1877. The latter was already strongly committed to the restoration of the Order in England and Ireland and declined.

So only France, because of its political climate, remained as a possibility to promote the Montreal plan. In fact, the French were strongly divided on the religious question. The Constitutional laws of 1875, which established a president and a bicameral parliament, left the field free to a political confrontation. On one hand, Monarchists, attached to traditional religious values, were favourable to a union of Church and State. On the other hand, the Republicans were hostile to denominational private schools, to Church interference in politics, and to the temporal power of the papacy. In fewer than three years, the Republicans, supported by popular suffrage, attained the administration of the State. Jules Ferry, who was appointed Minister of Public Instruction in February 1879, received the mandate to bring forth a policy of state secularism and public education that focussed on the training of patriotic citizens imbued with Republican values. How far would Republican politics go? Would the religious communities, which had developed, thanks to the tolerance of former governments although not legally authorized, be suppressed? Catholics began to be worried. In Rome, the Franciscan General suggested to the Provincial of the Aquitaine Province, Father Raphael Delarbre, to think about emigrating to Canada. He wrote "This country would be happy to receive the children of Saint Francis who were once its first missionaries."

Father Delarbre would consider the idea, but only "in the event of imminent and almost certain danger of suppression. For if we are not suppressed in France, we are not yet in a position to send a colony abroad."

Events seem to have been competing for the restoration of the Order in Canada. Monsignor Édouard-Charles Fabre, the successor of Monsignor Bourget since May 1876, was on his way to Europe in 1879, for his *Ad Limina* visit. In August, he contacted the Recollects in Ghent; then the General of the Franciscans in Rome, in the autumn. As a result of these conversations, Monsignor Fabre sent a letter to the Provincial of Aquitaine formally asking him to send Franciscans to Montreal. In France, things were coming to a head. The Republicans had eliminated the representatives of religious communities from the Council of Public Instruction. They forbade certain communities to teach. They decreed the dissolution of the Company of Jesus. The decrees of March 29th, 1880, which obliged French youth to serve in the military, quickly prompted the Provincial of Aquitaine to repatriate young recruits in formation: novices went to England; philosophers to Andalusia; theologians to Holland. The Provincial of Aquitaine moved quickly. Certain, however, that the Republicans would not go so far as to vote for the abolition of the communities, he kept the Montreal plan in reserve.

2. Father Frederick Paves the Way

In June 1881, Father Frederick Janssoone de Ghyvelde's meeting with Father Leon Provancher, in Paris, opened new horizons. The first, Janssoone, was the Custodial Vicar of the Custody of the Holy Land. He was collecting for the holy places, for which his community were the official guardians since 1342. The second, Provancher, a retired parish priest continuing his study of insects in Cap-Rouge, was returning from a pilgrimage to Palestine. He was a fervent tertiary and was looking for a visitator for the Third Order in Canada. He persuaded Father Frederic to come and to take up collections. The plan appealed to the Order's authorities. On August 24, Father Frederick arrived at the Lévis train station. He had two mandates in his pocket: one, the Sacred Congregation of Propaganda had mandated him to establish the Good Friday collection for the Holy Land, in Canada; the other, his superiors asked him to visit the Third Order fraternities and to evaluate the possibilities of a restoration of the Order.

Frederick was 43 years old, of Flemish descent, and trained in France. He was a man of experience—he was co-founder of the Bordeaux friary—and he had the reputation of being a holy man. He was said to be much older than his age, with grey robe and beard according to the custom of Palestine. His friend Provancher welcomed him to Cap-Rouge. He introduced him to the Archdiocese of Quebec where he preached the great retreat of Saint-Roch, and then to his friends from Trois-Rivières—Monsignor Laflèche, the bishop of the place; Luc Desilets, parish priest of St. Mary Magdalen at Cap-de-la-Madeleine; and the other members of the Desilets's family. The people of Trois-Rivières welcomed Father Frederick with open arms. His calm, emaciated, austere figure won everyone's heart. Father Desilets wrote: "he incites the people to run after him. They literally fight over him." The Province of Quebec established the Good Friday collection. Monsignor Laflèche was open to the idea of establishing a Commissariat of the Holy Land in Trois-Rivières. In Rome, the Order's superiors enlarged the plan and instructed the Provincial of Aquitaine to begin a restoration of the Order in Trois-Rivières. Father Raphael Delarbre chose two fathers about forty years old, experienced, and with a solid spirituality: Simon Valadier and Augustin Bouynot. But the decision fell upon bad luck. Father Valadier died unexpectedly on December 9, 1881. His successor, Othon Ransan, then vicar at Loreto, was kept in Spain following the death of his superior. These setbacks delayed the implementation of the plan. In addition, Monsignor Laflèche's reluctance was moving in the same direction. He had approved the establishment of a Holy Land Commissariat, not that of a community. He believed his diocese was too poor to accommodate a mendicant Order.

Pressured by his superiors, Frederick knocked on Monsignor Fabre's door. What a cruel disappointment! The latter's response was a complete turnabout. He no longer wanted "to accept religious for a long time, if in fact this were to be possible at all. It was probable that it would be his successor, or rather one of his successors, who would perhaps see that day." Monsignor Fabre's refusal was understandable: he was struggling with serious financial problems. In fact, in 1866, Monsignor Bourget had begun, to the chagrin of the Sulpicians, the former lords of the Island of Montreal, to carve out parishes within the limits of Nôtre-Dame, the only parish on the island. The construction of the churches and rectories had cost a lot. Around 1882, Monsignor Fabre had contracted debts, from the 16 new parishes of the island, for the sum of $840,000. To this amount must be added various debts incurred by communities recently settled in his diocese. Monsignor Fabre pressed the rich into contributing. Special collections, appeals and bazaars continually appealed to their generosity. How could he open the diocese to a mendicant Order, under these conditions, without arousing the ire of certain people – and perhaps also that of the Sulpicians who were reluctant to share their flowerbeds in the gardens of the Lord with others. Frederick was disappointed, but not hopeless. He continued to put his hopes in his friends from Trois-Rivières. But the outbreak of war in the Middle East forced him to return to the Holy Land. On the 1st of May 1882, he left Canada.

He was only able to return six years later, even though he and Leon Provancher came up with a new plan each year. Some impediment always arose as an insurmountable obstacle: at times it was the inability of a superior to assess a situation. In fact, scattered throughout the world from Quebec City via Europe to Jerusalem, the players in this restoration plan were unable to orchestrate their efforts. A practical man, Father Raymond Caisse, spokesman for the Seminary of Trois-Rivières, was to succeed in this feat. During a pilgrimage to the Holy Land in 1887, he was struck by the poverty and simplicity in which the guardians of the Holy places lived. He was convinced that the Franciscans "who were preaching everywhere humility and temperance by their words and examples" would be the most effective instrument to combat extravagance and drunkenness—"these two great ills" that plagued Canada. He proposed his project to the guardians of the holy places, and they endorsed it without expressing the need for "any financial support from the bishop." On his return to his country, he obtained Monsignor Laflèche's consent for the establishment of a simple Commissariat of the Holy Land where some fathers and brothers could stay. Father Caisse also wrote to the General of the Order in Rome, who referred him to the Provincial of Aquitaine, who consulted his councilors. In the fall of 1887, the foundation of a Commissariat was accepted "unanimously and with resolve" by the Province of Aquitaine. On June 7, 1888, the General of the Order announced to Monsignor Laflèche that Father Frederick was on his way to Trois-Rivieres, and that he had been mandated to proceed with the establishment of the Commissariat "until it is possible to establish a regular community."

On June 14, 1888, Frederick arrived without any fanfare in Trois-Rivières, accompanied by the lay brother Lazarus Fromentin. The rector of the cathedral greeted him at the station, and, in the absence of the bishop, the canons welcomed him at the bishopric. The parish priest Désilets offered him hospitality in his rectory. On June 22nd, Frédéric inaugurated the refurbished chapel of Notre-Dame-du Cap. He preached a prophetic sermon on this occasion about the fate of this little sanctuary—the "miracle of the eyes"—which was happening and seemed to be sanctioned that evening in front of Father Frederick, the parish priest, Desilets, and a parishioner, Pierre Lacroix. Later, Bishop Laflèche donated a square acre plot of land, at the corner of Laviolette and Saint Maurice streets, so that he could build a Commissariat there. According to what Father Frederick himself said, "if times become better, his Excellency would like to see there, along with the Commissariat, a regular community of religious of our Order." Frederick knew that this was a pious wish. In the short term, Monsignor Laflèche, whose diocese was cut off in 1885 from its richest portion, Nicolet, to the south of the river, could not do anything more because of his lack of financial resources.

So it was that Father Frederic turned his eyes towards Montreal to establish the beginnings of a community. The tertiaries there were fervent, and their fraternities were dynamic. The Fraternity of Saint Francis had been established in the Notre-Dame-des-Anges chapel, at the corner of Lagauchetière and Chenneville since 1867. This was a former property of the Recollects that the Sulpicians had acquired from a Presbyterian community. The site included a church, a fairly large two-story house big enough to accommodate a dozen religious, and a piece of land bounded by three streets. The Sulpicians had made this chapel available to the tertiaries free of charge, but an agreement stipulated that the tertiaries would be obliged to buy these buildings for $20,000, on the day the Franciscans assumed the direction of the Third Order. It is in this that a "providential situation" and a sign of God's secret purpose was seen. It could also have been a very human event. In fact, for reasons that Father Frederick did not understand, Monsignor Fabre refused him permission to preach and to hear confessions in the diocese of Montreal that summer. And in the fall, when, at the request of a parish priest, he preached two large parish retreats, the administrator of the diocese, in the absence of Monsignor Fabre who was visiting Rome, granted permission only with strong reservations. To Frederick's questions the administrator responded: "Step aside as much as possible and leave Montreal as soon as possible (. . .) I'm not free [to say anything more]." The seemingly benevolent welcome that the Sulpicians offered him masked perhaps struggles for influence and power.

Frederick did not understand the source of this opposition and informed his superiors. They reminded him that his mandate was to go ahead with a restoration of the order. They insisted that he try to "found a novitiate in Montreal" and that he test "cautiously the terrain with the Sulpicians." Overwhelmed by the prevailing climate in Montreal, Frederic replied at the beginning of 1890 "not to send any religious to Canada" because "no Canadian bishop was thinking of accepting a First Order foundation at the moment."

3. The Convent on Richmond Street

His superiors did not let up. They had little choice. In July 1889, the Ferry government passed the Army Recruitment Act: all citizens, clerics and lay people, were required to do an active military service of three years, except the seminarians for the diocesan clergy who were only required to do one year. The government invoked the principles of brotherhood and equality which were enforceable by law. Catholics saw it as a ploy to stifle religious vocations. The superiors of communities tried to evade the law by dispersing the novices and the temporary professed to foreign houses, only to repatriate them about ten years later. The law exempted 18- to 30-year-old French citizens living abroad from military service.

Time was running out. They had to consider the competitors who were thinking of settling in Canada, such as the Capuchins who were preparing to contact Cardinal Elzéar-Alexandre Taschereau. The General of the Order immediately called on Cardinal Jean Simeoni, the Protector of the Franciscans. As Prefect of the Sacred Congregation of Propaganda Fide, on which the Canadian Church and all the missionary countries were still dependent, Simeoni was an influential character. He was head of the bureaucratic network through which honors and reprimands passed. He was not opposed with impunity. Simeoni agreed to intervene and plead in favor of the Franciscans' plan "to transfer their novitiate house from France to the archdiocese of Montreal." At the end of February 1890, a series of letters were directed to Montreal: Simeoni's letter to Monsignor Fabre, those of the General of the Order to Monsignor Fabre and to the superior of the Sulpicians. The Franciscans' demands were minimal: they would settle for a "hospitable dwelling" which could be simply a rented house and a small conventual chapel. Simeoni's intervention silenced the opposition. Monsignor Fabre saw in this "a command from heaven" and was "very happy to obey him." The Sulpicians were too. The religious authorities in Montreal suggested that a delegate be sent first of all to assess the situation, and then to discuss the number of religious, the sharing of resettling costs, and the adaptation of the Rule to climatic and cultural conditions. Would the Franciscans be able to handle money? Could they profit from the land? Could they accept alms in cash and receive money for their preaching? In short, would they have to follow their rule literally or, as in missionary countries, make the best of it?

In mid-April 1890, the General of the Order appointed Father Othon Ransan, Provincial of Aquitaine, to be the delegate. He acted promptly. On May 15, he left Paris with Friar Clair Rouqueyrol. He arrived in Quebec City on May 27, where he was welcomed by Father Fulcran Lacoste, who was based in Trois-Rivières since 1889, and a postulant from Trois-Rivières, Victor Gagnon. Father Ransan stopped in Trois-Rivières where he greeted Monsignor Laflèche, and then, of course, he visited the Commissariat erected in the summer of 1889 by Father Frederick. On May 29, he arrived in Montreal where the Sulpicians offered him hospitality.

Othon got to work right away. Housing was his first concern. The tertiaries offered to buy Notre-Dame des Anges and the adjacent properties. The Sulpicians opposed this claiming that the house and the land belonged to Notre-Dame parish. Father Joseph-Ulrich Leclerc, honorary canon and parish priest of Saint Joseph parish in the Saint Antoine district (Petite-Bourgogne), suggested renting a house at the back of his rectory. Father Othon found the building "poor, old, but in conformity with Franciscan poverty and sufficient for the moment." It could house about 15 religious. In fact, it was a collection of old houses, consisting of a ground floor and a second floor, built on the same plan. They overlooked an alley called Metcalfe which could not be accessed other than by two doors opening onto Richmond Street. The lease agreement, drawn up by Father Othon and signed on June 1st, specified that the religious would have the use of the court, the burden of compensating the former tenants, paying the taxes and carrying out the maintenance work, as well as the freedom to arrange the premises as they liked. They would also have a confessional in the parish church.

On June 9th, Father Othon took possession of the premises. He was at the same time architect, carpenter and painter. Renovations were promptly carried out. The parish priest Leclerc "collected floor planks, mortar, and locks." The lay brothers and the tertiaries were also involved. In ten days, the work was finished. Monsignor Fabre came to bless the friary on the Feast of St. John the Baptist in the presence of many religious, priests and tertiaries. The six Franciscans who were present knelt before his Excellency. In his speech, Father Othon traced their future road: "the role of the Franciscans had not changed: by the grace of God, they would be, as they had been two centuries ago, Friars Minor, missionaries, the friends of the poor and the little ones. They would announce to all, with brevity of language, blessings, virtues, sorrows and glory, according to the recommendation of their Seraphic Father."

II. Settling-in: 1890–1920

When they arrived in Montreal in 1890, the Franciscans had the impression that they had been transported to some medieval region. Monsignor Bourget succeeded in his gamble to re-Christianize his diocese. "The working class is really good here," noted Father Othon, "there are almost no cafes and few workers read the newspapers (. . .), they clutter the churches, do not go to the café, gather in front of the doors of houses to chitchat and smoke peacefully, and they respect religion and its ministers." The predominance of religion was evident in the institutions. In principle, the Church and the State were separated, but in practice Catholicism was the matrix that shaped the organization of society. The Catholic Church had the upper hand on education and social assistance, as well as on the main social institutions: the family, the school, and the parish. Workers' organizations were still undeveloped, and political clubs were beginning to expand in regions of Montreal where social gathering places brought together workers who were always fond of playing some euchre or of hearing a speaker. But clubs could also be a means to convey ideas that put in question the beautiful homogeneity of society. "This poor people is beginning to be worked on," Father Othon deplored. "The influence of Anglicanism, but above all the unjust and antisocial teachings of Europe, are feared to be next for this dear population."

1. *Territorial Expansion*

From the moment of their installation, the Franciscans, who were only three Fathers and some brothers, were overwhelmed. The chapel was too small. They lacked confessors, preachers for parish retreats and visits to the tertiaries, and teachers for the formation of professed friars. Jean-Baptiste Pelte, the guardian of the friary, pleaded for reinforcements, even if it meant closing a few houses in France. He would not hear that such a beautiful portion of the Lord's Vineyard should escape from the Franciscans. "Remember", he wrote to his superior, "how, in the political realm, France lost Canada." Reinforcements would come. But in the immediate future other problems were more pressing. Pelte, an impetuous southerner, was inclined to see adversaries everywhere; however, physically and mentally overwrought, lacking tact and judgement, he could not manage to control them. Overexertion and the unsanitary conditions of the place undermined the health of the strongest. Father Fulcran came within an inch of death twice and Brother Godefroy Guyot died at 19. Father Xavier Ricomes became dyspeptic, and Brother Mathieu Pontvianne withered away rapidly. Moreover, the parish priest, Leclerc, behaved more as owner of the places than as a trustee. He assumed rights which were the responsibility of the guardian of the friary and he demanded excessive compensation for minor services. The Sulpicians, courteous and generous as always, made sure, however, that the Franciscans did not invade their parish and did not take charge of the tertiary fraternities. On the other hand, the tertiaries, dissatisfied with the spiritual services offered by the Sulpicians, urged the Franciscans to take on the direction of the Third Order.

Pelte acted impetuously. Pressed by the tertiaries and worried about the uncleanliness of the premises, and without consulting the bishop, he decided to move into a new convent located on Sherbrooke Street. This decision unleashed a hurricane. The parish priest, Leclerc, having had his material interests and prestige affected, reviled the Franciscans in *La Presse* and in *La Patrie*. The Sulpicians, anxious to retain their influence, called on Monsignor Fabre, whose representative was then sent to Pelte who received him in a cavalier manner. Pelte relied on canon law to defend his positions. His temperament stirred up problems more than tempering them. Monsignor Fabre turned to the supreme authority, Cardinal Simeoni. Experienced bureaucrat that he was, the Cardinal placed the problem back on the General of the Order who, in turn, sent it back to Father Pierre-Baptiste Gimet, Provincial of the new Province of Saint Peter of France, which separated from the province of Aquitaine in 1892, and which now included England and Canada. In February 1892, Father Gimet decided to come to Montreal to investigate.

In the words of the friary's first analyst, who judged these events by the measure of his faith, what seemed a loss became a heavenly aid. A good diplomat, Father Gimet took control of the situation quickly. Monsignor Fabre, the Sulpicians and the parish priest, LeClerc, were accommodating. Father Pelte offered his resignation in complete serenity. They gave Father Gimet carte blanche on the condition that he not install a friary on Sherbrooke Street—doubtlessly Sulpician land. Once again, Father Leclerc came to the rescue of the Franciscans. He came across an old house, in good condition, situated on an undefined piece of land on Dorchester Street, which permitted construction and where the incline allowed levels of pathways to be developed. It was located in a residential and Protestant area. The view overlooked the lower town. High fences ensured the privacy of the residents. Its only flaw was to be valued at $40,000, a considerable sum for the time. But the tertiaries were keeping an eye on it; and the fraternities were willing to pay $2,400 to guarantee the mortgage. Marie-Anne Devins, widow of Thomas Tiffin and now a retired tertiary living with the Grey Nuns, was full of compassion for the poor Franciscans of Richmond Street, financed $8,000 and promised other donations. Her friend, Marie Perrot, widow of Thomas-Leon McConkey, contributed a few thousand dollars. On May 13, 1892, the Franciscans acquired a new residence. The small community moved there on May 25th. Monsignor Fabre communicated to the General of the Order his deep satisfaction: "Unity and peace now reign. The Very Reverend Provincial maintained a conduct worthy of praise, in this delicate circumstance, and was eager to settle the matter amicably."

Now the Franciscans had a suitable residence, a piece of land that lent itself to an expansion of the friary, and benefactors whose financial means could assure a vision for the future. From the fall of 1892 to the spring of 1901, the Dorchester Street location was a construction site. The length of the friary was doubled and a floor was added. The construction of a crypt-chapel was begun in the spring of 1893, a complete renovation of the friary in 1894, a college was added in 1896, a new wing in 1898, and an upper chapel in 1900. The guardian was guided by several principles: traditional poverty, minimal comfort, simplicity and good taste. Benefactors were not wanting. Mrs. McConkey alone contributed some $70,000, a part of which would be used for expansion outside of Montreal.

At the end of the century, St. Joseph friary was well established. It had a novitiate, a seraphic college, and a house of studies for philosophy and theology. The small number of personnel was varied: five oblates and three lay brothers to take care of the physical tasks; five novices of which three were clerics were trying out their vocation; 25 students residing at the college while taking courses at the Sulpicians; eight clerics attending the Studium. About ten fathers taught philosophy and theology and preached retreats. The surrounding population, first surprised and then curious, became fond of these "beggar monks." Catholics flocked to the friary mass; Protestants were generous—some even converted. The tertiaries liked to meet in the chapel and the public—clerics and lay people—rushed to devotional celebrations. The Franciscans popularized pilgrimages: they organized a trip for 900 women tertiaries to Sainte Anne de Beaupré on June 16, 1894, then 600 men, in full habit, on July 28; and then more than 1,000 faithful to Cap de la Madeleine on September 24th.

It was time to think about expansion. According to the Rule, all the categories of religious should not be present in the same house. If the harvest that was seeming to ripen came to fruition, the friary on Dorchester Street would again be too crowded. The future, however, just like the friars' insertion into Canadian society, did not receive any collective reflection. There were no committees, there was no expertise. The Holy Spirit and tradition sufficed. Franciscan friaries were urban institutions with a three-fold purpose. They served, first of all, for the formation of recruits by teaching theology and offering pastoral experiences in various apostolates. They were also communities of prayers, bringing together men of various social classes who provided an exemplary presence, for the sole reason that, in remembrance of Jesus, they loved to call one another brothers and obey one another. They were open to the public for prayer, participation in liturgical celebrations, and for the sacrament of reconciliation. Finally, they were points of departure for apostolic works outside the walls of the friary; the administration of these works was centered there. The Franciscan experience was mid-way between the contemplative ideal of monks and the active service of the more recently founded religious congregations. This testified to the importance of sanctifying actions, which in and of itself, was not an intangible value.

The fathers of the Franciscan restoration sought to establish themselves in the cities. Reviving what the Recollects had established in New France, they kept their eyes on the regions of Quebec and Trois-Rivières. But the circumstances were difficult. Outside of Montreal, urban development was limping along. Competition between religious communities was fierce in small-town Quebec. Moreover, the diocesan clergy were often reluctant to contend with these communities that depleted their vocations, faithful, and alms. The population did not like to have too many demands placed upon it. Monsignor Louis-Nazaire Bégin, Bishop of Quebec, informed the Franciscans in 1898 that: "The population has not risen significantly in the last twenty years, industry has not developed; our harbor is deserted; individuals' wealth is reduced, as in the past, to honest work. In the current situation, my diocese has all the religious personnel that it needs and is capable of feeding." Colomban-Marie Dreyer, named local superior in 1895, but with assignments equivalent to those of a provincial delegate, knew the situation well. He was a realistic man, cautious with good judgement; he did not belabour the issue, but he remained attentive to the situation and did not hesitate to force it every now and then.

He knew that he had two assets: the memory of the Recollects so dear to the heart of the episcopacy, and a frontline of tertiaries who were scattered throughout the dioceses and capable of paving the way for the Friars Minor. These emotive factors favoured the rapid expansion of the Order.

These assets led to the establishment of the Franciscans in Quebec City in 1900. The Franciscan Missionaries of Mary, their chaplain Louis-Honoré Paquet, and the Vicar General, C.-A. Marois, skilfully prepared the ground. In September 1900, Father Angel-Marie Hiral, a 28-year-old priest whom Father Othon Ransan had brought with him in 1890 while he was still only a student cleric, came to Québec. He had a mandate to proceed with the establishment of a friary. The dream of Monsignor Bégin, Archbishop of Quebec, would have been to entrust the Franciscans with a new parish he was thinking of establishing in the Le Palais district. The Franciscan Rule, however, did not encourage the Friars Minor to take charge of parishes. Monsignor Bégin then proposed that the friars take care of a simple religious service-center which was ready to open and would accommodate the faithful of Saint Roch parish living near the Le Palais train station and the banks of the river. While waiting for the center to become available, Hiral, who, like his confères, did not very much like the bishop's proposal, settled into a school in the Mont-Plaisant district, not far from Villa Manresa. With his companions—Fathers Alcantara-Marie Gin and Vincent Ducasse, Brothers Pascal Buisson and Dominique Thompson—he lived a regular monastic life and kept himself busy with various works: maintenance, preaching, visiting the tertiaries. The turn of events was to his advantage. In 1902, the plan for a religious center near the station fell through because of a misunderstanding between the mayor of the city and the vicar general of the diocese. At the same time, Monsignor Bégin entrusted the parish of Limoilou to the Capuchins, which had recently been created just like Saint-Roch. Released of the obligation to take charge of a religious service center, Hiral was free to move on his plan for a friary in the Upper Town. On June 18, 1901, he had acquired a magnificent plot of land, 218 by 230 feet, on the upper part of the Saint Sauveur escarpment. From this promontory, the St. Charles valley, the river, and in the distance the Laurentians could be contemplated. Hiral had financed his purchase with the funds left over from the widow McConkey's gift and with the tertiaries' alms. An unexpected gift of $20,000, given by Sophie Letarte, tertiary and widow of Octave Mignier, allowed him to begin construction of a friary which was inspired by the former Recollect friary of Saint Antoine in Quebec, and which was in accord with the norms put forth by Saint Bonaventure. On September 17, 1902, the friary dedicated to the Stigmata of Saint Francis was blessed. The philosophy house of studies was moved there. A wing was added in 1903 and, in 1904, a chapel was begun which was blessed on 11 April 1906. Quebec now had a complete friary.

The work in Quebec City had not finished before another began in Trois Rivières. Here too, the land had been prepared since the time of Father Frederick's first trip in 1881. Frederick had some sure and devoted friends. On a piece of land given to him by Monsignor Laflèche, he had erected a one storey house, 30 by 40 feet, which accommodated at most four religious. This Commissariat of the Holy Land had been little used since Father Frederick was often out of town for long times, either because of his ministry at the Cap or because of his preaching. The arrival of Brother Accurse Vervinck, in 1892, then that of Father Augustine Boyunot, in 1895, induced him to spend more time at the Commissariat. The three confreres lived in community while waiting for a friary to be established. There were, however, different opinions regarding the future of the land on which Frederick had erected the Commissariat. The community was thinking of a *Ritiro*. The Provincial preferred a house of formation: either a scholasticate or a seraphic college. Father Frédéric proposed his plan for a friary to Monsignor François-Xavier Cloutier, the successor of Monsignor Laflèche. The Bishop was hesitant for the same reasons that Monsignor Bégin was in Quebec City. His diocese was poor, and he did not want to hinder the development of the parochial system. He hesitated, and then he accepted with certain conditions: the pastor of the parish which was soon to be erected, would retain the direction of the Third Order; the friary chapel would remain closed on Sunday mornings and public holidays; the friary would be attached to the Commissariat and not elsewhere in the city; the Franciscans would not act in any way to divert accruements from the parish. These conditions were within the practice and the spirit of the Order. The Provincial Commissaire was delighted. In mid-June 1903, the friars blessed Saint Anthony's friary. The large chapel was built in 1906. In August 1911, 24 students registered at the seraphic college built adjacent to the friary.

So far the Franciscans had been able to avoid parish ministry. But the massive arrival of immigrants who settled in Western Canada or who rushed into Canadian cities exerted strong pressure on some diocesan churches. Hard-pressed bishops, short of diocesan priests, sent urgent calls to religious communities. In 1908, after three years of correspondence, the Franciscan Provincial accepted the invitation of Monsignor Emile Legal, Bishop of Saint Albert, to establish the friars in Western Canada. The Franciscans would be responsible for the parish of Notre Dame de Lourdes (in the municipality of Lamoureux), about fifteen miles from Edmonton, and for the service of a 3,000 square mile rectangular territory along the Saskatchewan River. The Provincial dispatched Fathers Berchmans-Marie Mangin, Arthur Rappart and Simon-Joseph Archambault, who were accompanied by two lay brothers. The chapter in August 1908 declared British Columbia, Alberta, and Saskatchewan to be Franciscan territory. It was decided to establish a residence in the Packing Plant area three miles from Edmonton (now North Edmonton), where there was a community of about thirty families which promised a great future. In the summer of 1909, on land acquired by Monsignor Legal, a residence 40 by 48 feet, composed of two wings at right angles was built. The basement was for domestic use. The ground floor consisted of a large hall which served as a temporary chapel. The upper floor was divided into seven cells which housed the community. The attic served for storage. All the fathers resided in the friary, but each one had to take on one or more jobs, in addition to being parish priest for the parish. In September 1911, the residence was declared a guardianate.

The cosmopolitan population made life difficult. Within the community there were ethnic differences, and the parish ministry raised the question of languages. In a canonical visitation, the Provincial gave directions: use of the faithful's mother tongue in private; use of Latin in the usual public prayers; use of one or the other language [English or French], in a fair proportion during parish ceremonies.

The development of Western Canada stimulated development in Montreal, which began to be a metropolis around 1910. Monsignor Paul Bruchési, Archbishop of Montreal, was also looking for priests. He was in favour of the plans for a second Franciscan friary in Montreal to free up St. Joseph friary where students, novices and preachers were crammed together. He imposed, however, a condition: The Franciscans would have to take over a parish in Rosemont. Sensing that the future of their community was in Montreal, the Franciscans accepted this proposal. In January 1911, they began religious services at Lasalle Park on Sundays and public holidays. In September, the founding parish priest, Angel-Marie Hiral, settled-in there. The parish was named St. Francis Solano in remembrance of the great missionary of Latin America. While awaiting the construction of a chapel, the Franciscans provided religious services in a school. Very quickly, St. Francis Solano became a thriving parish with a diversity of works.

And so it was in Trois-Rivières where Monsignor Coutier, in August 1911, entrusted the Franciscans with the care of Notre-Dame-des-Sept-Allégresses parish. Diocesan needs brought the Franciscans for better or for worse to engage in the parish ministry.

In October 1914, the Franciscans were able to begin the construction of Resurrection friary, in Rosemont, on "a fairly pronounced hillside, from where the view to the east and the south stretched to the river and beyond." The land they acquired with the help of a public appeal undertaken by the tertiaries was a large rectangle with a frontage of 124 feet. On November 25, 1915, the novices from Saint Joseph friary, singing *Veni Creator*, moved into the place. Resurrection friary, although first a novitiate, would soon lodge the theology scholasticate. During the winter of 1916, the illness of the parish priest and the departure of Father Xavier for France led the Provincial, due to the lack of available priests, to give back the care of Saint Francis

Solano parish to Monsignor Bruchési. Monsignor Bruchési accepted graciously, but he warned the Franciscans that he would entrust them with another in the near future, carved out from the same region on which they had built their novitiate.

2. Works and Services

In 25 years, the Franciscans had reconstructed the ancient network of Recollect friaries, where, like their predecessors, they gave themselves to ministry which did not take on fewer forms for its being centered on Word and sacraments. In the first place came the discrete ministry of friary confessions. There is an evident link between an attention to spiritual direction and the flourishing of vocations that Quebec was experiencing. These friaries were very active spiritual centers, where the faithful, being sensitive to the beauty of the liturgy and in search of the Word and the Eucharist, flocked on Sundays and feast days. They regularly followed the usual exercises: the months of Mary, Saint Joseph, the Sacred Heart and the rosary, the thirteen Tuesdays of St. Anthony, and all the typically Franciscan celebrations. On the eve of the feast days, in some friaries, the penitents kept a dozen confessors busy for hours on end. These friaries were also the home base of preachers who, while visiting the tertiary fraternities, also collaborated in parish ministry. The preaching responded to a wide variety of pious forms: triduums, parish retreats, occasional sermons, retreats to priests, religious and bishops, and talks to elite audiences.

The Franciscan apostolates spread all the more outside the walls of the cloister because of their corporal and spiritual works of mercy: assisting the poor and visiting the sick were their daily lot. Priests were also chaplains to religious or others. Clerics taught catechism in schools. Franciscans along with tertiaries began social works. The fathers of Saint Joseph friary took care of the Maison Sainte-Élisabeth, a refuge for the elderly, and of the Maison Ave Maria, a home for young girls.

The friaries also radiated their faith and their charity through writing. *La Revue du Tiers-Ordre et de la Terre Sainte,* which became *La Revue franciscaine,* was published; and after 1905, their English versions, *The Franciscan Review* and *St. Anthony's Record.* They also published works of piety. Father Désiré's *Le Manuel du Tiers-Ordre* had 30,000 copies printed. In 1915, the Franciscans had already published 20 volumes, 51 brochures, and 120 different leaflets.

The Franciscan's zeal overflowed at a very early time onto "the beaches of foreign lands." The Order of Friars Minor is a missionary order; in fact, the first missionary order in the world. As soon as St. Joseph Province reached a certain maturity, its members left on missions. The first to leave was Father

Maurice Bertin, founder of Saint Antoine friary in Trois-Rivières. French in origin, an ex-naval officer, he had decided during a stopover in Japan to return to restore the Order of the Friars Minor. He left Quebec in 1906 *en route* to Sapporo, Japan. Father Pierre Gauthier, a native of Montreal, and Brother Gabriel Godbout joined him in the spring of 1907. They founded the mission of Hokkaido, where, in 1910, Father Calixte Gélinas and later, in 1918, Father Urban-Marie Cloutier came to lend them a hand. Then, in 1909, other missionaries turned toward China where Franciscans were already at work. In 1915, there were 10 French fathers in the Province of China, four of whom had already stayed in Canada, plus three Canadian fathers and two lay brothers, one of whom was Canadian. The laity, whose missionary zeal was heightened by Father Frederick, still the Commissaire of the Holy Land, participated in this missionary apostolate by their prayers and almsgiving.

3. The Men

Who are the men behind these works? What spirituality animated them? The men who restored the Franciscan Order in Canada were French Observants. At first, they came in small groups to develop a domicile in case the political climate deteriorated in France, and also to meet the spiritual needs of Canadians. From 1890 to 1900, 36 came: 18 priests, 14 clerics and 4 lay brothers. The priests were in their forties and were well experienced. Some were just passing through, others stayed a few years, and a small number settled permanently. Their first concern was to set up a network of institutions capable of assuring a succession of friars: a seraphic college, a novitiate, houses of studies for philosophy and theology. Great foresight! In France the leftist bloc, divided on social issues, was united in an anticlericalism fuelled by the political action of certain religious congregations favorable to the nationalist and monarchical leagues. On July 2, 1901, Waldeck Rousseau forced a vote on the Associations Act in order unify the Republicans. This law decreed the abolition of religious congregations unless they were recognized by special law. Some 615 congregations eagerly requested this authorization. Most if not all requests were rejected. In reality, congregations were suppressed; their institutions, closed; and their members, banned from teaching. They were given alternatives: either to go into exile or to be laicized. In spring 1903, the Franciscans were ordered by the French government to evacuate their houses, except the Commissariat of the Holy Land (Paris). From April to September 1901, three waves of immigrants arrived in Quebec: some 35 religious, most of them students. They were put up in Quebec City or Montreal depending on the stage of their formation. This massive arrival explains the 11 ordinations of 1907 and the 12 of 1909. Canadian institutions provided the formation for the recruits of Saint Louis Province. But this system created problems.

Transportation was expensive; French students were moved from their homes to Canadian soil; Quebec lacked teachers and the premises were cramped. The community changed its strategy. In 1909, Father Angel-Marie Hiral was mandated to establish a novitiate and a scholasticate in Menin, Belgium. It was the end of emigration to Canada.

These emigrants all had their temperaments. Even in the 1950s, people remembered the "great airs" of Fr. Germain Desai, the bonhomie of brother Daniel and the craziness of Brother Seraphim Grandjean. All these religious were imbued with a strong Spanish conventual tradition brought into France by Joseph Areso. This tradition was inspired by the ideal of medieval monasticism and the letter rather than the spirit of St. Francis's Rule—regular religious life, total seraphic poverty and austere mortification. In actuality, until at least about 1910–1911, this asceticism meant dry bread at breakfast, a meticulous regime of visiting hours, use of the discipline three times a week between meditation and supper, shaving without a mirror, bathing in cold water and using an oil lamp. The peace of the cloister and its silence were sacred: the directives were "not to make too much noise either by speaking or by walking." In the friaries, religious fervor was encouraged and greatly emulated. Each friar tried to be the best presence in the world by witnessing to monastic love and being a spiritual presence to men. The holiness of Father Frederick was foremost, but it was not an exception. Father Joseph Ortscheid led "a cloistered life, without outside contact, given entirely to teaching, to being an austere presence at community exercises, and to keeping silence." Arsène de Servières, who died in the odor of sanctity, pushed obedience and poverty to the heroic. Humble Father Hilaire Usse also died with a reputation for holiness.

The fathers of the restoration did not come to plant a mustard seed in Canada. They came to transplant institutions and customs, to reproduce carbon copies of themselves into another environment and within another culture. It is within this tradition that the Canadian recruits were formed. On January 14, 1891, Louis-Napoléon Jacques, a native of Louiseville, became the first Canadian recruit. He received an oblate's habit. Leon Monette did the same on May 26, 1892. The famous Father Joseph Roy, of Sorel, the first Canadian priest since the disappearance of the Recollects, was ordained at Clifton on December 19, 1897. Recruitment took effect slowly because it takes time to form a priest: seven years in elementary school, six years in high school, a year of Novitiate, three years of philosophy and four years of theology, 21 years in all. Moreover, not just anyone went to the seraphic college, this hotbed for vocations. The guidelines were clear: "Make it difficult to come, easy to leave." The family's respectability and the health and the Christian life of the parents were taken into account. Children had to be at least 12 years old but rarely more than 17. And above all, they had to have "more than ordinary intelligence." Under these conditions, the seraphic college grew slowly: in 1908, it welcomed 22 students; 46, in 1912; and after 1917, it accepted a hundred students. Few of them became priests: barely a dozen of the 150 who attended the college from 1892 to 1910.

Fuelled by Europe and Canada, the community quickly expanded. The numbers in Canada were calculated to be 59 in 1903; 144 in 1909, 135 in 1918. Initially the community was concentrated in Montreal, but gradually it expanded through a network of friaries. In 1918, there were 28 priests in Montreal, 21 at Saint Joseph's friary and 7 in Rosemont. There were 23 friars in Trois-Rivières, with eight priests at the seraphic college and two at the Commissariat. There were a dozen in Quebec City. In Western Canada, the small residence in North Edmonton brought together five priests and four lay brothers.

4. Stewardship and Administration

The Franciscans did not touch money. They asked nothing for their services and they relied on public charity for their food and lodging. Hence the need for stewardship: lay trustees to look after their finances, brothers to collect alms in kind, and teams of zealous supporters in the workforce.

The Canadianizing of the community did not occur without creating internal tensions. Cultures collided. The French who were dominant everywhere established themselves as the judges of language and customs. Members coming from Great Britain—only six arrived in 1903—expressed a sense of national superiority and, as early as 1905, they petitioned to have an English-speaking friary in Montreal. Visiting hours, in the afternoons between times of community prayer, did not meet the needs of the faithful male clientele who would have preferred to meet in the evening. The Canadian religious complained about the late hour for suppers and about other foreign customs. More fundamentally, the Spanish tradition, interiorized by the French, was more attentive to individual austerity than to fraternal relations and work in common. It favored external observance of the Rule as a criterion for the selection of superiors. It preserved outworn ways of governing inherited from the *Six Wings of the Seraphim*, the classical handbook for religious superiors written by Saint Bonaventure. The Provincial Chapter, which represented only 5% of the priests and no lay brothers, was dominated by the General Visitor and the Provincial Minister. Every three years, the Chapter's main concern was the appointment of friars. Deliberations were done in secret and there was no consultation. In short the Chapter had little impact on the future of the community which was ultimately abandoned to the Definitory that consisted of the Provincial Minister's advisors. It fell to the Definitory to subdue the uncooperative friars. The government of the community, conceived by Saint Bonaventure essentially as having the authority to regulate traditions and to care for positions acquired, hardly reflected the ideal of fraternity, so dear to St. Francis, where the brethren would be equal but different; nor did it stimulate the enthusiasm of a young community. It tended to hold members of the community in "a kind of infantilism."

By choice the Franciscans worked among the poor and stuck to a traditional pastoral activity centered on popular preaching. They were therefore absent from the great debates of the hour on compulsory education, on French schools in Canada, on the place of women in society. They lived on the margins of Catholic social action which generated cooperatives, labor unions and Catholic social clubs. Their mission was elsewhere: to ensure a higher form of presence in the world and to foster in the people, through the Third Order, piety and zeal for all virtues. In 1921, 375 fraternities, bringing together 70,000 tertiaries in nine Quebec dioceses, and even in New England and Manitoba, testified that the Franciscans did not work in vain.

III. Expansion—1920–1955

The Franciscans in Canada were not yet established as an autonomous administrative entity by the end of the First World War. This situation calls for a few comments.

1. The Commissariat of Saint Joseph, 1920

Those who came to restore the Order in Canada came from the Province of Aquitaine—the only Province of the Strict Observance in France – which then counted 13 friaries in France and 3 in England. The rapid multiplication of friaries brought about a division of this Province. It was decided to divide in February 1891 and the decision was implemented during the summer of 1892. The [General] Definitory of the Order carved out the French Province. This included the friaries of Amiens, Paris, Lille, Roubaix, d'Épinal and Brieux in the north of France; those of Clevedon, Saltash and Sacot in England; and finally the Canadian settlement overseas. The Provincial was established in Paris. The first Provincial, Pierre-Baptiste Giment (1892–1895) had chosen the location of Saint Joseph friary in Montreal. His successor, Arsène-Marie Beix (1895–1898) had previously been the guardian of this friary and a preacher.

Through a curious turn of events, the epicenter of power in St. Peter's Province had gradually slipped to Montreal—probably in the undertow of the turmoil aroused by the French government's policy of secularism. The provincial Beix had given to Colomban-Marie Dreyer, who was named local superior in 1905, duties equivalent to those of a Provincial's delegate. Dryer was himself elected Provincial in 1905, but remained in Montreal until the end of his tenure in 1911. Because of his many foundations and his ceaseless activity, he acquired the title of restorer of the Order in Canada. But during his administration, tensions multiplied within the Province of St. Peter. The Canadians began to experience a certain intellectual and spiritual colonization, and the French hardly appreciated that Montreal had been established as the administrative headquarters of St. Peter's Province. Angel-Marie Hiral, Dreyer's beloved disciple, who had acceded to the Provincialate in 1911, followed in his path. He maintained the austere practices, kept the administrative office in Montreal and completed the construction sites started by his predecessor.

The First World War, which had interrupted regular communications between Europe and Canada, made it even more difficult to administer a religious province and to bring together friaries scattered in such remote lands. On March 19, 1915, Rome named Father Jean-Joseph Deguire, a Montrealer, Provincial of St. Peter's Province. Deguire, who had visited all the Canadian friaries in 1917, was only able to travel to France in 1919. He had experienced all the disadvantages of a Province cut in half by the Atlantic and experienced the difficulties of administering a community divided by ethnic and cultural tensions. The situation had become untenable.

At the end of the war, the situation was entirely new. The desire for national affirmation that characterized the Canadian government's policy within the Empire existed at all levels of society. More and more, Canadian men and women religious were opposed to external influences and were looking for a legitimate administrative autonomy. The Franciscan establishment, moreover, had reached a size that allowed it to think of emancipation. Everyone agreed. Gathered together in Montreal in December 1919, the General Chapter of Saint Peter's Province voted for the independence of Canada's houses. It elected a Definitory for the Saint Peter's Province with its administrative seat in Paris; but Father Deguire was appointed provisory delegate to Canada until Rome legally defined the Canadian establishment. The French members of the community enjoyed the right of option, except Father Dreyer who had to return to France. A dozen friars asked to be attached to the Province of Saint Peter; twenty more opted for Canada.

The next step was beginning to take place. The Canadian establishment was raised to the rank of Commissariat on March 23, 1920. It was given the name St. Joseph. Father Jean-Joseph Deguire was appointed Commissaire. Saint Joseph friary became the administrative seat of the new Commissariat because it was the first friary to be established and because it had the physical space.

2. The End of Large Foundations

From 1920, the Canadian Franciscans were masters of their own destiny. One would have expected that they would start to look at the world with their own eyes, but, quite naturally, they continued to perceive it with the eyes of French Observants. They saw their situation through the distorting prism of a medieval monastic ideal and the French political situation. Could it be otherwise? The Observants, who transplanted their institutions, customs and ways of seeing and feeling in Canada, formed them in their own image. This was, moreover, the case with the whole of Quebec Catholicism, which was strongly influenced by the most conservative elements of the French Church. Like the episcopacy and most religious communities, the Franciscans continued to see signs of a resurgence of paganism in the changed morals that had been caused by the expansion of an industrialized capitalism that reshaped the social structure, by an urbanization which undermined primary relationships, and by the new values and new conduct proposed by the mass media. The liberal elite's attempts to adjust the social organization to the new socio-economic structures were still perceived as Masonic plots to impose secularism. Only a few Dominicans strove to open Quebec Catholicism to the modern world, to introduce freedom as a value, to present the old educational question in new terms, and to raise another more recent question: the place of women in society.

In the eyes of Commissaire Deguire and his councilors, the autonomy of the Canadian foundation imposed a priority on the friars, namely consolidating the means for recruitment and formation. In this regard, the construction of a friary outside the Quebec-Montreal axis would be advantageous: a better distribution of recruits between the formation houses. The community set its sights on the Eastern Townships, to the great satisfaction of Mgr. Paul Larocque, Bishop of Sherbrooke. He looked favorably on the establishment of a Franciscan friary in the heart of a territory dominated by protestants and anglophones. Father Celestine-Joseph Demers, who was appointed guardian of the new friary, smoothly accomplished things. In the winter of 1920, he acquired a farm of 140 acres on a hill overlooking the village of Lennoxville. How beautiful a site on which to build a friary! The work began in September and progressed rapidly, thanks to the support of the tertiaries and pious souls, who saw to the financial problems. The workers themselves, in a medieval gesture, voted to give "60 days of work for the love of God and of St. Francis." In the fall of 1922, eight novices from Rosemont came to settle there. "The sound of hymns, the murmur of the psalmody, the calm of solitude," wrote a chronicler, "overpowered the explosion of the mines, the tumult of voices, the sound of hammers, and the feverish activity of workmen." Monsignor Larocque presided at the ceremony that dedicated the friary to Saint Anthony, and the crypt and the chapel to the Assumption of the Virgin Mary.

There was still a missing link in the network of Quebec friaries: a missionary college. As the Commissariat of Saint Joseph came of age, it began to think about expanding the Kingdom. Missionary activity was a tradition of the Order, a pressing invitation of the Papacy, a zeal that animated Catholicity, and a vocation that the Church of Quebec had just discovered. In the wake of *Maximum Illud*, the charter for missions promulgated by Benedict XV on November 30, 1919, the Quebec episcopacy decided (January 26, 1922) to found the corporation of Saint Francis Xavier Seminary, whose purpose would be the formation of priests for foreign missions. The Franciscans, who already had some missionaries in the Holy Land, Japan and China, were at the forefront of the Quebecois missionary movement, second only to the Oblates and the White Fathers. Their zeal brought them to serve the Maliseet Indian reservation—approximately 45 Maliseet families, at the juncture of the Tobique and St. John's rivers, in the Diocese of Chatham, New Brunswick. In 1921, Father Hugolin Padma Lemay had a residence built in Tobique. In 1926, it would become a friary dedicated to Sainte Anne. The Franciscans' care extended to some 800 Catholics dispersed in the surrounding small towns: Aroostook, Limestone, Red Rapids, Tilley, Plaster Rock and Blue Bell. Because of their preaching parish retreats, the Franciscans soon expanded into regions of Madawaska and Maine. In August 1924, the Petites Franciscaines de Marie of Baie-Saint-Paul came to lend their support by taking charge of the school and the hospital on the reservation.

Maliseet was a test ground. In July 1921, Rome's decision to grant the Province of Saint Joseph a mission territory in Japan opened up their horizons even wider. This territory was detached from the huge diocese of Nagasaki and attached civilly to Kagoshima and Okinawa. The first missionaries, Maurice Bertin and Urbain-M. Cloutier, left Sapporo in the fall to settle there.

Missionary expansion required an organizational administration: someone to channel the donations, a magazine to increase the faithful's awareness of the missionary work, and a college to welcome recruits. In August 1922, a few Franciscans established themselves in Sorel. A dozen aspirants joined them in September in a house provisionally arranged as a friary. Bonaventure Péloquin, Salvator Archambault and Dieudonné Massé provided courses; Justinian Mercier presided over the founding of the friary. He chose a site along the river at the entrance to Lake Saint-Pierre. The friary was dedicated to Saint Pierre-Baptiste, and blessed on the 6th of October, 1924; and the first guardian was Father Simon Archambault. In 1927, two students from the recruits of 1922 entered the novitiate in Lennoxville.

To the west of Montreal, a territory was developing which also challenged the friars' missionary spirit. In the nineteenth century, the Oblates had written an epic comparable to that of the Jesuits in New France. The Franciscans were already working there. For several decades they had served the parish of St. Francis of Assisi, in Edmonton, which, after having been redefined in 1924 by Monsignor H. J. O'Leary, had some 90 poor families of a wide variety of ethnic backgrounds. The Petites Sœurs Franciscaines de Marie were responsible for the parish school. From there, the Franciscans went forth to serve in various locations. That same year, Father Martin Dietrich opened Saint François Solano residence in Vancouver, which was financed by a "shower" announced in local newspapers. Three priests and two brothers made up the small community. The priests preached the thirteen Tuesdays of St. Anthony, the Stations during Lent, and the month of Mary in the little chapel on Broadway. They served St. Paul's Hospital which belonged to the Sisters of Providence, and they cared for the Japanese who had been entrusted to the Franciscan Sisters of Graymoor.

In fact, western Canada was still, in many aspects, at the stage of being colonized, and very different from Quebec and Ontario in regard to its way of life, its cosmopolitan character, its foreign cultural traditions, and its need for its own clergy. Thus in 1925, the Definitory decided to establish a seraphic college in North Edmonton. This foundation was entrusted to Father Hyacinthe Workman, superior of Saint Francis friary, who was then appointed director of the future college. Faithful Father Chicoine helped him and was given the title of director of students and prefect of studies and discipline. Father Workman proceeded with the construction of a wing, while Father Chicoine was concerned with the organization of classes, development of a curriculum, and getting textbooks. The courses would be bilingual, but English would be predominant, given that Francophones already had a seraphic college in Trois-Rivières. On September 29, 1925, the college welcomed about ten students, including four French Canadians, one German, one Polish, one Irish, one Scottish and one English Canadian. There was no question of imposing Quebecois customs on these students. The regulations provided for later morning rising than the college in Trois Rivières, a New Year's holiday in the family home, and various considerations consistent with the western Canadian mindset. The following year, 40 students were welcomed. This college would be closed in 1965.

3. *Wind in the Sails*

The period of large foundations was over. The Commissariat of Saint Joseph had reached maturity. The *Elenchus* (record of friars' status) of 1924 testified to this. At that time, the community had 263 members, including 95 priests, placed into eight convents and three residences. It had the vitality of the youth: the average age was 32 and only one member was over 62 years old. Its future seemed to be secure. Its preachers had made it known throughout Quebec. The Commissariat recruited its members in Montreal (11.6%) and Quebec (6.6%), in small towns such as Saint-Hyacinthe (4.4%) and Sorel (2.2%), and especially in rural parishes (65%). The 450 fraternities of tertiaries, which straddle the Canada-US border, were nurseries for vocations. About twenty members came from New England. The finances of the community were good. The religious respected discipline and led a regular conventual life.

The time was ripe. On the 1st of February 1927, Father Bernardin Klumper, General of the Order, promulgated a decree in which, after pointing out and commending the progress of the Canadian establishments, he raised the Commissariat to a Province. This was the highest status that a group of friaries could attain in the Order of Friars Minor. Even under the French regime, the Recollects had not been able to go beyond the status of a Commissariat. And to underline its confidence in the new Province, the Sacred Congregation erected an Apostolic Prefecture in the Japanese territory entrusted to the Province of St. Joseph of Canada. Monsignor Égide Roy became the Apostolic Prefect and Calixte Gélinas, the superior of the religious. The General Definitory appointed Ambroise Leblanc as Provincial.

The Province of St. Joseph was part of an Order which, at the time, had produced 148 saints and blesseds. Throughout the world, this Order included 99 provinces, 815 friaries, 19,074 friars of which 9,727 were priests, and 1,660,740 Secular Franciscan tertiaries. In this mosaic of the Franciscan family, the Province of St. Joseph was the youngest, but not the least. It was very much above average in the number of secular fraternities and tertiaries, above average in the number of priests and religious, and exactly average in the number of friaries. Few provinces had such an extensive and promising territory, such young and dynamic teams. Its weakness was to have come from a tradition where studies were neither valued nor understood as a prerequisite for Church works. In some liberal Quebecois environments, people laughed at the "ignorant fathers." Already, in February 1906, the Provincial, Colomban Dreyer, had lamented the fact that the Franciscans could not "make any outstanding personality available" to the intellectual world. Still brilliant minds were not lacking. Odoric Jouve had obvious talents as a historian; Hugolin Lemay was a great literary man; Marie-Joseph Ortscheid had earned his stripes as a jurist at the University of Paris; Bruno-Marie Rousselat was an outstanding thinker. Neither Dreyer nor his successor, however, had attempted to remedy this situation. And this carelessness may itself be a sign of another weakness in the Bonaventurian notion of government, perhaps even a weakness in the Order's tradition. Religious authority preserved, it did not innovate or orchestrate action, leaving the opening of new avenues to individuals' charisms.

One man addressed these weaknesses. That was Georges-Albert Laplante, advisor to the Provincial Commissary from 1923–1927, then a definitor from 1927–1933, and later Provincial three times. Self-taught, he felt deprived of university studies. He dreamed big and hated mediocrity. History had taught him about "the beneficial influence of the Lesser Brothers in all fields of human activity." His antennas detected fields of inertia and dynamic currents at work in the community and in society. His position as advisor allowed him to become an instigator, a facilitator who revealed to others their gifts, their energies and their needs to push themselves further. He intended to form an intellectual and spiritual elite who were able to adapt the Franciscan ideal to present times and to give themselves with competence to publishing, teaching and preaching. Under his impulse, on these points, the community shied away from the tradition of the Strict Observance. Thus the intellectual level of the community began to be raised by better teachers, by introducing all sorts of courses in formation programs, and by promoting the Franciscan tradition. A sign of future times was the fact that Emphrem Longpré, a Canadian Franciscan doing research in Quaracchi, the highest place of Franciscan studies, passed throughout Quebec in 1927. In the big cities, he gave lectures on Jean Duns Scotus, the 13th century Franciscan School, and the general characteristics of Franciscan philosophy. In Thomistic lands, these lectures created an uproar. Laplante was ecstatic. Rodrique Villeneuve, an Oblate [of Mary Immaculate] and professor of philosophy, and other Thomists, dismissed the Franciscan tradition. On December 7, 1927, in *Le Devoir*, Longpré boldly issued a strong rebuttal.

In other areas, however, the influence of the Strict Observance persisted. Ambroise Leblanc and the new definitory remain very attached to the habits and customs: the sense of poverty, discipline, austerity; the concern for observances, and the cult of appearances. The adaptation of Franciscan life to the climate, the culture and the Quebecois way of living would take time. Successive administrations kept the stride of former ones and looked out for opportunities to expand geographically and apostolically.

The circumstances served them well. The community had the wind in their sails. From 1927 to 1954, it recorded 197 ordinations, not to mention those for the Vicariate of Western Canada and those in mission countries. Recruits flocked to them during crises and war: a first high point was reached in 1933, and the 1942 record of 19 novices destined for the priesthood reflected the conscription crisis. Is this too facile a correlation? Should not the Marian Year of 1950 be credited with the copious numbers of entrants between 1950 and 1957? In the absence of thorough research, it is better to observe than to comment. Constantine-M. Baillargeon described very well the atmosphere of those abundant years:

> I entered the novitiate in 1937, when the scholasticate of Rosemont was filled to the fullest and was expecting to accept many more. In fact, the years 1938 to 1941 were, I think, the ones that produced the largest groups of newly ordained priests in our history. It was during those years, in my opinion, that the Province experienced the height of its vitality and its creative potential.

> For those of us who joined its ranks, this exuberance was a source of euphoria and confidence. We belonged to a spiritually robust enterprise, which, with its abundant and ever-increasing numbers, went from conquest to conquest. . . (*Entre nous*, May 1983:5).

What were these conquests? At the invitation of Monsignor Joseph-Alfred Langlois, Bishop of Valleyfield, the Franciscans settled in Châteauguay-Bassin in 1930. In 1931, they erected a chapel to serve the holidaymakers settled on both banks of the river Chateauguay. In the fall of 1932, they welcomed the first group of retreatants to the newly built retreat house of Christ the King. It was the first Franciscan house for silent retreats, but the fourteenth in Quebec. This work, which attracted 1,250 retreatants in the first year, filled Monsignor Langlois with joy. He found it "desirable that the laity of the diocese seek this solitude where God awaits them to speak to their hearts." In 1931, the Franciscans established a residence in Regina. This house would welcome aspirants to the priesthood. It was a sort of Major Seminary for the formation of local diocesan clergy. In 1933, the Franciscans got a foothold in Maine, in Biddeford, where vibrant Third Order fraternities eagerly greeted them. They acquired a modest property at the opening to Pool Road and then made arrangements to establish a seraphic college. Saint Francis College opened its doors in 1939. It served, as evidenced by its French-language directory, Franco-Americans, and was destined to form future Friars Minor. To meet the needs of the region, Saint Francis College soon became a liberal arts college (4 years of high school and two years of junior college) open to students of all nationalities.

Missions always remained a work dear to the hearts of superiors. In 1929, two missionaries, Barnabas Lafond and Henri Langlois, went to Tibet to care for the lepers. These were exceptional cases. Japan remained the preferred territory. From 1928 to 1933, the Province of Saint Joseph sent 33 missionaries. The territory that they were given included 55 islands on which two and a half million Japanese lived. The Prefect, Monsignor Egide-M. Roy had chosen Kagoshima as the mission center. These reinforcements allowed him to open several other centres and to establish various institutions. The Holy Congregation of Propaganda appreciated this. On January 17, 1937, it assigned the Prefecture of Urawa to the Province of Saint Joseph, and entrusted it to Ambroise Leblanc himself.

4. Fighting Poverty

During this time, events that arose in Quebec made demands upon religious communities and brought forth new charisms. In October 1929, the stock market collapsed. It was a crisis, followed by a depression, that dragged on until 1940. The birth rate fell. Unemployment peaked to heights never seen before. The middle classes felt their material condition threatened. The urban proletariat lived in misery. *La Revue franciscaine* recorded the consequences of the crisis on Quebec Catholicism: "In some centres of Montreal, we see a most heartbreaking decline in the people's religiosity (. . .) Practice decreases alarmingly in some parishes. This can easily be explained by the excess of misery, by Protestant propaganda and by people's ignorance of religion." Traditional Catholicism was crumbling. There was a state of emergency: a war started by physical misery was leading to paganism and communism.

But the State and the Church were taken up short. The State had not yet learned how to control economic cycles, and the Church, whose pastoral action was centered on the rural situation, was not familiar with urban realities. Both quickly strove to alleviate poverty through "direct relief" and public charity. The Jesuits, under the leadership of Joseph Archambault, who had a good sense of teamwork and communication, led the ideologues on the intellectual front. Among the Franciscans, whose preachers were poorly remunerated by the parish priests, holy poverty was more than ever in the spotlight. According to Father Julien Déziel, the community survived materially thanks to "brother *quêteurs*," the friars who collected alms in kind, from urban markets and rural parishes. "At least five of our brother quêteurs were more popular than all our preachers and they were loved—Friars Dominique Thompson of Quebec City, Pascal Buisson of Trois Rivières, Gratien Marcote of Rosemont, Daniel Vidal of Sorel, and Friar André Chevalier, St. Joseph friary's own quêteur until 1932 when he moved to the friary at Châteauguay." These friars had a real ministry: they blessed the sick, comforted the afflicted and assured benefactors of the community's prayers. Very poor themselves, the Franciscans put the Third Order fraternities to work to help the unemployed—especially St. Elizabeth, St. Francis and Ave Maria fraternities. Friaries distributed food. For years, thanks to the charity of a Montreal bakery, the doorkeeper at Saint Joseph friary distributed from 500 to 600 sandwiches each week.

Some Franciscans preached an annual retreat for the homeless in St. Anthony's Chapel, at the corner of the Lagauchetière and Plessis, which was an opportunity for the poor to renew their wardrobe, thanks to the "Cloakroom of the Poor." To counter the influence of the "Workers University," which the leaders of the Communist Party had just set up to propagate communist ideology, Father Ferdinand Coiteux, guardian of St. Joseph friary, and the preacher, Father Archange Godbout, looked after the residents of Belmont Refuge and those who were at Sister Bonneau's refuge. With the support of Monsignor Georges Gauther, Archbishop of Montreal, Father Godbout transformed Belmont Refuge into a Catholic Workers University. It published *La Fouine*, then *La Chandelle*, to refute Albert Saint-Martin's propaganda. Saint-Martin was one of the founders of the Workers University and, in his newspaper *Spartakus*, he denounced the exploitation of workers and the collusion of clergy and capitalists. Godbout was also not afraid to attend sessions at the Workers University, and even less to provoke opponents by contradicting them. One day, he debated with Gaston Pilon, a very popular speaker who was part of the Workers University, in Salaberry School auditorium in Montreal. The theme was: "The Existence of God." The priest was triumphant. Thereafter, he began a series of lectures in Sacré-Coeur parish hall, right in middle of "Faubourg Québec," close to the Workers University. Godbout adapted and refuted the arguments presented at the nearby university. He managed to convert his opponent Pilon. He also continued his preaching with new themes: the feminine awakening during 1934, help to senior couples in 1935; and, in 1941, by appealing for Camp Notre-Dame, for disadvantaged children, in Saint-Ligouri.

Godbout and the Franciscans who worked in poor locations based themselves on tradition. In *La Fouie*, they claimed to defend "the old morality of mutual respect and affection which was the happiness of our grandfathers." It was the same for other Franciscans, who, from 1927, directed the Temperance movement toward families. They continued to strive for the same goal: the re-Christianization of society's foundations. But the [Franciscan] promoters of the family movement—Bernardin Verville, Gilbert Laverdure, Richard Thivierge, Gonsalve Poulin—were animated by a more structured social thought rooted in Quebec's realities. They also used more modern means. In 1937, Gilbert Laverture began publishing the periodical *La Famille*, which had all the characters of a popular magazine. Gonsalve Poulin, who in Paris had rubbed shoulders with Canon Jean Viollet, the animator of the Christian Marriage Association, founded the Friends of the Family in 1939.

5. *New Apostolates*

Radically new apostolates, both in terms of the type of work and of the values that gave rise to them, were introduced into the community by a contingent of friars that had recently been sent to studies. Alcantara Dion, back from four years of studying psychology and pedagogy in Europe, began a career in education. He had worked with Father Gemelli, a specialist in experimental psychology; and his thesis was on "Authority and freedom in new and traditional schools." He had very strong ideas on education and on professional formation, both of which should make a man free and bring him to reach his fullness as a man and a Christian. The goal is less new than the means, which took into account the knowledge gained from scientific information about man and society. Alcantara's activity was multifaceted. He reformulated the principles that animated scouting in Catholic terms and he taught new theories at Laval University.

Coming from another horizon, the biblical exegete Adrien-M. Malo had all the gifts of a communicator: intellectual training, clarity of expression, the ability to use new and suggestive images, the desire to educate others. He taught Biblical exegesis at the Franciscan theologate in Rosemont from 1925 to 1960, and the Church's social doctrine at the Pius XI Institute from 1939 to 1951. Malo was interested in Catholic Action. He had good reasons since Pius XI had chosen Francis of Assisi as the patron of Catholic Action, a sign that the seraphic spirit should be at the base of every Christian apostolate. He was involved in scouting and in the Independent Catholic League. But above all, he wanted to be one of the thinkers of the movement. He published his reflections in a series of works: *Le Milieu* (1936), *L'Action catholique spécialisée* (1937), *L'Action catholique et les Œuvres* (1942), *Panorama de la spécialisation* (1944).

Another example of a new apostolate was Edmond Gaudron's publication of the journal *Culture*, founded in March 1940. Trained in Leuven, where he was the first Quebecois to get a doctorate, he had taught philosophy since 1932 at the scholasticate in Québec City, then at Laval University. Gaudron began his career just when the Quebecois were becoming aware of their distinct identity. Nationalist ideas were being articulated on the concept of State and on the modernization of institutions. Young people dreamt of separation—the essayist Dostaler O'Leary published a book on the subject. This nationalism worried Gaudron, an attentive observer of European nationalisms. Fond of peace, Gaudron had confidence in the innate goodness of man and taught that the future was for people who "have a global, pluralistic and welcoming vision of the world." For him, the political solution of English and French relations in Canada was through mutual knowledge and ongoing dialogue. The journal he launched did not defend any political thesis. It simply opened a forum for dialogue, where one "would observe the other through its cultural activities." *Culture* presented itself as a scientific journal. It offered its readers philosophical, literary, and political essays, and historical or sociological monographs. Until 1971, it strove to be a forum where Francophones and Anglophones, Catholics, Jews and Protestants exchanged ideas and opinions.

These new apostolates flourished in the post-War context. The war brought about more than a resumption of industrialization and urbanization. It interrupted the normal course of things. It was a crucible where new attitudes were forged. It promoted the emancipation of individuals who escaped the influence of family and parish, and it opened Quebec to the world. Montreal, with its banks and factories, its ethnic ghettos, working class and posh neighborhoods, its bourgeoisie, intellectuals, and proletariat foreshadowed the future of Quebec. This cosmopolitan city revealed a pluralistic society where the voice of the Church was no longer the dominant voice. The chaplains of Catholic Action underlined the decrease of faith and the increase of anticlericalism and religious indifference, the weakening of morals, juvenile crime, birth control, and the decline of religious practice in young workers.

In this context, the new apostolates born out of the crisis were expanding, such as Father Ildefonse Riopel's apostolate with the J.O.C. [Young Catholic Workers]. The family movement was increased. In 1942, under the impetus of Gonzalve Poulin, Les Amis de la Famille became the Family Institute and their periodical, *La Famille,* became their mouthpiece. First installed in the Maison Saint-Louis, near Saint Joseph friary, the Institute acquired a building on Rue Saint-Denis, where Poulin organized family weeks, led study circles, and had a library. The movement had branches with different works and publications of all kinds. It begot imitators. The Franciscans, however, failed in bringing the community to continue this activity. They let Gonzalve Poulin go to Laval University where he participated in founding the School of Social Service, the Family Service of Quebec, and the periodical *Service social.* The creation of a Family Institute attached to the University of Montreal and directed by the Franciscans proved to be a failure. In the 1950s, the Family Movement fell out of the Franciscans' hands. Soon they only had the honor of being its pioneers.

Alcantara Dion expanded his sphere of activity. His direction of the journal *L'Enseignement secondaire* and his positions with the Council of Public Education put him at the heart of the school system's reform movement. Through his writings and lectures, he influenced the whole movement. He was the mind behind home economic schools, the counsellor of the nuns who carried out the reform of the Pedagogical Institute, and soon he would be the adviser of bishops in pedagogical matters.

As for Adrien-M. Malo, Catholic Action was dear to him: he popularized the reading of the Bible, until then little encouraged by the Church. He propagated this interest through courses, lectures and using mass media. From 1942 to 1951, he taught at Radio College. In 1943, he founded the Catholic Association of Biblical Studies (ACEBAC) where, once a year, French-speaking teachers of Sacred Scripture met. At the request of the episcopacy, in 1953, the ACEBAC along with Fides published an original translation of the New Testament. Revised in 1959 the printing reached one and a half million copies in 1970. Father Malo's teaching were born from his writings: *La Charte du royaume chrétien* (1944), *Clartés d'évangile sur nos sentiers* (1947), *L'Épopée inachevée de nos Lieux Saints (1955), Le choc de deux amours* (1959), *Dialogue près d'un puits* (1965). His zeal inspired him to take up another apostolate: the direction of religious communities. He founded *La Vie des communautés religieuses* which he managed until 1960. This magazine, which presented solid insights into the religious life, remained under Franciscan direction for some time. In addition, Father Malo was actively engaged in the recruitment of vocations. He directed the vocation ministry by his participation in study weeks and he took care to form spiritual masters.

The war-time situation affected traditional apostolic activity in different ways. During the war, the Japanese missions were closed and Canadian missionaries, interned or expelled. Rome ordered them to be transferred to Japanese colonies in Lima and British Columbia. Rome also pointed toward Latin America. The Provincial of St. Joseph's Province, Damase Laberge, went there in 1944. He visited the Amazon – a territory that Rome intended for Canadians. He went to Lima where Calixte Gélinas and Urbain-Marie Cloutier were taking care of the Japanese colony and the natives. He presided over the founding of a residence that took over the parish of Saint Anthony in Lima, and which was officially erected in 1952. He also went to Tingo-Maria, capital of the province, Leoncio Prado, where Father Ludger Beaudet was setting up the parish of Saint Theresa of the Child Jesus. This trip clinched the involvement in Latin America. In June 1945, Rome erected the Apostolic Prefecture of St. Joseph of the Amazon and appointed Monsignor Damase Laberge as Apostolic Prefect. He moved to Indiana in 1947 to serve an inhospitable territory, infested with snakes and mosquitoes, and where tribes still in the Stone Age lived in about ten localities. With his colleagues, he proceeded to establish the usual mechanisms which civilized the primitive society—schools, dispensaries, churches, farms.

The S.O.S. for pastoral ministry did not only come from Latin America. Quebec's rapid urbanization created a problem for the episcopacy, who could not adapt the network of parishes to the population's movement. It lacked diocesan priests to take charge of the new parishes carved out of the thickening urban fabric. The bishops asked religious communities to come to the rescue. The Franciscans responded "present," They accepted the parish of Christ the King in Châteauguay, in 1929; and that of the Sacred Heart in Welland, Ontario, in 1940. In the same year, they also assumed St. Mary's in Baker Brook, New Brunswick. Then they accepted Saint John Vianney in Longueil in 1945; Saint Maxime in Sorel in 1946; Saint Jean de Brébeuf in Port Colborne, Ontario in 1952; Saint Vincent de Paul in Ottawa in 1953; Saint Patrick in Trois Rivières, and Lac Castagnier, Abitibi in 1954; and Saint Anthony in Niagara, Ontario in 1956. Taking on parishes required an accommodation of the Rule—the priests handled money. Parishes took the Franciscans into new pastoral activities. They wrote parish bulletins, directed study circles, such as the Cercle Ozanam in Trois Rivières or the ACJC [Association catholique de la jeunesse canadienne] circles, and dealt with the upkeep of churches; they founded social works, choir schools, parish councils, unions, Catholic Action movements and pious associations. As a general rule, Franciscan parishes were located in working class neighborhoods and brought together working families or disadvantaged populations. Their priest strove to develop a community, to strengthen fraternal solidarity and to raise awareness of people's dignity. In many other sectors too, religious communities had to overcome the shortage of diocesan priests. The Franciscans increasingly accepted to be chaplains.

Under the influence of Alcantara Dion—and probably also supported by the educational reform movement that was growing in Quebec—the community became increasingly involved in teaching. In 1950, it decided to build an "Externat Classique" [a classical college for day students] in Longueuil which was inaugurated two years later. In 1953, the Didace-Pelletier College of Arts and Trades was opened in Sorel. In 1958, the students of the seraphic college moved into ultra-modern premises built on the "hillsides" of Trois Rivières. Over the years, these institutions had absorbed the best-trained and most experienced members of the community.

Franciscans also had to adapt their ministry to the expansion of mass media—to radio in the 1930s and to television in the 1950s. They made their first forays into radio in the 1930s with Father Vincent Bélanger at CKVL and Ferdinand Coiteux at CKAC. In 1938, they were very successful with the show "Saint Anthony and the Sick." In 1942, the Friends of Saint Francis presented on CKAC a series of broadcasts on the Recollects of New France, on the occasion of the 300th anniversary of the foundation of Montreal. Starting from 1947 in Montreal, and 1951 in Quebec City, radio stations broadcast the morning mass from Resurrection friary in Montreal and from Alverna friary in Quebec City.

6. The Highpoint

From 1920 to 1955, the Province of St. Joseph experienced a large expansion. In 1954, it had 598 religious, including 311 priests, 124 lay brothers, 163 novices and clerical students. This was an obvious sign of a certain prosperity. That year 15 professed friars were ordained. The Province's 17 convents and 22 canonical residences were divided among 20 Canadian dioceses. In the United States, the community was in the dioceses of Manchester and Portland. In total, the Province served 38 parishes. It had been responsible for a Commissariat in Japan since 1936 and another in Peru since November 8, 1944. Some of its members worked in Egypt, Israel, and Jordan; others worked or studied in France, Italy and Switzerland. By number and activities, the Province of St. Joseph was one of the top ten provinces of the Order of Friars Minor. It had established an identity. It stood out from other provinces for its interests in studies. From 1942 to 1946, 54 religious were sent to institutes of higher studies in Canada, the United States and Europe. Twenty-seven of them were involved in higher education. An intellectual flourishing and an openness to modernity characterized this period. The community had also become Canadianized. It adapted its apostolates to Canadian realities, and some of its regulations to the mentalities and needs of the people here.

These adjustments were not always accomplished smoothly. The traditionalists, who lived under the illusion of being French observants of the Strict Observance, regretted the loss of former times. They blamed their superiors for sacrificing missions to education. They found the new apostolates little in line with the tradition from which they had emerged, and they kept a stern eye on the pioneers who were marking out other paths. But there was also a dynamic minority which, as in other places in the Church, was influenced by materialism and a type of hedonism that permeated the changing culture. Between these two extremes, an elite contingent was in search of a new synthesis of the Franciscan ideal and tradition of the Order with Canadian culture and the needs of the present times.

According to Constantine Baillargeon, the "Belle Epoque" was characterized by a great conviviality that favored a "conformity of convictions stemming from a more unanimous theology than today" and by "a solidarity created from working for the same cause, to work for a kind of great spiritual mechanism, both old and prosperous, of which one was proud." Basically, everyone shared the same ideas about dogma, morality and religious life. And Father Baillargeon added: "Every religious in the Province was a co-worker, a comrade and a brother of arms that we were happy to find." These sociological and intellectual conditions nurtured feelings of belonging, solidarity and fraternity. But to what extent would these favorable conditions weaken the awareness of being spiritual brethren in Jesus Christ and in St. Francis?

IV. THE TRANSFORMATION—1955–1990

In the middle of the 1950s, Quebec was in turmoil. It was a time of discussions, trial and error, and clashes. The Church was no longer able, even allied with the civil power, to impose a socio-political order. The pluralist voice of the city dominated. Modernity penetrated the urban masses ever more deeply. The decline in practice and the fading of faith were symptomatic. Traditional elites from many occupational groups were crumbling and tended to polarize into two social milieus: the bourgeois and the working-class. The emergence of an intelligentsia, linked to the development of universities, mass media and social movements, was a historic event. The members of this intelligentsia considered themselves to be the bureaucrats, in the service of political and religious powers, for social change. Whether they were clerics or lay people, they shared a common aim: to change the rules of a political game that was based on personal relations, local elites, sponsorship and leadership cults. They were preparing for the emergence of an urban society managed by bureaucratic powers.

The Royal Commission on Constitutional Problems, created by Premier Duplessis in 1953, became the forum where people, through their intermediary bodies, expressed their grievances. The Franciscan, Gonzalve Poulin, one of the initiators of the family movement, brought to the attention of the Commission members the issue of help for the poor—in more modern terms: the issue of social welfare. All the reports of experts and of public grievances pointed to a direction which was summarized by the members of the Commission: "Today, everyone admits that it is no longer possible for the state to avoid helping, because the aid of private enterprise is insufficient." The socio-political arrangements developed in the nineteenth century by the Church and the State were being challenged and, as a result, so was the role of the Church in society.

1. The Obsolete Belle Epoque, 1955–1966

The general agreement of intelligentsia and some classes of society on the end of the regime exploded in different societal projects where the Church was more or less involved in the power structures. Paul-Émile Léger, who was named Bishop of Montreal in 1950, undertook modernization at full throttle, but he set the parameters: maintain the power-sharing between Church and State, increase the State's participation in funding the social works of the Church according to rational rules, and clean up public morals. This ambitious program for urban Christianity, which maintained clerical paternalism, obsequious obedience to Rome, and a failure to integrate religious and linguistic protestors into the culture, aroused both enthusiasm and opposition. A debate began on clericalism which soon degenerated, at the beginning of the 1960s, into the Church's being put on trial.

Monsignor Léger was drinking from the well-springs of Rome. On the other hand, the laity were inspired by an intellectual revival of French Catholicism as conveyed by the writings of the Dominicans Congar and Marie-Dominique Chenu, and by the magazine *Esprit*, which reflected the experiences of worker-priests and the great missions of France. The priesthood conferred by baptism and the autonomy of earthly realities were theological notions that opened up new perspectives for the relation of the Church to the world such as a separation of church and State, a lessening of the role of the institutional Church, a non-denominational respect of individual consciences. The question of the modernization of the school system, which dominated the political debates from 1957 to 1966, polarized thinking and became the source of confrontation between the left and right. The extent of the malaise revealed a multi-faceted social crisis: how to assimilate modernity without destroying cultural identity? What power could best take over the fate of the nation? What type of institutions would best meet the needs of a population that was less and less homogeneous? The school debate was a big part of the cultural change. The death of Pius XII in 1958 and Duplessis in

1959, then the victory of the Liberal Party, led by Jean Lesage, in the general election of 1960, and Vatican II from 1962 to 1965 favored the forces of renewal. Quebec was experiencing the "quiet revolution." Civil society modernized its political institutions: the Quebec state took care of welfare and teaching. Religious society adapted its pastoral activity to a larger society that was becoming de-Christianized. Inclusive pastoral plans arose, which linked the whole of the diocese's pastoral activity (catechetics, liturgy, preaching, apostolates) and coordinated both secular and clerical services.

This new pastoral activity, begun in Saint Jerome in 1958 then in Montreal and in Saint-Jean in 1960, did not prevent the radical break that was beginning to take place between religion and large segments of the population. The consumer society introduced a civilization focused on money, comfort and leisure. A practical materialism and permissive hedonism settled on the population. The media became the vehicle of exotic ideas: the sexual revolution and the liberation of women. It proposed values and behaviours that became the daily bread of a liberalized population. The springtime of counterculture and religious sects began around 1966. Traditional Catholicism bore the brunt of this change. Outdoor demonstrations of faith diminished. Sunday practice collapsed in Montreal and was resisted only in some rural areas where the Church's traditional control continued. The divorce rate climbed, and the birth rate plummeted.

From 1955 to 1966, under the relentless blows of state bureaucracy and urbanization, society became non-confessional and non-clerical. The Christian framework was collapsing: parishes were no longer homogeneous milieus. The former militants of Catholic Action invested their energy in building the "City," a new society. Unions and cooperatives broke their ties with the Church. Clerics and religious returned to the secular state by the hundreds: once church officials, they became state officials. The symptoms of a de-Christianized society increased.

Vatican II aggravated the situation by bringing into question the Church's hierarchical equilibrium which governed the relations with clerics, religious and lay people. Society was witnessing a sort of levelling of status, roles and styles. Moreover, with the reworking of the 1917 Code of Canon Law, Rome was ceaseless in cutting back the privileges and the status of communities. In the post-war period, Rome had forced communities to coordinate their actions and to standardize their status by creating federations of religious institutes in each country. The overall pastoral plan, which enforced diocesan life, required an even greater mooring of religious communities to the parish and diocesan frameworks and, perhaps also, to an increased authority of the bishops over the communities. This orientation appealed to many Franciscans who were attracted to the active life and to some who had lost sight of the goal of individual perfection. Indeed, and this was the case for all communities, there was a need for a renewed theology of religious life. The new values—they were called creative freedom, freedom of conscience, personal decision, fraternal service—created a tension within communities between the development of the person and the demands of the community. This situation forced communities to rethink their witness, and their collaboration in the mission of the Church.

The evolution of Quebec Catholicism was the backdrop which shaped the Franciscans' own history. In 1948, Georges-Albert Laplante's mandate as Vicar-Provincial ended. He who was rightly considered the founder of St. Joseph Province had been at the center of power since 1920. His relinquishing of power coincided with the end of an era characterized by clerical paternalism, the Church triumphant, and a kind of management of Christianity. The same tensions were found in the Franciscans as in the Church of Quebec. There were generational tensions: the clerics in formation rejected the paternalism of their spiritual masters. There were tensions of adaptation: the newly ordained no longer accepted being thrown into action after having lived eight years in a vacuum. There were intercultural tensions: the West and the East of St. Joseph Province evolved in different ways. There were tensions in friaries: religious conformism and monastic regularity hindered fraternal life. Father Baillargeon strongly felt these tensions:

> . . . the Franciscan Province had evolved more quickly than we friars did. Tensions were felt between the groups assigned to teaching, to the Third Order, to parish ministry; rivalries were arising between our colleges. And sometimes less than kind things were written in *Entre nous* that showed large cracks in the monolithic bloc of a Province that Georges-Albert had established. The ageing of religious, the aftermath of the quiet revolution, the influx of friars returning from Europe produced increased ideological factions. When in 1966, I became Master of Clerics in Rosemont, I knew beyond a doubt that the Belle Epoque of the Province was over. . . (*Entre nous*, May 1983:7)

Some problems were quickly resolved. In 1955, the Definitory undertook an in-depth review of the specific legislation of Saint Joseph's Province. To promote spontaneity and fraternal life, it gradually softened regulations concerning discipline, keeping silence, and rigorous schedules. Religious life, once predominantly conventual and ascetic, was released from its outmoded and obsolete observances.

In the same year, the Minister General of the Order of Friars Minor decreed a change from Commissariat of Christ the King to the erection of the Custody of the Christ-King of the Friars Minor of Canada. The new custody brought together the four provinces of western Canada: Manitoba, Saskatchewan, Alberta and British Columbia. It had four friaries, two residences, two colleges, a novitiate and a retreat house. It had 68 friars, including 40 priests; and it served seven parishes. The mother house was in Cochrane, Alberta. This separation, long desired by the West, was necessary. Western Canada was a very different world from that of Quebec. The population comprised more than 25 different ethnic groups, which tended to retain their languages and customs. It was poor and spread over vast territories. This situation presented difficult challenges for preaching and parochial organization. In a sense, the West was still a mission country that had its own needs and its own mentality. An administration located in Montreal and inclined to view and govern in a Quebecois manner was not very suitable for forming members for the West, or for preparing apostolates adapted to this milieu. Autonomy was recognized as desirable, and finally granted:Fidèle Chicoine wrote that instead of maintaining an ineffective and paralyzing centralization, it was better to promote a decentralization that generated new energies, new talents and a revival of life.

The reform of 1955 liquidated a past, but it did not light a beacon for the future. It did not bring about those "timely substitutions" necessary to maintain community cohesion around a collective ideal nor express a Franciscan identity in a new lifestyle. The active life tended to be autonomous and the quest for personal sanctification was diluted by the euphoria of works.

> Father Hervé Blais observed that, in its own way, the Province of St. Joseph became a small pluralistic society. . . . The old order had disappeared, and various ideals appeared, which did not unanimously rally the friars (*Chroniques et documents*, July 1977:167).

In the recently attained field of education, the community suffered a setback, even though its achievements had been remarkable despite the thousands of difficulties it had faced. With teachers and financial resources in competition with a vigorous public sector of education, the community had to close Collège Didace-Pelletier (Sorel) in 1965; then its "Externat Classique" day school in Longueuil in 1967; and the seraphic college in Trois Rivières in 1968. Preaching was also transformed. Triduums and parish retreats attracted fewer and fewer faithful and those who attended questioned the traditional sermon. The establishment of an annual session of pastoral input in 1961, by the Provincial, Fulgence Boisvert, did not stop the crisis.

More disturbing in the long term were the signs of the community's accelerated ageing. Apart from a few exceptional years, notably the years 1950–1955, recruitment was on a downward phase, as was the recruits' rate of perseverance. At the same time, the mortality rate began to take an upward swing. Starting in 1957–1958—perhaps even a little earlier—the community was no longer able to replace its dwindling numbers. The following table illustrates this:

SIGNS OF AGING

	Total Number	Ordained	Deceased
1940–1944	55	40	14
1945–1949	35	23	29
1950–1954	48	38	20
1955–1959	34	27	29
1960–1964	22	24	32
1965–1969	5	13	37

The radical re-questioning of the community's future was accompanied by agonizing questions about its survival. The sources of recruitment had dried up by 1967. The returns to the secular state multiplied: 5 in the 1950s, 20 in the 1960s and 16 in the 1970s. Mortality wrought even greater havoc: 10 deaths in 1962 and 16 in 1967. Territorial redistribution (autonomy of the Franciscan Vicariate of Korea in 1969 and the erection of the Province of the Holy Martyrs of Japan in 1977) brought about a loss of 74 members. The strength of the community melted like butter in the sun. From 1962 to 1988, it would decrease by more than half, 525 to 236. And those who remained were old, so much so that soon the retired friars would be more numerous than those that were working.

DISTRIBUTION OF SOLEMN PROFESSED BY AGE, 31 DEC. 1988

Age group	Number of professed	Percentage
90–100	4	1,85%
80–89	29	13,43%
70–79	54	25,00%
60–69	63	29,17%
50–59	45	20,83%
40–49	14	6,48%
30–39	6	2,78%
20–29	1	0,46%
Total	216	100%

2. In Turmoil, 1965-1990

Like most communities, Franciscans walked in a thick fog. The superiors solved problems on a day-to-day basis and gradually took up fail-safe positions. They remained attentive, however, to calls from the world that would "produce new fruit on old tree." For lack of friars, various works were abandoned. The magazine *Culture* disappeared in 1970. The summer camp at Mont-Tremblant was sold in 1971; the house for silent retreats was closed in Amos in 1974; the friary in Biddeford was closed in 1975. One by one, the works that made the community proud disappeared.

It was a time when the vineyards of the kingdom were recycled to produce fruits better suited to a new way of insertion in the world and to pastoral care in general. Unable to decide on collective objectives, the Franciscan community became a pluralistic community, a place where there was a remarkable expansion of individual initiatives. In search of educational endeavors that were suited to more promising ministries, a large number of religious went to universities, where the faculties of theology and social sciences adapted their programs for professional training. From 1965 to 1977, 70 Franciscans returned to studies for at least one year. More than 50 opted for specialization in pastoral ministry or catechesis.

The new apostolates depended on individual choice and charism. Here are some examples: Leander Poirier, professor of scripture at Rosemont's studium and colleague of Adrien-M. Malo, assumed the direction of the Catholic Bible Society (SOCABI) from 1968 to 1972 and commented on Biblical readings weekly from 1969 to 1979. Roger Saint-Arnaud worked in the large mission of metropolitan Quebec from 1967 to 1970; then he was in pastoral service for the diocese from 1970 to 1972 and finally he accepted to serve at Centre-Dieu in Place Fleur-de-Lys. In 1971, Évariste Lessard chose to live with the destitute of Saint-Sauveur, Quebec. With some companions, he set up a team to renovate houses, and then, over the years, he established various agencies and support services. From the activity of this small group of social activists, a great achievement came forth: La Maison de Lauberivière, a dwelling place for poor people.

In 1971, under the impulse of Gilles Bourdeau, a "Fraternity of Prayer" was born in Lachute on the site of a former pilgrimage site, *La Grotte*, dedicated to Our Lady of Lourdes. This fraternity was to favor contemplation as the pivotal point for its vision and its daily activity, and it would take on a project which allowed it to return to its point of reference and direction. Various experiences arose in relation to this "Fraternity of Prayer," such as the *Feast of Tents* in 1976, 1977 and 1978 (a spiritual camp for young people aged 18–25), also such as *La Source* which existed since 1978 (contemplative life inspired by St. Clare but seeking a new style of community and insertion). It is to this "Fraternity of Prayer" that the Franciscan novitiate was grafted after 1978. All the young friars in St. Joseph's Province of Canada had to spend a prolonged period there. Gilles Bourdeau, who was at the heart of this initiative, became Provincial in 1987.

In Lennoxville, Damien Côté and Roger Poudrier began a modest Franciscan hermitage in the former friary, which the novices vacated in 1964 and which had been converted into a student residence. The new guardian, Raymond Mailhot, had a larger vision. He inquired about the diocese's spiritual needs and renovated the building for groups of retreatants. On 21 July 1979, some 30 people participated in a silent retreat. The "Burning Bush"—which was the name of this new institution—caught on and welcomed priests, religious, and the married or single working poor in search of spiritual renewal. In the same year 1979, Camp Notre-Dame of Montreal was also revived in Saint-Liguori de Montcalm, with a very Franciscan form of animation. Here, there were no sermons, but rather the witness borne by a peaceful welcome, a particular view of life and acceptance of people, and a way of being present in the world. This was the type of testimony given by Armand Picard who had been working for years in a popular daycare center.

In 1980, after twenty years of extensive study on sects and new religions in Quebec, Richard Bergeron and a team of collaborators set up the *Centre for Information on New Religions* (CINR) to help people cope with the serious consequences of this problem. The CINR was a place of intellectual critique, spiritual discernment and psycho-social help for people involved in the new sects. The CINR's interventions were based on evangelization and education in the faith for a secular and pluralistic world. In the fall of 1989, the CINR celebrated its fifth anniversary, a witness to the vigor of its founder.

After having left their colleges, the Franciscans did not forsake their apostolate of teaching. Léonce Hamelin, René Bacon and Richard Bergeron were regular professors at the University of Montreal's Faculty of Theology. Marc Renaud and George Marcil also taught philosophy at the university level. Odoric Bouffard, Constantin Baillargeon, Gilles Norbert, Mario Cardin worked at the college level, and Réal Prévost taught arts in high school and Victor Dionne instructed in pastoral animation. Others, such as Jacques Gosselin and Regent Raymond practiced as psychologists; and Marie-Albert Baril practiced as an architect.

These and many other examples are all signs of an astonishing individual creativity, even if they do not indicate a profound revival of Franciscan life. Nevertheless, the decrease in numbers and the ageing of the friars were slowing down the overall activity of the community. "The Province is always doing something," observed the Visitor General in 1984, "but it is obliged to do less." This demographic data created many challenges: establishing services adapted to friars aged 36 to 45. This was more than a question of downsizing; the community leaders' concern was to maintain "a balance of activity, and to assure the friars mutual assistance and determination to live the mission of the Friars Minor in a meaningful way."

New forms of ministry and the decreased activity required a reorganization of community life. In 1968, a new type of implantation emerged: the "fraternities of insertion," also called "small fraternities," which were intended to function in particular milieus. Six small fraternities arose in the space of four months to relocate teachers who had worked in CEGEPS and priests who had been at the University of Montreal. Then there were a dozen more. These fraternities had a twofold purpose: they brought together a small number of people—from three to ten—and they had a "projet de vie," that is, "a particular way of conceiving and living their religious commitment" (Pierre Bisaillon). Some were directed to bringing others to Franciscan life, others provided lodging for young itinerants, still others worked with the disadvantaged, etc. In fact, in 1987, the Visitor General of the Order, Fr. Thierry Gournay, described three types of fraternities:

1. The institutional fraternity. It was a former friary where priests continued to welcome the laity who were consoled or who celebrated reconciliation. These fraternities provided a visibility to the city's collective conscience.
2. The fraternity of presence in a particular milieu. Members lived their vocation of *Lesser Brothers*. They led a hidden life, without fanfare, in the daily sharing of the simple life of the little ones of this world.
3. The parish fraternity. It brought together friars involved in parish ministry and stimulated by a larger community.

There was a passion to experience life in fraternity, but it was difficult to realize. There was no predetermined model: it was necessary to be attentive to the Gospel, Saint Francis and the history of the Franciscan Order. And how, in the isolation of the fraternities, could a sense of belonging to a religious order be maintained? The quality of fraternal life varied greatly from one fraternity to another, either because it was profoundly shared, or because friars simply lived alongside one another. Due to the shortage of active friars, leaders were struggling to build fraternities that were strong enough to give life and meet the needs of the community.

3. In Search of an Identity

Among the Franciscans, the spiritual animation of the community was traditionally vested in the guardians of the friaries and the Provincial. The latter circulated letters that were read during meals and on which the guardians commented at length and frequently. Other mechanisms, such as canonical visits, chapters of faults where everyone confessed his breaches of the rule in public, monthly and annual retreats all extended the superiors' animating role. With the publication of *Entre nous* and then, *En bref*, community bulletins where everyone could express himself freely—at his own risk, of course!—the letters from the Provincial became less frequent. In the 1960s, the democratic spirit which had penetrated communities and the severity of the crisis led community members to want to take their spiritual animation into their own hands. The Provincials' circulars were no longer read during meals. Chapters every three years, formerly co-opted by a tight-knit group, became the place where the community collectively tried to read the times and orient its destiny. In 1966, for the first time, Chapter preparation saw several committees created to look at pastoral work, the renewal of Franciscan life, and studies and formation. In 1969, the editorial team of *Entre nous* dedicated ten issues to chapter preparation. The friars were able to exchange thoughts on a new lifestyle and apostolic commitment. This became a base for research, for in-depth study, and for evaluation.

But we do not democratize an Order that was more than seven hundred years old, in one fell swoop! The former notions of obedience internalized in the conscience stifled the desires for democracy. In the name of prudence, the Chapter fathers avoided confrontation and stuck with practical problems. Above all, the discussion of Franciscan life, an issue that had always divided the Order, was avoided. The results of these chapters were disappointing. They brought up disagreements and worsened tensions more than rallied the friars.

The breath of the Spirit seemed to set free individual charisms and swept away community goals. The title of *La Revue franciscaine* proclaimed: “Franciscanism in 1969 takes on a new skin.” There was a strange story about an invertebrate that left a shell made up of a mixture of religious clothes, cloisters and outworn customs to become a chameleon, in a habit in a friary, or in a Roman collar for official ceremonies, or in what-not for intimate meetings. The “service of others” now animated its activity and, driven by evangelical freedom, its daring behavior gave it “the appearance of the unique and exemplary wisdom of God.” Freed from “a fear inducing austerity”—a rag that he left in a locked cupboard behind the closed doors of the friary—he lived a life of hope in small fraternities. “A Franciscan is not a monk, but an apostle in the world.” Of course, he always tips his hat to Lady Obedience and before Lady Poverty, but to only to discuss with the first, and to get a handout from other. This description of the Franciscan did not have the official character of a provincial circular. It did not have the endorsement of a majority of the friars. But this new “general rejection,” by its tone and by its brutal rejection of the past, testified, however, to a serious crisis of membership.

The province of St. Joseph was less and less a uniform and coherent reality, and Franciscan life gave rise to many interpretations. This outburst of ideal and action was expressed in a constant search for the meaning of the Franciscan vocation, of lifestyle and of a policy of action for the present times. The chapters, open since 1975 to all solemn professed members, took place in a public forum. The chapter members organized themselves in a way that allowed reflection and sharing information. They respected the equality of the brothers, the diversity of functions, particular charisms, and they promoted individual responsibility. The chapters became places of healing, but did not rally a majority of friars, nor succeed in choosing the means or the people who could realize the objectives that were decided upon. In fact, the fate of the

Franciscan Province seemed to escape the community, so great was the rupture in the western world between culture and the Gospel, and so rapid was the change of society in Quebec.

EPILOGUE—A NEW BEGINNING

Like the Quebec church, the Franciscans also experienced the change of Quebecois society in the tug between making accommodations for today and remaining consistent for tomorrow. Even in 1984, the Definitory failed to propose a synthesis for Franciscans apart from a rereading of the Gospel, the history of the Order and a reading of the present times. This impasse incited the community to move forward. The whole community started to listen to itself and society. It permitted itself to journey collectively. It enlisted the help of an external resource, the Jesuit Alfred Ducharme. For three years, in meetings, in committees and in annual get-togethers, all the brothers looked clearly at their experiences to arrive at forceful ideas, priorities, and lines of action. In May 1987, the Chapter ratified the results of this reflection in a document entitled "Provincial Project, 1987–1993."

This project was rooted in the Order's traditional core values: 1. Contemplative life; 2. Fraternal life; 3. Solidarity with the poor, and thus the commitment to justice and peace; 4. Mission and Evangelization. These values are a given. These values came from the gospel and its interpretation through the history of St. Francis. But they were not just a return to the past. They were reformulated in ways of fraternal living that were adapted to the Quebecois society and to the rhythm of modern life. They were reincarnated in a common plan, that had matured collectively, and was centered on four priorities that the brothers brought forth from the works that vied for their commitment. Two priorities concerned fraternal life: the reception and formation of recruits, and the revitalization of the community fabric. These priorities were intended to give substance to community life and an appeal to their witness. Two other priorities concerned the building of the Kingdom: the presence among young people, and the spreading of the Franciscan message. These two priorities called for a lifestyle, attitudes and deeds "that illustrated the vision that Francis lived, for the world today."

What then was a Franciscan in 1990? Simply a contemplative and a man of action, attentive to God's action in himself, in others and in the world. He did not live in a monastery, but cohabited—in a friary or fraternity—with brothers in a community that fed him, supported him and committed him to maintain fraternal relationships with all created beings. His habitation and schedule included times for silence, contemplation, prayer, and other times for fraternal life, and also for building the kingdom. His charism was to create places in the world where men could discover brotherhood and where the unloved were greeted with the warmth of love. He lived with the poor, partook of a consumer society, lived in solidarity with the unfortunate with all their hopes and their plans. His lifestyle was a challenge to everything that oppressed human beings and nature. His deeds were the many stones that rebuilt "the Church of Christ" into a just society, respectful of life and its environment.

Bibliographic Guidelines

The Franciscans have written extensively about the history of their community. Hugolin Lemay's bibliographies bear witness to this, even if they stop in 1938. This present bibliography is not intended to be exhaustive; this would be a colossal undertaking. It is a guide for the reader who wants to know with what materials this work was written and for researchers interested in deepening one or another aspect of Franciscan life in the Province of St. Joseph of Canada.

I. Manuscript sources

The community archives are kept in Montreal, at Resurrection friary (5750 Rosemont Blvd.)[2] Except on rare occasions, we did not consult them for the preparation of this book. Father Hervé Blais, archivist, gave a very useful description in « Présence franciscaine au Canada. Inventaire des sources documentaires conservées dans les archives de la Province Saint-Joseph du Canada », *in* CD, vol. 28, no. 2, juin 1975; 184–197.

II. Periodicals

Journals and newsletters written for the general public, Secular Franciscans or members of the community are found in the community's annals. They contain documents, accounts, correspondence, newsletters and studies. The entirety is a very rich source of information to reconstruct the universe of the Franciscans. We have used this documentation extensively.

Almanach de S. François, 1917–1949; 1956–1959, Ann.
Cartons violés, 1932–1940. Mens.
Chronique franciscaine, 1941–1945.
En Bref, 1966–. Mens.
Entre Nous. Bulletin de liaison. Janv. 1965–. Mens.

---

2. As of October 2022, Resurrection friary on Rosemont Boulevard was relocated to: 6455 rue Louis Riel, Montreal, QC. H1M 1P1, where some of the archives are stored; others were placed in storage elsewhere.

Franciscan Review, 1905–1963. Mens.
Missions franciscaines, 1924–. Mens.
Nos Cahiers, 1936–1939. Mens.
Nouvelles et Documents, 1937–1969. Mens.
Revue franciscaine, 1891–. Mens.
Souvenir, 1952–. Irr.
Studium, 1946–1969, Trimes.
Trois, 1935–1940. Hebd.

III. General Works

There is no general synthesis of Canadian Franciscan history. The monumental history of Mgr. Hiral by Father Paul-Eugène Trudel gives an overview of this history, from the arrival of Father Frédéric Janssoone to 1915. Two other publications—*Studium 25* and *Notre Province a cinquante ans*—give general insights into the various aspects of Franciscan life. The material and articulation of the "Historical Overview" presented above are drawn from these works. In addition, statistics are compiled from the community's yearly censuses. The title of these censuses varies over time: 1. *Elenchus Fratrum Minorum*, 2. *Table de famille*, 3. *État de la Province Saint-Joseph.*

Baillargeon, Constantin. « La Vie fraternelle à la belle époque » *in Entre Nous*, vol. 18, no. 1, mai 1983 : 5–8.
Brouillard, Carmel, « Les Franciscains au Canada », *in* AF, 1938 : 19–45.
Chicoine, Fidèle. « Les ministères effacés des Franciscains », *in* CD, vol. 38, no. 1, janvier 1985 : 33–38.
Héroux, Barthélemy. « Notes pour servir à l'histoire de la province Saint-Joseph du Canada », *in* ND, vol. 17, no. 3, octobre 1962 : 237–245. Aussi ND, vol 18, no. 1, février 1963 : 80–85 et no. 2, juin 1963 : 184–187.
Légaré Romain. *Une spiritualité toujours jeune.* Montréal, Les éditions Saint Louis, 1943, 38 p.
[Lemay, Hugolin]. *Vingt-cinq années de vie franciscaine au Canada, 1890–1915.* Montréal, Revue du Tiers-Ordre, [1916]. 335 p.
[Poirier, Léandre]. *Notre Province a cinquante ans.* Numéros spéciaux de CD. vol. 30, no. 1, juillet 1977 et no. 2, novembre 1977. 328 p.
Poirier, Léandre. « Le Frère franciscains dans l'Église d'aujourd'hui », *in* ND, vol. 19, no. 2, juin 1964 : 124–134.
[Poirier, Léandre et Saint-Pierre, Bertrand]. *Cahier-souvenir du 75ᵉ anniversaire de la seconde restauration franciscaine au Canada, 1890–1965.* Numéro spécial de ND, vol. 20, no. 3, février 1966, 222–347.
Poisson, Joseph-Hermann. « J'aurais tant voulu … mais », *in* AF, 1940 : 72–76 (la vocation de frère convers).
Projet de Province 1987–1993 des Frères mineurs de la Province Saint-Joseph du Canada. Document du chapitre. Montréal juin 1987. 50 p.

Rapport de Province, 1984–1987. Province Saint-Joseph du Canada. Document du chapitre. in En Bref, vol. 21, no. spécial 2, avril 1987. 44 p.
Rapport du comité d'étude sur le vieillissement et les secondes carrières. Montréal, 1970 et 1971.
Rapport du visiteur général de la Province Saint-Joseph du Canada. Document du chapitre, in En Bref, vol 21, no. spécial 3, avril.
Studium 25. Numéro spécial de la revue *Studium*, déc. 1946 : 181–556.
Trudel, Paul-Eugène. *Mgr. Ange-Marie Hiral.* Montréal, Éditions franciscaines, 1957–1961. 5 tomes parus.

IV. Biographies

The collection, *C'était mon frère*, compiles the obituaries of community members. It is a very rich source for getting a glimpse from within of the Franciscan universe and of understanding the diversity of the friars' apostolates. Researchers will also be able to consult the bibliographies of Hugolin Lemay in 1916 and 1933, the records contained in *Studium* 25 (1946) for personal information.

Baillargeon, Constantin et Légaré, Romain. *Le Bon Père Frédéric.* Montréal, Éditions paulines, 1988. 415 p.
Bougé, Yvonne, *Valentin-Marie Breton.* Paris, 1958, 288 p.
Bouffard, Odoric et Légaré, Romain. « Georges-Albert Laplante », *in* CD, vol. 28, no. 1, juin 1976: 9–32.
Lamontagne, Onésime, éd. *Ils étaient des nôtres.* Préface du T.R.P. Hervé Blais, o.f.m. Montréal, Éditions du Bon Père Frédéric, 1953, 122 p.
Parent, Édouard. *Éphrem Longpré. Héraut de la Primauté du Christ et de l'Immaculée.* S.l., 1985. 324 p.
Saint-Pierre, Bertrand et Poirier, Léandre. *C'était mon frère ... Soixante-quinze ans de vie franciscaine au Canada, 1890–1965.* Montréal, Librairie Saint-François, 1965. 477 p.
Saint-Pierre, Bertrand et Poirier, Léandre. *C'était mon frère ... Supplément I, 1965–1976.* Montréal, Archives des Franciscains, 1976. 232 p.

V. Friaries and Residences

Specialized monographs must be supplemented by general works. Thus, Father Trudel's *Mgr. Hiral,* gives a lot of very reliable information about the foundation and beginnings of the first friaries.

Bisaillon, Pierre. « Nos petites fraternités, 1968–1987 » *in* CD, vol. 41, no. 1, janvier 1988 : 3–26.
Bourdeau, Gilles, « Une fraternité de prière : démarche et projets », *in* CD, vol. 25, no. 2, juin 1972 : 15–19.
Déziel, Julien. *Maison du Christ-Roi, Châteauguay : 50 ans d'évolution, 1932–1982.* Châteauguay, 1983. 95 p.

Guilbault, Jules-Marie. *Cinquante années de vie franciscaine à Québec, 1900–1950.* Québec, Les Franciscains, 1950. 126 p.
Jouve, Odoric-Marie. *Les Frères mineurs à Québec, 161–1905; simple coup d'œil historique.* Québec, Couvent des SS. Stigmates, 1905, 159 p.
Laplante, Clarence, « Maison Saint-Antoine de Pittsfield », *in* CD, vol. 37, no. 1, janvier 1984 : 34–40.
Légaré, Romain. *Les Franciscains en Abitibi.* Montréal, 1978. 64 p. Extrait de CD, vol. 31, no. 1, janvier 1978.
Léger, Grégoire. « The First ten years of Pert Hospital", *in* CD, vol. 26, no. 2, juin 1973; 14–20.
Les Franciscains à Trois-Rivières. Cinquante années d'apostolat. 64 p. Numéro spécial de la revue *Le Souvenir*, vol. IV, no. 2.
Poirier, Léandre. « La Vie d'une grande fraternité. Chronique de Rosemont 1972–1975 » *in* CD, vol. 28, no. 2, juin 1975 : 119–126.
Sylvestre, Florent. « La Vie au couvent Saint-Joseph », *in* CD, vol. 24, no. 1, janvier 1971 : 11–19.

VI. Parishes

In the "Historical Overview" above we have only listed the parishes led by Franciscans. And we will not be able to devote a separate chapter to them when we speak about the "Fields of apostolate" where they worked. Studies are often lacking or are too incomplete. However, the following writings can be usefully consulted.

Anonyme. « Notes historiques. St. Patrick's Parish, Trois-Rivières », *in* ND, vol. 22, no. 1, février 1967 : 89–90.
Buisson, Augustin. « Histoire religieuse de 'Église canadienne-française dans la péninsule de Niagara », *in* NDD, vol 18, no. 1, février 1963 : 7–15.
Chicoine, Fidèle. « Fort Saskatchewan, Alberta, 1922–1925 », *in* CD, vol. 35, no. 1, Janvier 1982: 10–15.
Cormier, Grégoire. Un Jubilé d'Or de fondation : la paroisse Notre-Dame-de-la-Merci. Aroostook Junction, N.B., 1926–1976 », *in* CD, vol. 29, no. 2, décembre 1976 : 129–132.
Cormier, Grégoire. « Adieux è Andover », *in* CD, vol 34, no. 2, juillet 1981, 129–131.
Cormier, Grégoire. "Jubilé d'Or à Maliseet, N.B., 1928–1978 », *in* CD, vol. 34, no. 1, janvier 1979 : 35–37.
Godmer, André-M. *Esquisse historique de Baker Brook; jubilé d'argent de la bénédiction solennelle de l'église, 1928-1953.* Edmunston, 1953. 57 p.
Houle, Jean-Jacques. « Les 25 ans de la paroisse Saint-Maxime », *in* CD, vol. 34, no. 1, janvier 1979 : 7–9.
Léger, Grégoire. « Limestone Siding, Tilley, Andover," *in* ND, vol. 19, no. 3, octobre 1964: 301.

[Lemieux, Wilfrid et Turcotte, Rufin]. *Saint-Jean-de-Brébeuf. Port Colborne, Ontario. Ma paroisse.* Port Colborne, Imprimerie Gagné Ltée, 1968. 96 p.

Poulin, Gonzalve. *Notre-Dame des Sept-Allégresses, 1911–1961 : Un demi-siècle de vie paroissiale.* Trois-Rivières, 1961. 93 p.

Poulin, Gonzalve. *Paroisse du Sacré-Cœur. 1919–1969.* Welland, Les artisans, 1969. 94 p.

Poulin, Gonzalve. *L'église Saint-Vincent de l'avenue Stanley.* Ottawa, 1969, 42 p.

Poulin, Gonzalve. *La Paroisse Saint-Maxime de Sorel, 1946–1971.* Sorel, Imprimerie des Franciscains, 1972. 73 p.

Simoneau, Octave. « Chronique paroissiale. Our Lady of Perpetual Help, Châteauguay," *in* ND, vol. 18, juin 1963: 180–182.

Chapter Six

Franciscans and Education[1]

Noël Bélanger

The history of education in Quebec has unquestionably established the active and continuous presence of the Church in the work of education. In a privileged way, secondary education and the preparation of youth for higher studies benefited from the contribution of diocesan clergy and communities of religious men and women. It would not be until the mid-20th century that there were alternatives to the traditional classical program and that a public secondary educational system was created which would also lead to the doors of the university.

It is in this context, that the Church's presence in teaching should be understood as a substitute for a state which was timorous and destitute. Generally speaking, there were no educational institutions left other than those under church authority the purpose of which was to prepare the succession of priests and provide society with religious leaders.

The Franciscans' questioning the *purpose* of their educational institutions must be placed at the center of any discussion about the Franciscan' presence in education.

The *purpose* of Franciscan educational institutions must be placed at the center of any discussion about the friars' presence in education. During the last century, the Friars Minor established educational institutions in Quebec, and in some local churches, mainly to prepare young people for the Franciscan priesthood. The evolution of these institutions occurred in accord with their *purpose* in such a way that to put this in question or to hint at all of expanding this primary vocation would be a threat to their very existence and would be a contradictory factor for the community.

But there is more to it than this. We also have to consider the "Franciscan ideal," the raison d'être of a friar in particular. What is an authentic Franciscan? Why does he exist? Where does he draw his inspiration? What is the source of

1. Bélanger, Noël, « Les Franciscains et l'éducation », in Hamelin, Jean (dir.), in *Les Franciscains au Canada, 1890–1990,* Sillery, QC, Septentrion, 1990; pp. 209–250.

his action? It is always necessary to refer to Francis himself and to the Rule left to his sons, where he urges the non-contradictory and seamless union of action and prayer. Let us hear what Father Carmel Brouillard had to say:

> The Franciscan is a man of work and prayer. It is in the former that he draws the courage and understanding that precede the latter. His life becomes harmoniously hierarchized to the extent that he attains the intense reality that enflamed Francis's existence: Love. Love best explains and sums up the spirit that guides him (. . .) Love forms the center of Franciscan theology and mysticism; it underlies the great Franciscan masters' philosophy.[2]

The individual Franciscan friar even comes to ask himself what should be undertaken as an apostolate in accordance with his profound vocation. In other words, can Franciscan involvement in education, with no direct link to the recruitment of subjects itself, be justified? Father Odoric Bouffard, who for many years was an administrator and professor of literature at the Seraphic College of Trois-Rivières, wrote:

> I must admit that throwing myself into preparing for a retreat or a sermon freed me from a certain guilt complex. We heard that teaching literature was not priestly. So, I gladly left the mine fields of literature to rest on the shores of the Sea of Galilee.[3]

This very real tension, strongly articulated by some individuals, became amplified as the 20th century progressed, as Quebec society gradually became secular, and as religious vocations became increasingly rare. The Second Vatican Council proposed to the Church a renewed missionary pastoral care based on the four main axes of faith instruction, community, liturgy, and social commitment. This is the context from which we will consider a hundred years of Franciscan presence in education. It is a hundred years of a system that was intended exclusively for the recruitment and renewal of the community's workforce. It placed an immense effort on training high-quality teachers and educators to pursue educational goals that became too grand for a community of missionaries and preachers. Many wondered whether investments in the field of education were really in keeping with the traditions of their Order.

---

2. Brouillard, Carmel. "Les Franciscains au Canada », in *Almanach de saint François,* 1938, p. 43.
3. Bouffard, Odoric. "Bio-bibliographie du P. Odoric Bouffard, o.f.m., » in *CHRONIQUES ET DOCUMENTS* vol. 35, no. 1, janvier 1982: 18.

1. THE "REPRODUCTIVE" SYSTEM

The birthplace of the Canadian Franciscan educational work must be placed in Montreal. The first Seraphic College was established there on the feast of the Presentation of Mary, November 21, 1892. At that time, it was in embryonic form, in a modest house on Dorchester Street, but it grew in the following years. Insufficient, it was replaced in 1896 by a newly built small two-story college that lodged students until 1916. This could be called the "Montreal phase" of the Seraphic College. During these twenty years, the students received free academic training at the College of Montreal.[4] Franciscan poverty thus found among the Sulpician educators "truly distinguished apostles who distributed the benefits of a formation inspired by the purest classical tradition."[5]

In September 1911, fifteen years after the humble beginnings of Montreal's Seraphic College, a branch opened in Trois-Rivières, in the former Commissariat of the Holy Land which had been expanded to accommodate 25 students in the preparatory class. After a rather shaky start, the number of students grew to the point where a new building was required. As early as 1914, Bishop F.-X Cloutier of Trois-Rivières had blessed the first stone. Until the 1915–16 school year, the Trois-Rivières branch had organized only the first three classes: Preparatory, Latin Elements, and Syntax. In September 1916, the Seraphic College reached a decisive stage in its evolution: the Montreal house was closed, and all classes were transferred to this new location.

The Seraphic College located on Laviolette Street was a brick building that, in addition to the ground floor, consisted of three floors, the rear of which overlooked a modest courtyard surrounded by a row of poplars and a high wooden fence. Built to accommodate some 120 students, the Seraphic College was an institution whose goals were defined in the *Yearbooks*:

> The Seraphic College is not a boarding school or a home of education that prepares students for different careers. Nor is it a simple small seminary intended to provide priests for the needs of a diocese. (. . .) It is a special college, a kind of small novitiate, with the aim of increasing the number of Franciscan missionaries in Canada and in the missions.

---

4. Translator's note : The Collège de Montréal, still located in downtown Montreal, is a former Roman Catholic minor seminary, founded on June 1, 1767 as the Petit Séminaire of Montreal by the Sulpician Fathers. Cf. Collège de Montréal—https://en.wikipedia.org/wiki/Coll%C3%A8ge_de_Montr%C3%A9al

5. Chicoine, Fidèle. "Collèges : Sources de vocations franciscaine", *in CHRONIQUES ET DOCUMENTS*, vol. 36, no. 1, janvier 1983 : 4.

> To meet this end, it accepts children, rich and poor, who show serious indications of a vocation to Franciscan life. By a special education given by the friars themselves, it trains these children in the science and virtues that are suitable for such a holy state.[6]

From the beginning, the purpose of the Seraphic College was explicit and unambiguous: to select and prepare recruits for the Franciscan Order by which the College became, effectively, a reproduction center. Its only function was to be the reproductive organism of the Franciscan Province of St. Joseph in Canada for the Franciscan Order. Thus, in the foundation plans, there was no intention to participate in the instruction and direction of French-Canadian youth, as other colleges or small seminaries did. In short, "one of the first tasks of the Franciscans upon their arrival in Canada was to set up a centre to ensure their increase and continuation; and this was the Seraphic College."[7]

By establishing such an institution, the Friars Minor introduced the "small community seminary" or "small religious seminary" to Quebec. It was referred to by other communities as *the Juvénat* or the "Juniorate." The Franciscans were the only ones to use the poetic name, Seraphic College, for this house which not just anyone entered. The annual admission and the readmission of students was strictly monitored. It was necessary to express explicitly the intention to become a Franciscan. Indeed, it was designed according to the model of European institutions to train young aspirants to the priesthood, apart from the influence of other young people, the world and the family. The Seraphic College offered a six-year course of studies which extended from elementary Latin to rhetoric.

A former and illustrious student of the Seraphic College in Trois-Rivières left a beautiful account about the living conditions found there between 1929 and 1935. The friars, living close to the students, helped to create a very intense family climate in which one's spiritual, sporting and intellectual life could flourish:

> I spent five years at this college, marvelous years as much for physical and moral health as for intellectual training. I was very happy to have spent so much energy on fascinating tasks; I experienced so many intellectual pleasures.[8]

The historian Trudel's testimony is enforced by his assessment of the *cursus studiorum* (the same as the Sulpicians' with which the first students at the

---

6. Bergeron, Cécile. *Le Collège Séraphique des Trois-Rivières : 1952–1968*, Thèse à l'Université de Sherbrooke, 1971, p. 37.

7. *Ibid.* 42.

8. Trudel, Marcel, *Mémoires d'un autre siècle*, Boréal Express, 1987, p. 89.

Seraphic College in Montreal were formed), the rich library (more than 5,000 volumes), the excellent preparation of teachers, and rigorous and very high intellectual demands.[9]

After completing Rhetoric, the Franciscan aspirant spent a short year at the novitiate in Sherbrooke to learn more about Franciscan life.

> Religious life begins here. For a year, the young man who responded to the divine call will apply himself to the sublime task of sanctification. He is an apprentice who strives to handle the instruments of his trade, who seeks in silence and peace to understand what rules him and his intimate secrets. The Franciscan novitiate is located on the edge of Sherbrooke on Lennoxville Road. The décor is beautifully grandiose and impressive.[10]

Having exchanged his secular clothes for the habit and cord, and having been advised by the master, who directs him in this new life, the young man follows another European model adopted by all men's religious communities. He began to study philosophy—scholastic philosophy, to be sure—in a "clericat" called the Philosophy Studium.[11] This was located in Quebec City. Being a scholastic meant focusing on studies required to train him as a future cleric. The three-year course was sanctioned, like Rhetoric, by the baccalaureate exams awarded by Laval University since 1933. Let us take a look at the life led within this institution:

> A day of study with the Franciscans is arranged to assure the demands of both the future scholar and priest, to harmonize them proportionately so that the importance of knowledge and piety emerge equally.
>
> The tranquility of the cloister, the competition that exists between these young students, as well as their fraternal accord promote this long assimilation of learning, philosophy (. . .).
>
> The best literary and scientific periodicals are provided to keep them informed of current schools of thought.[12]

After three years of philosophical studies, the Franciscan student was directed to the Theology Studium located in Montreal, on Rosemont Boulevard. An excerpt from the 1921 chronicle described the first night spent in this rural environment in these terms:

> We are going to bed. No street noise: no cars, no horses, no shouting, especially no locomotives with their gaspy and rowdy rattle, no heavy

9. *Ibid.* 84.

10. Brouillard, Carmel, *art. Cit.,* p. 26.

11. Built by Father Ange-Mary Hiral in 1900, this *Studium* was in the Friary of the Holy Stigmata.

12. Brouillard, Carmel, *art. Cit.* Pp. 28–29.

> wagons going back and forth under our windows. In the distance we only hear the muffled lowing of some solitary cows, the barking of dogs, or the seductive sound of some neighboring tram.[13]

In this institution, the routine differed little from that of Quebec; however, the atmosphere did. The scholastic student made irrevocable vows; he embarked directly on the path leading to the priesthood, through a succession of sacred orders and advanced theological and ecclesiastical learning. The General Constitutions of the Order recommended a keen dedication to the masters of the Franciscan school. In Rosemont, this fidelity to the Franciscan intellectual tradition was openly welcomed. To give an idea of this formation house's quality, the friary's rich library should be mentioned—more than 30,000 select volumes—as should be the valuable teaching staff responsible for the training of future Franciscan priests. A few notable names were: Fathers Georges-Albert Laplante, Leonard-M. Puech, Adrien-M Malo, Guy-M Brisebois, Léandre Poirier, Emmanuel Boisvert, René Baril, Léonce Hamelin, Thaddée Matura, Lucien Lapierre and Laurent Boisvert. More particularly, in the field of Holy Scripture, Father Malo successfully enriched the library and created a Biblical Museum. Father Matura, for his part, helped to open the scholasticate to ecumenism and the emerging liturgical movement.

It is worth noting the atmosphere of *freedom* that prevailed in Rosemont. It helped to spread trust, understanding, and a cohesion among the members of the Order, which were contagious, according to Father Léandre Poirier:

> The Studium was without a doubt a school of learning for us. It was above all, I would say, a school of trust that united students with their master, and the master with the students. Our union was, I dare say, universal. It had nothing of this simple affinity of temperament or this meeting of interests which would not have brought us together; rather, that very type of union would have multiplied the interest groups into a divided community. Had we suppressed the common ideal that attracted us all, the ideal of the priesthood which shaped our wills to consent joyfully to the work which it imposed, none of those memories that I have just evoked, these memories deeply etched in us, could have been printed here. It is rather the elevation of an ideal that brought us to remove all obstacles to the fraternal life that we were already living.[14]

The Order of Friars Minor does not only include clerics. It welcomes any individual who aspires to a religious life as a lay brother. In August 1946, Father

---

13. *Studium*, vol. 1, no. 4, Numéro-Souvenir, 1946: 203.
14. *Ibid.* 192–193.

Osias Vandandaigue, who was helped by Father Anastase Mailloux and Brother Jean Moreau, was asked to organize a school to prepare young people under the age of 18 for religious life. The former missionary college in Sorel was adapted for these aspiring lay brothers. Known as the Didace-Pelletier School, the institution initially accepted between 15 and 20 students. Intensive recruitment brought this number to 43 in 1951. This was an unequivocal sign that a new building was needed. It was built on the friary grounds and officially inaugurated on January 18, 1954. It provided a training modelled on the Schools of Arts and Crafts of the province of Quebec. The program included the acquisition of basics, specialized internship training in workshops and, of course, a solid introduction to religious life. Lay brothers well trained in their professions, such as Eugene Bilodeau and Wilfrid Soucy, were responsible for the internships. The school provided the community with the qualified personnel needed in the Canadian friaries and in those of the mission countries.

In order to meet the needs of the district, the school's management established secondary education in June 1959; and in June 1961 it became Didace-Pelletier High School. It did not survive the decline in vocations and the redevelopment of the school system any more than the classical colleges. Uncertain of the future and facing increasing operating costs, the Franciscans closed their school in June 1965 and the following year opened their premises to the Carignan Regional School Commission.

2. HELPING LOCAL CHURCHES

Edmonton

It is usual to present the Franciscans especially as a missionary and preaching community. But the need to assure its succession prompted the Friars Minor to establish foundations outside Quebec, that is, in western Canada and in the eastern USA.

As early as 1921, the specific apostolic difficulties encountered by the Franciscans who were established in the west since 1908 suggested the establishment of a Seraphic College. One thinks, in particular, of the problems of multiculturalism and various cultural traditions that made it imperative to recruit an indigenous clergy. It was not until 1925 that the Definitory decreed the establishment of a Seraphic College in North Edmonton, where the Franciscans had been in charge of a parish and a few other places scattered throughout Alberta. On May 17, 1925, Archbishop Joseph O'Leary of Edmonton, assisted by Fathers Bérard Norbert and Fidèle Chicoine, blessed the foundation stone of the future St. Anthony of Padua College.

The course of study was to be bilingual, in accordance with Rome's instructions regarding the Canadian priests' ability to minister in both official languages. In fact, the majority would be given in English, because recruitment would be mainly among English-speaking candidates and also a French-language college already existed at Trois-Rivières. Further adjustments were necessary to meet the particular conditions of western students who were recruited from a wide range of social and cultural backgrounds. Greek was removed from the classical course and replaced by German. The disciplinary regulations of the Seraphic College of Trois-Rivières were relaxed to correspond to the climate and habits of this part of the country.

The evolution of North Edmonton's Seraphic College was not smooth. Its very existence was called into question a few times. After only a few years, the College had to close its doors temporarily; it reopened in the 1930s with a revamped program and a more diverse enrollment. The College retained its primary purpose, namely the recruitment of Franciscan vocations; but, by conforming its programs and its teachers' qualifications to the Department of Education's requirements, it was accredited as a preparatory institution for Calgary and Edmonton dioceses' seminary, and for secular studies in the Province of Alberta's university.[15]

In 1965, after forty years of good work, in often ungrateful conditions, St. Anthony's College had only 12 students. It closed its doors permanently, due to the lack of students and vocations. The Franciscans, responsible for pastoral service in the parish of Our Lady of Lourdes (sic),[16] continue to live in the house, whose dormitory has been converted into a library. Uncertainty reigned over the future of the institution.

Biddeford

A double motive animated the Franciscans when they made plans for a foundation in Biddeford: to establish a residence for Franciscan preachers, and to establish a Seraphic College for the recruitment of Franciscan vocations from French-speaking Catholics in the USA, from Maine and elsewhere in New England. The first brochures, written in French, underlined the primary purpose of the work, that was to develop religious vocations, while not excluding the concern of preparing students for any other professional orientation.

Biddeford was chosen because of its strong Francophone presence at the time. In addition, many Franciscans in the French-Canadian Province had

---

15. *CHRONICS AND DOCUMENTS*, 30, No. November 2 1977: 223; *CHRONICS AND DOCUMENTS*, 36, No. 2, July 1983: 17.

16. Translator's note : in fact the friars lived in the friary and continued their services in St. Francis of Assisi Parish; some friars also taught in the Catholic public school system and were later involved in its administration; and around 1968 and thereafter others were involved in teaching at St. Joseph's Seminary and establishing Newman Theological College.

been recruited from Franco-American centers such as Biddeford. The College opened in November 1933, with 13 students. The six-year curriculum corresponded generally to Quebec's secondary education, and with the equivalent American high school and junior college. The teaching staff consisted of 4 friars who were helped by a layman teaching mathematics.

The evolution of the Friars' presence would be inversely proportional to the college's progress. The more notable one was, the more modest would be the other. A few figures illustrate this. During the first decade, there were between 3 and 6 friars; between 1940–1949, from 10 to 16; between 1949–1960, from 18 to 24 friars. Then came the years of decline. The presence of lay people increased in proportion to the withdrawal of friars and the increase in student numbers. At the peak of student enrollment (736), in 1969–70, there were only 14 friars, compared to 52 lay teachers and administrators. The first lay president was elected in 1967.

Meanwhile, in response to the growing enrollment, which became mixed in 1967, the campus had greatly expanded and was covered with pavilions, including Frederick Hall and the College Library. All of these investments were valued at more than $5 million. It was a far cry from the humble beginnings of Rhodes House, the friars' first residence on St. Francis College's campus in Biddeford. By 1969, it had become increasingly clear that the community no longer had the human and financial resources to bear the enormous weight of such an institution. To maintain their identity, the friars tried to distance themselves from the college, which had become increasingly removed from their primary objectives. By 1955, St. Francis College had become an American liberal arts college. The concern for French culture and priestly vocations, without being neglected, had naturally ceased to be a priority. On a personal level, Father Luc-M. Chabot believed that preaching suited him more than the administration of a growing institution now oriented exclusively to college level students. For his part, Father Frédéric Bélanger, who was devoted to the college and personally identified his work throughout these decades with its history, had high hopes for the College. He believed in the [Franciscan] community's ability to ensure the institution's full development. There was a tension that would be found amplified in the future plans and direction of Trois-Rivière's Seraphic College.

In 1975, the Franciscans handed over responsibility for the College to a secular corporation. If we can talk about a close relationship between the Franciscan community and Biddeford College, we cannot speak about a strong identification with the College. The friars willingly admitted that, apart from Biddeford College, there would always be the possibility of other occupations: preaching, retreats, parish ministry, service to religious communities. Within the Order, there was on one hand, this continual tug-of-war between teaching and administration; and on the other hand, pastoral work that was considered more essential.

Nevertheless, it was with regret that most of the friars, who had intimately known this work, left Biddeford. This was not only the end of the Franciscan's educational work, but also the end of the presence of friars from the Canadian Franciscan Province of St. Joseph in New England.[17]

3. Intellectual influence

It is readily accepted that the Franciscan Order does not get the accolades that are usually attached to Dominicans, Jesuits or Sulpicians, who are closely associated with university teaching and research. It was during the 1920s, however, that the Franciscan community really began to get interested in education and the difficulties related to it. Until then, the friars had been mostly concerned with their own continuance. They began to consider that any apostolate, in order to be effective, had to take into account the progress of modern culture:

> From an asceticism that was not interested in the acquisition of knowledge, religious life moved to the cult of doctrinal preparation, so necessary to exert the influence it wanted on its environment.[18]

Beginning in the 1920s, several Franciscan clerics' intellectual commitment was confirmed by university degrees or graduate certificates. Who was responsible for this impulse given to studies? According to Father Georges-Albert Laplante, it was the first provincial of the Canadian province, Father Ambrose:

> Recognition that is not usually given to Father Ambrose, but which belongs to him, is the fact that he boosted studies. To what do we attribute this unforeseen direction? Was he influenced by questions of efficacy? Maybe. Did he and his subjects feel the lack of basic training? Did his refined sense bring him to foresee the rapid advancements in learning that were developing in our country, from which he was keen enough to perceive the warning signs?[19]

We should recognize a bit of Franciscan humility in this acknowledgement, and we should also attribute to Father Laplante some of the credit that

---

17. Marcil, George. "Franciscans in Biddeford, Maine, 1933–1975," In *CHRONICS AND DOCUMENTS*, 29, No. 2, December 1976: 31 ff.; see also Laplante, Clarence, in *CHRONICS AND DOCUMENTS* 36, No. July 2, 1983: 19.

18. Gaudron, Edmont. "The study curve at home. For the history of our intellectual life," in *CHRONICS AND DOCUMENTS* 30, No.2, July 1977: 229.

19. student residence complex *Ibid.* 230.

he so generously bestowed on Father Ambrose. He was himself a wise councilor for Father Provincial from 1927 to 1933, before being elected Provincial in August 1933. When he was re-elected in October 1936, 23 clerics had taken university courses or were about to complete them. The field of study extended far beyond the ecclesiastical sciences (theology and philosophy) to the increasingly popular studies in pedagogy and social sciences which were mainly oriented toward the family.

This attraction to studies was transmitted by the older to the younger friars who discovered an atmosphere that they were not accustomed to, an atmosphere of renewal where the appreciation for knowledge and informed action was increasingly transmitted:

> You do not go to university for two, three or even four years without coming back desirous to imitate what you have admired; or without becoming aware of the work required to continue in this environment. That continuity, which was evident particularly in the advanced studies, contributed to the formation of a group of men, a group that could even be said to be homogeneous, in the sense that everyone felt the need to fulfil a deep sense of intellectual and moral duty.[20]

The Friars Minor's intellectual outreach has been beautifully shown by several friars who committed their lives and devoted their energies and talents to the service of their Order, their country, and even the international community. A first name comes immediately to mind: Father Marie-Alcantara Dion (1897–1949).

He was precisely the kind of public man who got around and was known to everyone because there was no boundary or limit that he could not overcome. A confrère described his many activities:

> Let's not count the hours spent in university chairs and laboratories, committee and commission meetings, study days and school camps, preaching in churches and in open air, in consultation and in every kind of spiritual ministry.[21]

What immediately strikes us about this man of diverse activities are his deep desire and his spontaneous response to all requests made of him as a friar, priest, and scholar. This man was both a thinker and a man of action, resolutely modern in his commitment to experimental research, but deeply respectful of wisdom-proven traditions. Here is one among many testimonies

20. *Ibid.* 233.

21. *T.R.P. Jean de Circulars Capistran Cayer 1948–1949 and T.R.P. Herve Blais 1949–1954* n°. 4, 95–96.

which demonstrated his capacity for synthesis, this ability to create something new while relying on tradition:

> We would like to make better known the exceptional work of this priest, to whom the pedagogical problems of Europe and America are familiar to the friends of the "Guides." One of the merits of Canadian Catholic Scouting will undoubtedly be to create a new synthesis, all the richer because it confronts the problems of education with the bold new look of youthful America while carefully safeguarding traditional values.[22]

Father Dion began his career at the Seraphic College of Trois-Rivières in 1924 teaching English and supervising students. From 1925 to 1929 he was responsible for Rhetoric, a position he would take up on his return from Europe in 1933. Was he the ideal teacher that some saw regarding the breadth of his knowledge, his clarity of mind, his gift of analysis and methodical demonstrations? He certainly brought to his tasks a meticulousness and a seriousness that some students sometimes feared, at least during exams. Historian Marcel Trudel recounts his own personal experience:

> Each quarter ended with a session of written and oral examinations. Ah! These examinations were taken in front of the whole class and invited teachers, or even sometimes presided over by the prefect of studies. For a while, it was Father Alcantara Dion [who examined us]. After graduating with a doctorate from the University of Milan (a title alone that terrified us), Father Dion was short of word, rarely smiled; and when he did, we thought it was a ruse. Presiding over the oral exam, he opened his "Li'l-Book" at random and indicated a paragraph: "Translate!" We immediately began to stutter. If we were getting it wrong, he encouraged us to continue as if we were right; we would go from one stupidity to another, to the point of ridiculousness. Then, he would say to us coldly, "Do you understand what you're telling me?" After an experience or two like that, we learned to take on the challenge, we learned the game. So goes education: as in sports, training should not be an easy thing.[23]

It is surprising to learn that this man, nourished by apostolic ambitions, turned to education out of religious obedience. From 1929 to 1933, Father Dion attended Sacred Heart University in Milan, an intellectual center renowned for the revival of scholastic studies and for its work in educational, social, and industrial application of experimental psychology and medicine. His four-year stay ended with the defense of a doctoral thesis in philosophy entitled: *Authority and Freedom in New and in Traditional Schools.*

---

22. Lamy, Albert. "Canada's New Scout Lessons" in *The Guide*, March 1940: 57.
23. Trudel, Marcel. *Memories. . .*, 85.

Father Dion's responsibilities at Trois-Rivières' Saint-Antoine Seminary were only part of his multifaceted activities that often took him to the United States, Latin America and Europe, where he was consulted by various associations and universities, or gave conferences, annual courses, etc. In his own country, this Christian humanist became "the soul of Catholic Scouting and Guiding in Canada;" others will add that he was the "brain behind the Canadian episcopacy."[24] But it is especially in the field of secondary education that Father Dion's power of thought and action were put to work. In 1935, he became a full education professor in the Faculty of Letters at Laval University. He held other important academic chairs at the Graduate School of Family and Home Education and the Institute of Family Studies. In 1941, he was appointed Director of Studies and Professor at the Normal School of Secondary Education at the University of Montreal. He also served on several committees and subcommittees of the Department of Public Instruction.

This man was sought from all sides; he increased his lectures and radio talks to audiences of young people, adults and educators all of whom were fascinated by the ideals and the truth he offered them. In education, an area with which he was particularly familiar, he was at ease in inter-related subjects: pedagogy, psychoanalysis, mental health, fine arts, Catholic Action, secondary education, youth movements. His personal contribution to the reorganization of *Secondary Education* alone deserves a lengthy mention; in any case, it should be said without hesitation that he helped make this magazine a prestigious advocate for Quebec's Classical colleges.

But this was only a small part of the written work that Father Dion exercised in his apostolate of the pen. This is clearly evident in the five hundred or so articles of a biobibliography presented at the University of Montreal in 1946.[25] From his immense work, we remember above all those twenty-six lectures, given at Radio-College and published under the title *Orientations*.[26] This remarkable synthesis of Christian educational principles and formulations became a classic for Quebec's youth in secondary schools who were looking for a light to direct them to better professional and Christian lives.

Was this great and seemingly inexhaustible mind a monolith, impervious to the doubts and weaknesses common to most humans? We might be surprised. There was a depth of anguish and shyness in him: "Father had, extraordinarily, the absolute sense of God and the relativity of every creature."[27] In 1940, this international academic wrote:

---

24. The expression would belong to Bishop Papineau, Bishop of Joliette, who used it in a letter to Father Ephrem Longpré.

25. *Bio-bibliography P.R. Marie-Alcantara Dion.*

26. *Guidelines*Shownal, Pax And Editions Bonum, 1945, 267 pp.

27. The phrase is from the Father Odoric Black.

> People do not know what is most burdensome to me, what requires the most exhausting and terrible efforts; it is teaching university—I have an unconquerable aversion and terror of it. A single class exhausts me more than a week's work. But that is a secret between God and me.[28]

This admired man sometimes had complaints made against him, some of which caused him a great deal of pain. He was sometimes criticized for a certain *elitism* in the choice of Franciscan vocations. He was the source of diverging views about the greater importance of intellectual abilities in assessing the criteria for vocations. This attitude resulted from a personal evaluation of secondary schools whose level he aimed to raise and which he said were "cluttered with undesirable elements."[29]

This man was also sometimes accused of being too involved with extraneous works detrimental to the friars' primary concerns regarding education and apostolates. Was his large outreach preventing him from serving the Province's cause, as he could and should have done? At any rate, we must recognize that Father Marie-Alcantara Dion always remained an authentic Franciscan friar, unquestionably professionally competent, an orderly and prayerful man, whose life greatly illustrated what was possible and realizable in a well-rounded Franciscan:

> He lived the Franciscan Rule and absorbed its spirit. He had a great love for the Seraphic Father and was proud to belong to his religious family. This sentiment filled his works. His Franciscan pedagogy of love and trust greatly influenced the country's educators.[30]

Ahead of most of Quebec, he was involved in almost everything that arose in the world of education of his time. What things would not have happened, were it not for him? How many things would have been profoundly different?[31]

Let us turn now to another friar, Father Fernand Porter. After his classical, philosophical and theological studies in the Friars Minor's institutions, he did a doctorate in theology at the Catholic University of America (1943–1945) and advanced studies in pedagogy at the Institut Catholique of Paris (1953–1954). On his return from Europe, with a graduate degree in pedagogy, he assumed the post of rector of Longueuil's Classical Externat. It was a real challenge, according to a witness of the time. In this institution, which was

---

28. *T.R.P. Jean de Circular Capistran Cayer and T.R.P. Herve Blais* N°. 4, 104.

29. *Ibid.* 107.

30. *Ibid.* 111.

31. These questions are those of the Lucien Labelle era on Father Marie-Alcantara Dion, in handwritten notes dated June 9, 1989.

trying to find its way, Father Porter was a workaholic. He had to teach several subjects, including religious studies, the philosophy of education, English, and history where he tended to be given to romanticism and providentialism. This teacher was able to inspire and revive. He was, however, unable to lead his colleagues. One of them wrote:

> Had he wanted to do so, it would not have been easy. We had become too accustomed of making fun of our rector's little manias of accomplishing broad directives. Father Fernand may have understood the situation.[32]

This teacher, who knew how to appeal to the pride and sensitivity of the college student and who had a sense of awe and the sacred, had already been presented as the disciple of Father Marie-Alcantara Dion. Was there a reason to do that? In this regard, a colleague said: "Fernand would have learned the fascinating power of the realm of the mysterious from his master, the late Father Alcantara."[33] This description is both attractive and ambiguous. If there is a connection between the two individuals, it would be in intellectual concerns, particularly research. Indeed, Father Fernand Porter was a researcher whose major work, *L'Institution catéchistique au Canada: Deux siècles de formation religieuse,* would be discovered and appreciated a few years later as both original and important. The Dominican Benoît Lacroix gave an account of the work and stressed its relevance:

> We need to have a historical sense and be objective to understand how fundamental this small book is. (. . .) The author has chosen a subject that may at first glance seem pedestrian, even useless; but it is quickly apparent that it contains in embryonic form the story of the Canadian person's religious formation, the very way in which Catholic ideas entered into our earliest populations, and how religious sentiment was able to dominate our lives for so many centuries.[34]

From September 27 to 29, 1984, a symposium was held at Laval University organized by members of a research program entitled: "A Socio-Cultural History in French America (1534–1984): Catechetical Production." For young researchers, Father Porter's work was still a relevant contribution

---

32. New Year's Eve, Paul. "P. Fernand to wear. Notice Biographical" in *CHRONICS AND DOCUMENTS,* 38, No. 2, June 1985:169.

33. *Ibid.,* p. 169

34. Quoted by Raymond Brodeur, "Who produces the catechisms? in Raymond Brodeur and Jean-Paul Rouleau, Dirs, *An unknown in the history of culture. The production of catechisms in French America,* Sainte-Foy, Ed., Anne Sigier 1986, p. 1.

to the history of catechisms and its practice. Addressing Father Porter, guest of honor at the inaugural session, the group's spokesperson said:

> This work's fundamental qualities make it valuable and of inestimable interest to the members of this research program (. . .). And, it is for this reason that we have come to pay tribute to its author tonight.[35]

The organizers of these sessions compiled the meetings' papers into a book. It is called: *Une inconnue de l'histoire de la culture. La production des catéchismes en Amérique française* (Anne Sigier Editions, 1986, 480 pp.). It was dedicated to Father Porter, "a pioneer in socio-cultural history of catechisms in America."[36]

This honor, which underscores the value of Father Porter's best-known work, should not cause us to forget his abundant written works, even if they are of unequal quality. They include five books, more than 300 articles, and some thirty duplicated manuscripts which had a smaller circulation. His long collaboration with *L'Enseignement secondaire au Canada* and his *Perspectives pédagogiques au Canada français* reveal his taste for the history of French-Canadian educational practices and his gifts as a compiler.

The vitality of intellectual life within the Franciscan Order is not limited to the friars we have just mentioned or to their personal work. Moreover, to have such an active and fruitful career, every researcher, every thinker, must rely on considerable material and human support. If Father Marie-Alcantara was able to play such a decisive pedagogical role, it is because he was excellently assisted by Father Fernand Porter and, later, by Father Lucien Labelle. If magazines such as *L'Enseignement secondaire au Canada, La famille* and *Culture* became so popular, it is thanks to the mobilization of an army of more or less anonymous collaborators behind the charismatic leaders.

One thing is certain, those who attended the Seraphic College were not slow to recognize what they owed to Fathers Rodrigue LaRue and Irénée Saint-Arnaud in Latin and Greek classics and to Fathers Yves Gaudreau, Augustin Buisson, Odoric Bouffard and Claude Héroux in French literature. The alumni of Longueil's Classical Externat also fondly remember the extent of Charles Bélanger's culture, Paul Sylvester's versatility, and Pierre Bisaillon's solidity. In philosophy, Fathers Edmond Gaudron, Constantin Baillargeon, Édouard Parent, Marc Renaud and Claude Giasson seem to have been the most renowned. We have already listed the names of the professors who have most marked the students' intellectual and spiritual life at the theologate from 1920–1967.

---

35. Rouleau, Jean-Paul. "I'm Fernand Porter. sound Work" in *CHRONICS AND DOCUMENTS*, 38, No. 1, January 1985: 10. This is a passage from thes at the opening night of the catechistic production symposium, September 27, 1984, at Laval University.

36. *An unknown in the history of culture. . .* , ix.

How can we not mention here the figure of Father Leonard-Marie Puech who, from 1935 to 1954, was Master of Students in Rosemont and an incomparable professor. Shortly after his death in 1984, Constantin Baillargeon compiled a memorable profile from which we can take large excerpts:

> Fr. Leonard was a gifted man. He possessed an unusual physical resistance and ability to work, it was assumed he would one day attain a high degree of excellence. And, he did. He read Latin and Greek at first glance and fluently spoke Provençal, his native language, French, English, Italian, Spanish and even some German. But what was most remarkable about him was his theological knowledge, which, every year, astonished the new students who took advanced theology. His *De Deo uno et trino* was excellent. But his De *Christo* and his *De homine christiano* were even better. And of the two it was the *De homine christiano* that was the more exciting. Inspired by St. Paul and St. John, it was solid, enticing, and spiritually nourishing. . . . Certainly, over the years, one or another aspect of this theology has aged and lost its luster: it must not be forgotten, Fr. Leonard taught before the biblical and Franciscan renewals. But the fact remains that, such as it was, his thought was of a superior quality. It flowed into a powerful synthesis, so vibrant with life that its listeners felt they were seeing it created and evolve before their eyes. He actually thought in front of us! This explains why his teaching had such a profound impact: it was a recitation! As for the professor's stature, I will sum up what I think by saying that I place Fr. Leonard among the five or six great masters that I have met at the three universities I attended. . . . In spirituality alone, Fr. Leonard's qualities could have made him a shining star, but this was lost in the stratosphere. His peasant origins . . . were a counterweight and grounded him with a realism which was not diminished by his rustic bearing. It was this peasant realism that made him draw, for his spirituality lectures, from St. Vincent de Paul, a peasant like himself, from Fr. Chevrier, founder of the Prado, and even from Fr. Lacouture, whose concrete and practical spirit he admired. Even if the synthesis between these elements and his theology was never completely made, the fact remains that the unexpected juxtaposition of his two poles of thought made Fr. Leonard's spirituality an original composition that strongly marked the students who passed through his hands. . . . To complete Fr. Leonard's portrait, a word remains to be said about his temperament, for he had quite a character. Given the wealth of his abilities, he could not help but be a little on the domineering side. . . . But was not his occasional crankiness compensated for by his genuine hospitality, his constant care to encourage and promote his students' personal abilities, and his real compassion for these young friars' ordeals? It was indeed good to live at the Rosemont scholasticate during Fr. Leonard's reign. This great master, despite his gruff airs, was at root a tender and fraternal man, and in this he was an authentic son, though of

a unique type, of the Little Poor Man of Assisi. Combined with his outstanding intellectual abilities, these aspects of his character made Fr. Leonard a master educator and builder emeritus of the Franciscan Province of St. Joseph of Canada (cf. *CHRONIQUES ET DOCUMENTS*, vol. 38, no. 11, janvier 1985: 64–65).

To take stock of intellectual life, as it is currently being experienced in the Friars Minor community, we doubtlessly have to mention the circumstances which led to diversifying the Province's intellectual activity. Thus, greater attention should be given to the position of Franciscan clerics in liturgical, pastoral and catechetical action, particularly in the local church and diocesan councils, regional pastoral secretariats, ecclesiastical tribunals, etc. Should we not see in this a generous and fervent response to the Church's need to be inserted at this time into the world?

4. Scouting[37]

Scouting was born in England. Its founder, Lord Baden Powell of Gilwell, was a cavalry officer who served in the Imperial Army during the South African War at the beginning of this [twentieth] century. Having had to endure a rough siege in Mafeking, he decided to use young people as scouts. This experience revealed to him the generosity and know-how that young people can show when one has confidence in them.

As much a military man as he was, he was horrified by war: to him, it was nothing but a stupid and cruel killing of brothers. He had the idea to work at training scouts to promote peace. A brilliant educator, he devised a system of instruction capable of harmonizing the authority and freedom necessary for the normal development of young people. This gave them a sense of honor and responsibility and directed them towards a zealous dedication of energies which were too often poorly used for lack of a good cause to serve.

Baden Powell founded his first Scout troop in 1908. It was the beginning of a movement that in a few years would spread to all the countries of the world and become the largest educational movement ever known in the history of mankind, apart from school education.

The founder of Scouting was profoundly religious. His works bear witness to this. But as he was a faithful member of the Church of England, his initiative at first seemed somewhat suspicious to several Roman Catholics. His system was accused of being tainted by naturalism. Pope Pius XI, who was

37. This section on Scouting is taken from Bernardin Verville, o.f.m., « Le scoutisme et les Franciscains canadiens », in *La Revue franciscaine*, vol. 80, no. 8, October 1965: 270–272.

very concerned about training young people, was personally interested in the problem. His conclusion settled the question.

Shortly after its appearance in England, Scouting crossed the Atlantic and spread rapidly in Canada among our English compatriots. From that time on, Father Robert Moore, an English-speaking Franciscan, became interested in it. The first Catholic Scout troop in Canada, some say in the British Empire, was born in 1914 in Montreal under the patronage of the *Alverna Catholic Association*. It was named the 52nd *Alverna* troupe of Montreal. M.T. Taggart Smyth was the Honorary Scoutmaster, Mr. Daniel-R. Cartier was the leader, and Father Robert Moore was the chaplain. Two other troops were to be born under the same patronage: the 56th *Iona* and the 60th *Marist* troops, both of Montreal. When Father Moore enlisted as a military chaplain, Father Ethelbert Sambrooke succeeded him.

There are evident similarities between Scouting and the spirit of St. Francis. When Canon Cornette undertook to expand Catholic Scouting among French youth, he went to Assisi to meditate in a mystical Franciscan atmosphere on this project. It is therefore understandable that the sons of St Francis were drawn to this method of training which strives to instill in young people the taste of a simple life, the love of nature, joy even in difficulties, and a chivalrous spirit of service to others.

In 1928, Fr. Vincent Bélanger, vicar at the parish of Notre-Dame-des-Sept-Allégresses, introduced Catholic Scouting to the diocese of Trois-Rivières. His intuitions in particular should be praised and his pragmatism helped him as much as his intuition. His influence on Quebec Scouting is undeniable. It is no exaggeration to say that his idea of Catholic Scouting left its mark on the federation that was to be born a few years later. Father Vincent had become a diocesan chaplain but left Trois-Rivières in 1933 due to illness; then, because the troops had multiplied, Fr. Flavien Vary succeeded him; and shortly after, Fr. Marie-Alcantara Dion, also a Franciscan, replaced him.

For Fr. M.-Alcantara Dion, scouting was an incomparable method of education. From 1934 until his death, which occurred suddenly in November 1949, he dedicated his remarkable talents, his vast pedagogical knowledge, and all his generosity of soul to perfecting and expanding Catholic Scouting and even more to Guides. He organized the first training camps for leaders and chaplains, and, through his writings, he was able to get Scouting accepted in educational institutions. In 1935, with the encouragement of Cardinal Villeneuve, he worked to unite the various diocesan groups of Scouts in the province. This was the *Federations of Catholic Scouts*, which was attached to the *Boy Scout Association* of Canada and thereby received official international status. Two years later, he did the same for the women's branch: the Catholic Guides. He surely is not totally responsible for these negotiations, but he was certainly a leading voice, as he was later in revitalizing the spirit of the two federations. Even the *Boy Scout Association* was happy to draw inspiration from his always lucid thinking.

In 1950, the Quebec episcopacy called on Father Bernardin Verville to replace Father M.-Alcantara Dion, as Assistant General Chaplain of the Federation of Scouts. (A Jesuit priest was appointed to the Girl Guides). He found that the Federation was already firmly established with a sound doctrine. He only had to continue the work that was so well begun, while at the same time leave more things to lay leaders to intensify their sense of responsibilities as committed Catholics. They were more and more called upon to replace chaplains overwhelmed by ministerial needs. At the 1955 International Gathering of Scouts (called the International Jamboree) in *Niagara on the Lake,* where 10,000 Scouts gathered, he was appointed General Chaplain for French-speaking boys, and virtually all Latin American language groups. A greeting was obtained from His Holiness Pius XII for all the Catholics and the highest dignitaries of the Canadian Catholic Church came to officiate, including the Apostolic Delegate. In addition, he was involved in negotiations with the *Boy Scout Association* which were extending the Quebec Federation to all French-speaking Scouts in Canada.

In 1960, the *Federation of Catholic Scouts* celebrated its twenty-fifth anniversary of being established. The event was the subject of a memorable religious and civic festival in Quebec City. At the same time, Commander Roger Brien, editor of the international magazine *Marie,* published a special issue entitled "Mary and Scouting." The Franciscan authorities considered that, after this crowning recognition of twenty-five years of work, the time for retirement had come. With the assent of the episcopacy, the role of Assistant General Chaplain passed into other hands.

The Franciscans named above were not the only ones dedicated to the cause of scouting. Several others became involved with the movement. Four names deserve special mention: Fr. Fernand Porter who, as secretary, worked closely with Fr. Marie-Alcantara Dion, and the Fathers Lucien Labelle, Zoël-M. Robert, and Télesphore Lacroix, all of whom successively held the position of chaplain at the Federation's headquarters.

Scouting is also indebted to the Canadian Franciscan Province for a special sort of temporal support. St. Louis House, presented to the Third Order, housed the Scouts' headquarters free of charge for several years, and in 1948 the former Family Centre on rue Saint-Denis was ceded to the Federation of Scouts on exceptionally advantageous terms.

This, in short, was the Franciscans' contribution to the development of the Catholic Scout movement in our country. It was a movement which gave birth to or nourished many priestly, religious, and missionary vocations, among fostering numerous other benefits. The Canadian authorities of the *Boy Scout Association* saw fit to recognize these services rendered to the cause of scouting. On November 22, 1960, His Excellency, Major General Vanier, Vice-Regent and Chief Scout of Canada presented the *Silver Wolf* award to Most Reverend Father Fulgence Boisvert, Provincial Minister, at a ceremony in Rideau Hall, Ottawa. This decoration was the highest honor bestowed by the World Scout Organization.

This account only mentions the Franciscan contribution to the Scout movement; it recognizes, however, that other personalities, clerics and lay people, hold a place in the history of Canadian Scouting and merit to be recognized. Among these personalities one name stands out: that of the late Jean-Marie Bureau from Trois-Rivières, whose collaboration with Fr. Vincent Bélanger and Fr. M.-Alcantara Dion was so close that, in this case, it would be unfair not to mention him with them. He and others have earned the recognition of Scouting in Canada.

5. The Broken Dream

The first sign of intense intellectual life in the Canadian Franciscan Province of St. Joseph, as we have seen, was the abundant harvest of university degrees and then the large influence of many excellent thinkers who devoted their lives to the apostolate of truth. The fervor of this climate, within the Franciscan Order, was the prelude to an evolution that was taking place in the field of education in Quebec, especially at the level of classical colleges. Quebec, indeed, was beginning to perceive that the traditional ideology behind the selection and admission of students, the lack of democratization, and the elitism of the curriculum was inadequate for the needs of the time and corresponded less and less to the social reality. The educational reform of the 1960s was being undertaken to address these problems.

How was the Franciscan Province of St. Joseph involved in this new endeavor? In 1946–47, it felt the need to open a branch on Gouin Boulevard, in Montreal, to teach the elements of Latin. The experiment was repeated on a completely different scale in 1949, when, at the request of Bishop Anastase Forget of Saint-Jean-de-Québec, they decided to establish a Classical Externat in Longueuil. This initiative was supposed to meet the needs of the youth of the South Shore who, for various social reasons, could hardly think of attending the Seminary of Saint-Jean. In principle, the institution was supposed to follow the model of diocesan seminaries. Its promoters envisaged it to be the crowning achievement of the groundbreaking work undertaken by the Franciscans in Côteau-Rouge.[38]

38. Chicoine, Fidèle. « Collèges: sources de vocations franciscaines » in *CHRONIQUES ET DOCUMENTS*, vol. 36, no. 2, juillet 1983 : 20.

But how could a decision to increase the investment in education be justified to the friars at a time when the shortage of candidates was becoming more and more evident? Father Provincial explained, thus:

> There was a need to maintain a staff in colleges to ensure a succession; a need to adopt an effective long-term policy of replenishment so as not to deplete the meagre resources of this ministry.[39]

This long-term replenishment policy proved to be very unpopular among the Franciscans. One of them observed that the "investment in education will always be judged in the courts of Franciscan opinion as a waste of the priesthood."[40]

In 1950, the Classical Externat rallied a dozen friars to teach about 400 students. This already indicated the importance of the large presence of lay people in the institution. Living and studying conditions in Longueil were particularly difficult, especially in the early days. Pierre Vallières[41] painted a very severe picture of his *Alma Mater,* which he frequently reported in his rhetorical [writings]. According to him, everything seemed to be makeshift: the state of the premises, the furnishings, even the teachers.[42] Should such a version of things be taken as is? Father Paul Sylvestre commented on Vallières's comments:

> Pierre Vallières, [. . .], did justice to educators such as Father Flavien and the one he calls Charley [Charles Bélanger]; but he was blatantly unfair to Father Fernand [Porter]. Moreover, his description of the Externat in its beginning days is far from flattering, but it seems fair enough to me.[43]

---

39. Quoted by Cécile Bergeron, *Op. Cit.,* 68.

40. *Ibid.* 68–69.

41. Translators Note: Pierre Vallières, an alumnus of the Externat, entered the Franciscans but left after a couple of years. He became a journalist, first for *Le Devoir*, and then for *Cité Libre*, and in the early 1960s became involved with the FLQ (*Front de liberation du Québec*). He was arrested and imprisoned for his involvement with FLQ activities: the robbery of a Montreal cinema, the death of Thérèse Morin killed in the bombing of a shoe manufacturer, and the death of a fellow FLQ member, Jean Corbo, who died while placing a bomb at the Dominion Textile factory. He was arrested in 1966 and, while in prison in 1967, wrote *Les nègres blancs d'Amérique (White Niggers of America)*, an autobiographical account describing his journey to independence and socialism. In 1970, his life-imprisonment charges for murder having been appealed and reduced, he resumed his career as a journalist and writer. After the October 1970 FLQ kidnapping and murder of Pierre Laporte, the Deputy Premier of Quebec, he renounced the FLQ's violence and endorsed the Parti Québécois' route of legal advancement.

42. Vallières, Pierre. *Nègres blancs d'Amérique*, Éditions Parti Pris, s.l.n.d., pp. 170 et suiv.

43. Sylvestre, Paul. « P. Fernand Porter. Notice biographique » in *CHRONIQUES ET DOCUMENTS*, vol. 38, no. 2 juin 1985 : 168.

Significantly, as the number of students increased, so did the involvement of lay people become more important in the institution, which was gradually moving towards being uniquely collegial education. After eighteen years, the institution was prospering and rendered a loyal service to the south shore's community. In 1968, Father Pierre Bisaillon made the transition, he became the new general director of what was now known as *CEGEP Édouard-Montpetit*.[44]

What was the point of the Franciscan presence in this great college on the south shore of the St. Lawrence? Among many others, the following testimony seems to us to express a particularly serene portrayal of a detachment worthy of the sons of Saint Francis:

> The Franciscans, through Longueuil's Classical Externat, have served as a transition in building-up the region of the city. They had a transitional role that allowed the city to take charge of a well-established institution. Throughout history, Church institutions had been present everywhere, especially in this transitional role and interim function. The Classic Externat of Longueuil was one more shining example of the many achievements on the coat of arms of Saint Joseph's Province.[45]

The evolution and then finally the sale of Longueuil's Classical Externat took place without causing too many painful clashes or deep splits within St. Joseph's Province. Is this perception correct? What is certain is that this was not the case with the Seraphic College in Trois-Rivières when, around 1950, talks began to make it an institution more suited to the mentalities and needs of the time. As we know, this house was the work par excellence of the Friars Minor. It was a vocational college, the only institution designed exclusively to recruit Franciscans in Eastern Canada. As a result, special ties united the College to the Franciscan community: "The College is the reproductive centre of the Order and this specific function helps to strengthen the tie uniting the College and the Franciscan Province."[46]

At a time when Longueuil's Classical Externat was fighting for life and abundantly draining the increasingly scarce material and human resources, and at a time when Biddeford College was also trying to respond to America's population explosion by asking for at least a dozen friars every year, we began to talk about transforming the Seraphic College—a project that also required heavy material and human investments—to accommodate pedagogical ideals.

---

44. Chicoine, Fidèle. « Collèges : sources de vocations franciscaines », in *CHRONIQUES ET DOCUMENTS*, vol. 36, no. 2, juillet 1983 : 20.

45. Sylvestre, Paul. « Dix-neuf ans de service à l'Externat classique de Longueuil » in *CHRONIQUES ET DOCUMENTS*, vol. 30, no. 2, novembre 1977 : 28.

46. Bergeron, Cécile. *Le Collège Séraphique des Trois-Rivières : 1952–1968*. Thèse à l'Université de Sherbrooke, 1971, p. 155.

Moreover, at the same time, classical colleges as a whole began to question their place in the educational system. The creation of the Federation of Classical Colleges in 1953 tried to respond to this need.

The diverse plans for a new Seraphic College did not meet with agreement. Tension arose between the Franciscan Province and its reproductive center, the Seraphic College. The latter considered [by the Province as] a Provincial institution, because of its very purpose, merited a review by the Franciscan authorities concerning its proposed values and objectives. From its founding until the 1950s, the College had undergone no profound transformation, no structural change. Now, the social context of the mid-20th century called into question the relevance of minor seminaries. Some teachers attached to the traditional conception of vocation—a divine call—wanted to keep as an admission criterium the desire to become a Franciscan or at the very least a priest. Others, more open to psychological data, sociology, and theology, without denying the divine aspects, took more account of human mediation. In an advanced Christianity society, early human mediation—a Christian home and an appreciation of the priesthood—nurtured the desire to be a "Father" from childhood or the beginning of adolescence. But could not a college that welcomes young people with a good Christian education also become a fruitful human mediation for priestly vocations in an undeveloped Christian society? Moreover, in the age of the laity, the Franciscans would not be wasting their time if they trained committed laymen!

It was in this direction that Trois-Rivière's new Seraphic College sought to readjust its own objectives. This was done first through the admission of students: slowly and subtly placing more emphasis on moral, intellectual and Christian skills and psychological balance than on the desire to become a Franciscan priest.[47] This is apparent in the *Yearbooks,* starting in 1956, especially in the corrections made to the 1960 edition. It was achieved mainly through the house's ability to meet both the needs of contemporary students and those of the entire Franciscan community. Indeed, the reasons given for justifying new renovations can be summed up as follows: the Laviolette Street college was inadequate to meet the needs of the Franciscan Province, which should see to its own [formation and] renewal; there was a need to provide better educational facilities for Franciscan students who were "inferior" to graduates of other colleges; they needed to present themselves attractively in competing with the classic sections of public schools.[48]

On January 24, 1956, the Provincial Definitory agreed to build a new college in Trois-Rivières. The overall concept had to respond to some

47. *Ibid.* 159.

48. *Ibid.* 64–65.

educators' convictions that the future construction would not only open the way to an increased clientele, but above all would provide more appropriate training for young people and the contemporary world. The man behind this project was Father Lucien Labelle. When he returned from Paris, where he had trained in psycho-pedagogy, he was offered the positions of either Director or Prefect of Discipline. He opted for the second position, convinced that his training and daily contact with students would allow him to be a psycho-educator—and not just a simple pawn or room supervisor. He summed up his guiding principle in a simple formula: "If we form true Christians, we will have a harvest of vocations."

Concretely, the institution was to materialize on Trois-Rivières' hillsides, in a mixed [environment] and was meant to be an out-of-doors and innovative boarding school. The formula is worth thinking about:

—*mixed*. The precise formula assumes that a couple with their children would take charge of the residential pavilions,
—*outdoors*. The boarding school would include a set of residential pavilions in one area of the campus and a group of service buildings in another area. Daily activities would require going outdoors;
—*innovative*. On one hand, the students would participate in the cultural life of the city and, on the other, the campus would be a cultural center for citizens.

In short, the pedagogical plan was inspired both by the principles of active pedagogy and scouting. The approach was strictly psycho-pedagogical and no longer philosophical-pedagogical. It combined the pavilion system and the team system:

> Around a single central block, which included common services, were scattered the residential pavilions. Teenagers lived there, divided into mixed teams. The youngest had a special more age-appropriate diet; rhetoricians were freer. Cardinal Mercier College (in Belgium) was the model that Father Labelle followed very closely in planning the concept.[49]

Certainly, at the time, this project was novel in Quebec's educational circles. What the reformers wanted was to create personalized living environments, which rejected the idea of a huge boarding school that imposed mixing different age groups and the same academic schedule for all. This concept, one suspects, would not be unanimously accepted by the Franciscan community, or even by the faculty of the Seraphic College. Father Fernand

49. *Ibid.* 99.

Porter, supporter of a "small traditional religious seminary" and provincial definitor, found major flaws in this "Christian college" project. According to him, such a living environment would be an unfortunate reconstruction of the family where discipline and the exercise of authority would be threatened; dimensions of original sin would have to be kept under surveillance; the masters would be responsible only for teaching; and we would be proposing humanism without ascetical [discipline]. In short, we would be adopting an inadequate pedagogical plan that was contrary to the Franciscan mentality.[50]

Fathers Porter and Labelle were the leaders of both trends. They were the two voices which probably expressed "much deeper and more encompassing convictions than pedagogical principles." This struggle led to the expression and confrontation of two divergent spiritualities, two antagonistic ways of considering the human being.[51] The two issues would confront each other over a period of fifteen years, during which personality conflicts sometimes dominated the clash of ideas. In fact, only four pavilions were built. Until 1968, only students in the Elementary Latin and Syntax and some of the students in Methodology were able to live in premises which the project had proposed.[52]

For all practical purposes, from 1963, the Seraphic College was no longer a single unity. As the Seraphic College Committee undertook a three-year investigation into the future of the institution, it became less and less in control of its own destiny. It gradually lost its initiative and, in successive stages, it fell under the sway of the public sector, which was also experiencing its own educational revolution. The premises of this college, "modern" like all the others of its time, were made accessible to the future CEGEP which was at that time organizing itself according to the June 1967 law. Finally, all the buildings were acquired by the Government of Quebec, which assigned it to the University of Quebec in Trois-Rivières.

Conclusion

"A beautiful broken dream": this is probably how we can describe the final fate reserved for Biddeford College, Longueil's Classical Externat and, especially the Seraphic College in Trois-Rivières. Along with these institutions, the pedagogues had dreamed of seeing a blossoming of renewed Christian humanism. It is probably futile to ask ourselves if the authorities of St. Joseph's Franciscan Province knew how to assess properly the human and material resources required to embark on projects of this magnitude. It is certainly

50. *Ibid.* 86 ff.
51. *Ibid.* 90.
52. *Ibid.* 136.

more illuminating to defer to the conclusions of the Committee for Studies formed by the Provincial Chapter in 1963.

During a survey that lasted almost three years, the committee tried to place its analysis in the context of Vatican II and within the changes that affected all of Quebec society. The three elements—churches, society, and Franciscan vocations—were the guiding threads of its reflection.[53] The future was seen in an inclusive way. Thus, it was not the fate of a particular college that was considered, but rather the whole Franciscan activity in education. It was felt that a Franciscan commitment to education and colleges was in accordance with the Franciscan vocation. At the same time, it was also thought that owning a college was harmful to the witness of Christian fraternity, which was so characteristic of the Franciscan vocation. In this sense, the possession and administration of colleges was no longer a desirable possibility for the Franciscan Order.[54] Finally, did this mean that the Franciscans were to withdraw so submissively from an environment that they had attained with such a great struggle? In a text dating back to 1964, Father Odoric Bouffard felt that the Franciscans had to understand the urgent need to live in their time, to be of their time:

> There is no point in moaning about a lost past, which perhaps becomes romanticized over time. It is no use resting on our laurels. We must move forward, fall in line with the Church of John XXIII and Paul VI. This Second Vatican Council Church shouts out: "Christians, adapt to the world of today. Make yourself modern souls, sensitized to the modern values of technical efficiency, of scientific advancement. But also, and this is your role as Christians in the world, bring the knowledge and love of Jesus Christ to this atomic and interplanetary civilization. But how can you be heard if you do not speak today's language? How are you to reach people, if you appear to them entrenched in a medieval civilization or the times of the crusades."[55]

Such a message was clearly heard. It resulted in no longer owning or administering colleges for which the state was now responsible, but in accepting more specifically priestly functions and tasks in the parishes and in school environments, after appropriate studies in pastoral care, liturgy, and catechetics. University teaching should be continued by theologians and philosophers who would carry on the long tradition of friars trained in the best universities in the world.

53. *Ibid.* 179.
54. *Ibid.* 183.
55. Bouffard, Odoric. "Bio-bibliographie du père Odoric Bouffard … », p. 23.

What perspective can a Franciscan friar have of a world that has asked such sacrifice and adaptability? In wisdom and serene humility and with a Franciscan spirit, it seems appropriate for us to view this as though: "Everything had grown up around us; but, basically, not exactly without us."[56]

Bibliographic Guidelines

The history of Franciscan involvement in education is still to be written. It will be a long and arduous undertaking. Certainly it is necessary to examine: the archives of the Seraphic College and the Philosophy and Theology scholasticates, the too few testimonies of professors which are recorded in *Studium* 25 (1946) and in the *Almanac of St. Francis,* and the obituaries of the most eminent professors. For the time being, one can profitably read:

Bacon, René. « Le P. Emmanuel que j'ai connu au scolasticat de Rosemont », in *Chroniques et Documents*, vol. 33, no. 2, juillet 1980 : 121–124.

Baillargeon, Constantin. « Témoignage sur le P. Léonard Puech (1902–1984) », in *Chroniques et Documents*, vol. 38, no. 1, janvier 1985 : 63–66.

Bergeron, Cécile. *Le collège séraphique de Trois-Rivières, 1952–1968.* Thèse présentée à l'École des gradués de l'Université de Sherbrooke, 1971. 221 p.

Boisvert, Emmanuel. « Le Père Adrien-Marie Malo », in *Chroniques et Documents*, vol. 31, no. 2, juin 1978 : 139–174.

Bouffard, Odoric. « Le T.R.P. Georges-Albert Laplante, père de notre Province", in *Chroniques et Documents*, vol. 29, no. 1, juin 1976 : 11–32.

Bouffard, Odoric. « Marie-Alcantara Dion, 1897-1949. Un chef de file et sa synthèse franciscaine », in ND, vol. 17, no. 2, juin 1962 : 133–143 ; no. 3, octobre 1962 : 246–252.

Bouffard, Odoric. « Père Emmanuel Boisvert (1908–1980) », in *Chroniques et Documents*, vol. 33, no. 2, juillet 1980 : 110–119.

Chicoine, Fidèle. « Collèges, sources de vocations franciscaines », in *Chroniques et Documents*, vol. 35, no. 2, juin 1982 : 143–150 ; vol 36 : no. 1, janvier 1983 : 3–14.

Chicoine, Fidèle. « Aux débuts du Collège séraphique d'Edmonton », in *Chroniques et Documents*, vol. 30, no. 2, novembre 1977 : 217–223.

Labelle, Lucien. « P. Odoric Bouffard, 1908–1985 », in *Chroniques et Documents*, vol. 39, no. 2, juillet 1986 : 114–142.

---

56. Gaudron, Edmont. "La courbe des études chez nous. Pour l'histoire de notre vie intellectuelle », in *CHRONIQUES ET DOCUMENTS* vol. 31, no. 2, juillet 1977 : 237.

Laverdure, Gilbert. « École Didace-Pelletier. Historique et État actuel » in ND, vol. 14, no. 2, juin 1957 : 183–198.

Marcil, George. « Franciscans in Biddeford Maine, 1933–1975 » in *Chroniques et Documents*, vol. 29, no. 2, décembre 1976 : 133–178.

Monfette, Prudent. « Collège séraphique (Nagasaki). Fondation 1931 », in *Chroniques et Documents*, vol 36, no. 2, juillet 1983 : 22–25 ; vol. 40, no. 1, janvier 1987 : 3–10 ; no. 2, juillet 1987 : 79-90 ; vol. 41, no. 1, janvier 1988 : 27–39.

Poirier, Léandre. « Témoignage sur le P. Emmanuel Boisvert », in *Chroniques et Documents*, vol. 33, no. 2, juillet 1980 : 119–120.

Puech, Léonard-Marie. « Récit autobiographique », in *Chroniques et Documents*, vol. 38, no. 1, janvier 1985 : 59–63.

Sylvestre, Paul. « P. Fernand Porter. Notice Biographique », in *Chroniques et Documents*, vol. 38, no. 2, juin 1985 : 162–171.

Permissions

The following images are published with permission:

Jean-Baptiste Scotin, *Le Vray portrait du tres Religieux Didace Pelletier*, début XVIIIe siècle. Encre sur papier, Québec, Musée de la civilisation, Collection du Séminaire de Québec.

François-Xavier Habermann, *Vuë de la Rue des Recolets dans la haute Ville de Quebeck*, c. 1775. Encre et aquarelle sur papier vergé, 36 × 49,7 cm, Québec, Musée de la civilisation, Collection du Séminaire de Québec.

[Diplôme d'agrégation et d'affiliation spirituelle donné à Jean-Baptiste Perreault, marchand aux Trois-Rivières, par le révérend père Hyacinthe Berrier, provincial des Récollets de la province de Saint-Denys en France], 1758. Feuillet, 34,5 × 25,6 cm, Québec, Musée de la civilisation, Fonds d'archives du Séminaire de Québec, Documents Faribault, n° 233.

Anonyme, *Portrait du frère Louis Demers*, début du XIXe siècle. Huile sur toile, 82,3 × 65,8 cm, Québec, Musée de la civilisation, Collection du Séminaire de Québec, 1991.85.

Anonyme, *Portrait du frère Alexis Demers*, début du XIXe siècle. Huile sur toile, 80,9 × 64,9 cm, Québec, Musée de la civilisation, Collection du Séminaire de Québec, 1991.84.

Joseph Légaré, *Le Freère Louis, Récollet*, c. 1830. Huile, gouache, papier collé sur bois, 31,7 × 22,2 cm, Québec, Musée de la civilisation, Collection du Séminaire de Québec.

Georges Delfosse, *Première messe chantée sur les bords de la Rivière-des-Prairies par le R.P. Denis Jamay*, 1908. Huile sur toile, 429,26 × 223,52 cm, Montréal, Cathédrale Marie-Reine-du-Monde.

Attribué au Père François (Jean-Melchior Brekenmacher), *Le Père Emmanuel Crespel*, c. 1755. Huile sur toile, 81 × 64,6 cm, Québec, Musée national des beaux-arts du Québec, 1958.187.

Anonyme, *Portrait de Louis Hennepin*, 1694. Huile sur toile, 40,64 × 37,47 cm, St. Paul, Minnesota Historical Society.

James Pattison Cockburn, *Père-Dieu*. Aquarelle sur papier, 15,20 × 23,80 cm, Québec, Collection du Monastère des Ursulines de Québec.

Anonyme, *Moine capucin*, [portrait présumé du père Joseph Denys]. Huile sur toile, 80 × 67 cm, Québec, Collection du Monastère des Augustines, Hôtel-Dieu de Québec.